Challenging Sports Governing Bodies

Challenging Sports Governing Bodies

Adam Lewis QC, Barrister, Blackstone Chambers

Jonathan Taylor, Partner and co-head of International Sports Group, Bird and Bird LLP

Nick De Marco, Barrister, Blackstone Chambers

James Segan, Barrister, Blackstone Chambers

Bloomsbury Professional

Bloomsbury Professional Limited
Maxwelton House,
41–43 Boltro Road,
Haywards Heath,
West Sussex
RH16 1BJ

ISBN: 978 1 78043 988 4

Typeset by Compuscript Ltd, Shannon
Printed and bound in the United Kingdom by CPI Group (UK) Ltd, Croydon, CR0 4YY

Preface

In 2002, Lord Woolf wrote the following words in the *Foreword* of the first edition of *Lewis & Taylor, Sport: Law and Practice*:

> Sport has changed. A relatively few years ago the idea that there would be any demand or need for a book devoted exclusively to law and practice in relation to sport would have been regarded as surprising. Those involved in sport would then probably have been of the view that the more limited the interaction between the law and sport the better.

The changes that Lord Woolf went on to describe, in particular as a result of the commercialisation of sport, have only intensified in the 14 years thereafter. Barely a week goes by without reports of legal disputes in various sports making headline news. Hundreds of smaller disputes, at every level of just about every sport, some involving very large sums of money and others being determined with no costs or fees at all, take place outside the glare of the media spotlight. Thousands of sports people, administrators, lawyers and arbitrators face novel and often complex disputes throughout the year.

Yet whilst the law and practice in sports have increasingly developed certain common themes and principles, the area remains one of change and development. Even some of the fundamental issues covered in this book, such as the supervision of the courts over sports governing bodies, and the extent to which those bodies can require participants by means of arbitration clauses, to determine their disputes within the sport, have been the subject of recent important developments as well as criticism.

The purpose of this book is twofold. First, it updates those key chapters of *Lewis & Taylor, Sport: Law and Practice* that concerned sports disputes (in particular parts D1 and D2 of the 3rd edition). Secondly, by concentrating on disputes, it aims to provide an accessible and practical handbook, not only to the busy legal practitioner involved in those disputes, but also to sports administrators, agents, managers, and commentators, as well as to students of sports law.

The book is divided into 14 chapters reviewing the circumstances in which challenges can be brought against the actions of sports governing bodies, how and where to bring those challenges, the standards of review that courts and arbitral bodies shall apply to decisions of those bodies, the various causes of action which can arise and the remedies that are available. As such, *Challenging Sports Governing Bodies* should provide those interested and involved in the sector with an invaluable handbook to guide them through every stage of a sports dispute. The law in this edition was as stated in June 2016.

Adam Lewis QC
Jonathan Taylor
Nick De Marco
James Segan

London, June 2016

Contents

Table of Statutes

Table of Statutory Instruments

Table of Cases

F

G

H

I

J

K

L

M

N

O

P

Q

R

S

T

Y

CHAPTER 1

Introduction

1.1   Sport is important to a large number of people, for different reasons. Many people play or watch a large range of sports for recreation. Some people compete at an amateur level. A few make their living from competing at sport, at least for some years. A very few compete at an elite level, nationally or even internationally. Others involve themselves in the organisation of sport, whether as a referee or an umpire on the field of play, or as a manager or coach on the sidelines, or in an administrative capacity. Some are paid, and some do it voluntarily.

1.2   Other people, and businesses, make a living from the commercial exploitation of sport. Some of them, such as promoters and event organisers, develop and stage events that the public can attend in return for an entrance fee. They may also employ or engage the services of players to participate in the event, or may contract with clubs to participate in the event, which may themselves employ or engage the players. Some make and sell the products, or own and rent out the facilities necessary to play the sport or to stage the event. Others provide broadcasting, webcasting, publishing or other services that allow those not able to attend the event nevertheless to 'consume' the product, in return for some direct or indirect fee. Further people and businesses pay rights fees to the sports governing body or participants in the sport in return for the additional valuable commercial opportunities that arise in relation to the event, such as the privilege of being associated with the event, a club or a player, through sponsorship, official supply arrangements, merchandising, publication, travel and ticket arrangements and corporate hospitality. Others may act for players or clubs, or seek to invest in them.

1.3   All of these people and businesses are affected by how the particular sport's governing body or bodies choose to run the various aspects of the sport. Those governing bodies have principal responsibility for defining and regulating how their sport is played, and for promoting and encouraging participation and investment in their sport, by preserving and enhancing the features of the sport (a physical and mental contest, played openly and fairly on a level playing-field, with an uncertain outcome) that make it attractive to its participants, the general public and therefore potential commercial partners. Sports governing bodies take a number of forms, and the extent of their power and influence varies from sport to sport. In some instances, there are a number of bodies that have different responsibilities within the same sport, including in some cases separate bodies, organised as businesses, that create and stage events or competitions under the sanction of another governing body. In almost all instances, there are national and international bodies. What sports governing bodies have in common is that they are composite bodies with a membership of others involved in the sport, and they control the organisation of a particular element of the sport or the commercial exploitation of it. The expression 'sports governing body' is used here to cover these disparate organisations, but it does not extend to businesses such as clubs, promoters, or the owners of facilities. The 'actions' of sports governing bodies for the purpose of the analysis here cover the rules they adopt to govern players and clubs and others, their decisions applying those rules, and their treatment of commercial activities not necessarily covered in the rules but arising out of the competitions that they organise and/or sanction. The contexts in which these actions arise cover a wide spectrum: rules are made by sports governing bodies to address many different matters, often unique to the particular sport, and their decisions range from disciplinary rulings in relation to conduct on the field of play by an individual amateur, to the sale by an international association to an international broadcaster of broadcasting rights to televise a professional competition, for many millions of pounds.

1.4   The courts, and arbitral bodies established by sports, provide a number of mechanisms of varying efficacy for reviewing the actions of sports governing bodies that are perceived to be wrong, unfair or unlawful. Those mechanisms, termed 'causes of action', are the same as, or are at least based on, causes of action that are used in areas other than sport. There is no general legislation in the UK in relation to sport, such as in France. There is no single authority in the UK to deal with sports disputes. However, particular causes of action have been used in the sports context more often and more readily than others, and the courts have developed principles that are specific to sport and that can be carried forward to inform the examination of later sports cases.

1.5   Whether this process is sufficiently developed to allow one to describe the courts and arbitral bodies as applying a law of sport[1] may be of more academic than practical interest. Equally, it is arid to suggest that the courts' and arbitral bodies' approach to the application of the law to sport should not be addressed as a distinct topic. People and businesses are affected every day by the actions of sports governing bodies. They and their advisers need guidance on the particular ways in which the courts and arbitral bodies have approached analogous cases in the past, in order to evaluate what steps they should take and whether to challenge the action at issue.

1 See Beloff, Kerr, Demetriou and Beloff, *Sports Law* (2nd edn, Hart Publishing, 2012), Ch 1; Gardiner, O'Leary, Welch, Boyes and Naidoo, *Sports Law* (4th edn, Routledge, 2012), Preface and Ch 2. The question is of more relevance in the context of the decisions of international sports arbitral bodies such as the Court of Arbitration for Sport.

1.6   This book seeks to provide those affected by the actions of a sports governing body with a road map for deciding whether to bring proceedings, against whom or what, and where, and to provide sports governing bodies with guidance as to the possible consequences of their actions.[1] After this introductory section, Chapter 2 considers the broad range of *factual* circumstances in which challenges have arisen to the actions of sports governing bodies. This allows those deciding whether to mount a challenge, to identify similar situations that have been addressed by the courts and arbitral bodies, providing a starting-point for the evaluation of their own circumstances. Chapter 3 then seeks to assist in the identification of an appropriate cause of action and appropriate respondent. Chapter 4 addresses forum: when a challenge should be brought in the courts, or before arbitral bodies, or elsewhere. Resort to the mechanisms described in this and the following chapters by its nature comes after a 'decision' has been made by the sports governing body, and often internal remedies allowing a challenge to that decision have to be exhausted first before turning to the courts or to arbitration.

1 This book is based on the relevant chapters in the wider text, Lewis and Taylor, *Sport: Law and Practice* (3rd edn, Bloomsbury 2014). Other chapters in that text provide more details in relation to specific aspects of the application of the law to sport.

1.7   Chapter 5 touches on whether the decisions of sports governing bodies should be regarded as public or private for the purposes of challenge, including the applicability of the Human Rights Act 1998, and the extension to sports governing bodies of the EU free movement obligations, which are generally applicable to the state and not to private bodies. Chapter 6 addresses the varying degrees of review applied by the courts and arbitral bodies, which have traditionally expressed reluctance in many instances to intervene in the specialist decision-making processes of sports governing bodies, where those bodies have a jurisdiction expressly conferred upon them by the applicable rules.

1.8   Chapters 7 to 12 deal with the ways in which English courts and arbitral bodies have adapted or applied particular English law causes of action (grounds of review based on control of the sport, contract, tort and restraint of trade) in the context of challenges to the actions of sports governing bodies,[1] and provide a summary of the European law causes of action (free movement and competition law). Chapters 13 and 14 address the remedies available, and various procedural aspects of challenge.

1 See generally Beloff, Kerr, Demetriou and Beloff, *Sports Law* (2nd edn, Hart Publishing, 2012), Ch 2; Gardiner, O'Leary, Welch, Boyes and Naidoo, *Sports Law* (4th edn, Routledge, 2012), Ch 3; Anderson, *Modern Sports Law* (Hart Publishing, 2010), Ch 2; Lewis and Taylor, *Sport: Law and Practice* (3rd edn, Bloomsbury, 2014) section D.

CHAPTER 2

The actions of sports governing bodies

A ACTIONS AFFECTING A SPECIFIC INDIVIDUAL PARTICIPANT

2.1   There are many different individual participants in sport. First and foremost there are players, but there are also clubs, coaches, trainers, and managers. There are individual owners in sports such as horse and greyhound racing. There are also other individuals, such as agents and promoters, who are not directly involved in the playing of the sport but who nevertheless participate in the sense that they contribute to the structure of an exciting sport capable of generating revenue from the public's interest. A decision of a sports governing body in the application of its rules may directly[1] relate to and impact upon a specific such individual or club. The individual may seek to challenge the validity of the application of the rule, or the validity of the rule itself.

1 In the main, any challenge would be brought by the individual to whom the decision related. However challenges may be brought by a club affected by a decision against one of its players (see for example *Sankofa and Charlton v The FA*, 12 January 2007, Comm Ct Simon J), or by another participant complaining that a party had been inadequately dealt with by the governing body (see *Sheffield United v FAPL* [2007] ISLR-SLR 77, where the club complained that the FAPL had not deducted points from West Ham following their rule breach).

(a) Doping

2.2   The misuse of drugs in sport has given rise to a number of cases in the courts, and very many more before governing bodies' internal tribunals and external arbitration bodies such as the Court of Arbitration for Sport and (in the UK) the National Anti-Doping Panel. The introduction of the World Anti-Doping Code, with its adoption of an international review system involving ultimate recourse to CAS, has meant that since 2003 there have been few doping cases in the courts, and many before CAS and domestic arbitral panels. In the main the cases before the courts have involved individual players who have been sanctioned by sports governing bodies for the use of performance enhancing or recreational drugs, seeking to challenge the legality of those decisions or the underlying rules.[1] There have been challenges both to the validity of a particular doping decision and to the jurisdiction of the sports disciplinary body to make it.

1 See for example Dwain Chambers' unsuccessful attempt before the 2008 Beijing Olympics to challenge the British Olympic Association's bye-law under which athletes with doping convictions were banned for life from Team GB (*Dwain Chambers v British Olympic Association* [2008] EWHC 2028 (QB)). Chambers' application for an interim injunction based on restraint of trade, breach of competition law, and irrationality failed on the grounds that he did not have a sufficiently strong argument on the merits, that the balance of convenience was strongly against the application since he was seeking to displace the status quo and exclude another athlete, and that it was made after considerable delay. However, four years later, before the 2012 London Olympics, the BOA bye-law was overturned on a different basis when CAS upheld WADA's decision that the BOA bye-law was in breach of the World Anti-Doping Code, because a signatory could not adopt additional sanctions for doping offences to those imposed under the World Anti-Doping Code (*British Olympic Association v World Anti-Doping Agency*, CAS 2011/A/2658, award dated 30 April 2012).

2.3 The validity of particular doping decisions has been challenged in the courts and before arbitral bodies on the basis that it was not open to the disciplinary body to conclude that a doping offence had been committed because there had been a failure to follow prescribed procedures in taking, storing or testing the relevant sample,[1] or because the governing body had failed for some other reason to prove the presence of a prohibited substance in the sample of the player. Particular doping decisions have been challenged on the basis that the disciplinary body acted in a procedurally unfair manner or was biased,[2] or on the basis that it reached an unreasonable or disproportionate decision.[3]

1 See for example *Paul Edwards v UK Athletics & Ors* High Court (Queen's Bench Division), 29 November 2013, Case No: HQ13X01923, 2013 WL 8467444; see also, *Gasser v Stinson* QBD 15 June 1988 Scott J; and *Modahl v British Athletics Federation* QBD 28 June 1996 Popplewell J; CA 28 July 1997; HL 22 July 1998; QB 14 December 2000 Douglas Brown J, [2000] All ER (D) 2274; and 8 October 2001 [2001] EWCA Civ 1447, [2002] 1 WLR 1192.
2 *Modahl v British Athletics Federation*, see n 1, *Wilander and Novacek v Tobin and Jude* (see para **2.4**, note 1), and *Flaherty v National Greyhound Racing Club Ltd* [2005] EWCA Civ 117.
3 CAS jurisprudence has established that in theory at least CAS has a residual jurisdiction to set aside the mandatory sanctions set out in the World Anti-Doping Code where the result mandated by the Code is so disproportionate as to be shocking to the conscience. This will rarely be the case, but for a recent application of this principle domestically, see *The Football Association v Jake Livermore*, 8 September 2015 (mandatory one year suspension for taking cocaine where the panel found no significant fault or negligence, reduced to no suspension on proportionality grounds given the exceptional circumstances of the case relating to the player's depression as a result of the death of his child). The proportionality of doping sanctions has also been attacked on competition law grounds, amongst other things before the European Court of Justice, see para **2.4**, note 2.

2.4 The rules empowering disciplinary bodies to impose a sanction in doping cases, and their application in given cases, have been challenged on the basis that they are in unreasonable restraint of trade[1] and on the basis that they are contrary to the European free movement rules or competition rules.[2] Jurisdiction has also been challenged on the basis that a sports governing body could not appeal against its own tribunal's exoneration of a player, or that the wrong sports governing body was attempting to impose the sanction for the doping offence.[3] There have also been challenges in the context of horse and greyhound racing to decisions that the animal was doped and to the sanctions imposed on individuals as a consequence.[4] There has been an attempt to prevent publication of pending anti-doping proceedings.[5]

1 *Gasser v Stinson*, 15 June 1988 Scott J; *Wilander and Novacek v Tobin and Jude*, ChD, 19 March 1996 Lightman J, (1996) Times 8 April CA and [1997] 1 Lloyd's Rep 195 Lightman J and on appeal [1997] 2 Lloyd's Law Rep 293 CA.
2 *Meca-Medina v Commission* CFI 30 September 2004 (T-313/02) [2004] ECR II-3291, [2004] 3 CMLR 1314, In *Meca-Medina* two swimmers challenged the legality of a two-year ban imposed by FINA for a positive finding of nandrolone on the basis that it infringed European free movement and competition law. In August 2002, the European Commission and the CFI rejected the challenge on the ground that anti-doping rules are necessary for the protection of the integrity of the sport and therefore fell within a 'sporting exception' to European law (see Commission press release IP/02/1211, August 2002). The CFI upheld the Commission's decision. The Court of Justice however overturned the CFI's decision that there is a 'sporting exception' taking such rules of the sport itself outside competition law, and held that those rules are just as much subject to the requirement that they be justified as any other rule of an association governing access to an occupation, but that, on the facts, the ban was in all the circumstances proportionate.
3 *Korda v ITF* [1999] All ER (D) 84, revsd [1999] All ER (D) 337, CA 25 March 1999.
4 *R v Disciplinary Committee of the Jockey Club, ex p Aga Khan* [1993] 1 WLR 909.
5 In *Spelman v Express Newspapers* [2012] EWHC 355 (QB) Tugendhat J 24 February 2012, a rugby player unsuccessfully attempted to injunct disclosure of his doping case. In a number of libel cases, the sporting context has been central.

(b) Misconduct on the pitch or serious breach of the rules of play

2.5 A second major area of activity for internal disciplinary bodies that has given rise to challenge in the courts or arbitral bodies involves the improper actions of players while playing the sport. The decisions of internal disciplinary bodies in this context have been challenged, for example in circumstances where the player alleges that the process has been procedurally unfair, that irrelevant considerations have been taken into account, or that the decision or sanction is unreasonable or in restraint of trade. The range of such actions is wide, but broadly divides into on-field violence and actions affecting the integrity of the competition.

2.6 There have been a number of cases involving challenges to the way in which the sports governing body has dealt with on-field violence or a sending off[1] or abuse.[2]

1 See for example *Sankofa and Charlton v The FA*, 12 January 2007, Comm Ct Simon J. The violence may not always be during the course of play: see *Football Association v Evra and Chelsea Football Club* (2009) International Sports Law Review 1, SLR1-9, FA Regulatory Commission, 12 December 2008.
2 Some forms of abuse may also lead to criminal proceedings: see for example *R v John Terry*, Westminster Magistrates' Court, 13 July 2012.

2.7 There have also been a number of cases involving challenges to the way in which the sports governing body has dealt with cheating,[1] or race- or match-fixing,[2] or a breach of playing rules particular to the sport.[3]

1 See for example *World Motor Sport Council v Renault, Briatore, Symonds* 21 September 2009; *Smith v Nairn Golf Club* [2007] CSOH 136, 2007 SLT 909, GWD 25-420; *European Rugby Cup v Williams* (2009) 4 International Sports Law Review 122, ERC Appeal Committee, 24 August 2009; *European Rugby Cup v Richards, Brennan, Chapman and Harlequins* (2010) 1 International Sports Law Review SLR9-43, ERC Appeal Committee; and *Brennan v Health Professions Council* [2011] EWHC 41 (Admin), (2011) 119 BMLR 1 (QBD Admin).
2 See for example *McKeown v British Horseracing Authority* [2010] EWHC 508 (QB), 12 March 2010.
3 See for example *Briggs v Professional Combat Sports Commission* [2012] WASAT 57, 27 March 2012 and [2011] WASAT 30, 18 February 2011.

(c)   Bringing the sport into disrepute or breach of specific rules of conduct

2.8   Misconduct does not always take place on the pitch. Most sports governing bodies have power to discipline players or other participants for actions that bring the sport into disrepute,[1] or for breaching their specific rules of conduct. Internal decisions sanctioning players or other participants for such misconduct off the pitch may be the subject of challenge on similar grounds to decisions in respect of misconduct on it. The type of conduct that falls into this category is obviously again wide, and ranges from comments on social media to involvement in criminal actions.

1 General rules prohibiting bringing the sport into disrepute are open to criticism as being insufficiently certain and governing bodies must take care not to misuse them. Roy Keane was sanctioned by The FA for bringing the sport into disrepute when he admitted in his autobiography that he had deliberately set out to injure Manchester City's Alf-Inge Haaland, in revenge for a perceived slight three years previously. The sanction was for writing about it, as opposed to the original offence, and it was reported at the time that Roy Keane considered relying on his right to freedom of speech to resist The FA proceeding against him in respect of his admission. In the event he did not do so.

2.9   Such challenges include players refusing to train or play,[1] participants breaching specific rules covering them or acting with a conflict of interest,[2] and participants disobeying an instruction of, or inappropriately criticising, the governing body. A growing number of cases involve participants being disciplined for inappropriate comments on social media.[3]

1 See for example *Currie v Barton* Scott J 26 March 1987; CA 11 February 1988, Times, 12 February 1988.
2 See for example *Bland v Sparkes (for the Amateur Swimming Association)* (1999) Times, 17 December, CA.
3 The development of social media has led to a significant number of players being disciplined for comments on Twitter or Facebook, both in relation to governing bodies and to other players. The FA has fined players such as Rio Ferdinand and Ashley Cole significant sums for such comments, both arising out of the criminal and disciplinary proceedings against John Terry for allegedly racially abusing Anton Ferdinand. In August 2014, The FA revealed that that since 2011 it had imposed fines totalling around £350,000 for social media-related offences. The highest fine to date has been £90,000, imposed on Ashley Cole for using foul language on Twitter. As yet no challenge to such disciplinary proceedings has gone beyond the internal appeal processes.

2.10   Such challenges have also included participants being convicted of or charged with criminal offences,[1] or giving inaccurate evidence to the police or a court.[2] They also include breach of rules against inappropriate sexual relationships between coaches and athletes, as well as of child protection rules.

1 See for example *Colgan v Kennel Club*, Cooke J, 26 October 2001; and *Fallon v Horseracing Regulatory Authority* [2006] EWHC 1898 (QB), 28 July 2006, [2006] All ER (D) 427.
2 One of the charges made against the football players' agent in the *Stretford* litigation (*FA v Stretford* FA Appeal Board (Peter Griffiths QC); *FA v Stretford (Disciplinary Proceedings)*, 22 December 2008).

(d)   Assumption of exorbitant jurisdiction

2.11   In most instances, any challenge is to the way that a decision in respect of a particular player is taken (for example on grounds of breach of the rules, procedural unfairness, taking into account the wrong considerations or unreasonableness), or to the validity of the rules on the basis of which the decision is taken (for example on the grounds of restraint of trade, or breach of competition or free movement law). In addition, however, there have been challenges to the appropriateness of the particular governing body assuming jurisdiction over the matter at all, on the basis that the matter is properly dealt with by a different body.[1] There have also been challenges to the assumption of jurisdiction by *any* sport governing body.[2] A challenge may be based on the individual circumstances of a particular case, or as to the validity of rules assuming jurisdiction over a class of people.

1 See for example *Roach v FA* [2001] 9(3) SATLJ 26.
2 See for example *Davis v Carew-Pole* [1956] 2 All ER 524.

(e)   Denial of access to the sport at all

2.12   Apart from suspending participants for disciplinary offences, addressed above, sports governing bodies also control access to the sport in the first place. They make decisions which have a fundamental effect on the ability of the player to pursue his recreation, or his business, in the way that he chooses. The decisions are generally made in the context of an application for a licence or other authorisation to take part, and are often based on the perceived lack of fulfilment of entry criteria (such as health and physical fitness,[1] passing an examination,[2] or payment of a bond). Challenges have been mounted to such decisions, on the basis that the refusal of access was discriminatory,[3] in breach of contract, procedurally unfair, and/or in unreasonable restraint of trade or breach of the competition law rules.[4]

1 *Wright v Jockey Club*, Sir Haydn Tudor Evans 15 May 1995 (1995) Times, 16 June. See also *Hall v Victorian Amateur Football Association* [1999] VCAT AD 30, [1999] 7(2) SATLJ 66; and *Keefe v McInnes* [1991] 2 VR 235.
2 *Fraser v Professional Golfers' Association* [2008] CSIH 53.
3 *Nagle v Feilden* [1966] 2 QB 633, CA.
4 *McInnes v Onslow-Fane* [1978] 1 WLR 1520; *Phoenix v Fédération Internationale de l'Automobile and Formula One Management* [2002] EWHC 1028 (Ch).

(f)   Denial of access to a particular competition or level of participation; ineligibility and non-selection

2.13   Once a player has become a participant in the sport, he may nevertheless be prevented from taking part in a particular competition or from playing at a particular representative level or for a particular team, or may simply not be selected. The rules, and decisions, of sports governing bodies in this context may also be susceptible of review, although the courts have been slower to intervene in this context than in others, at least when the decision relates to an evaluation of the player's standard of performance.[1] Where the grounds for exclusion are technical rather than performance-related, the courts may be more prepared to intervene.[2]

1 *Cowley v Heatley*, Browne-Wilkinson V-C, 22 July 1986, (1986) Times, 24 July.
2 *US Swimming v FINA* CAS Atlanta 96/001, award dated 22 July 1996, *Digest of CAS Awards 1986–1998*, (Staempfli) p 377; *Andrade v Cape Verde NOC* CAS Atlanta 96/002 and 005, awards dated 27 July 1996 and 1 August 1996, *Digest of CAS Awards 1986–1998* (Staempfli), pp 389 and 397.

2.14   The courts or arbitral tribunals are also prepared to intervene where an improper restriction has been placed on the player for other reasons, for example a requirement that a player only play for a particular team,[1] prohibitions on grounds of nationality, ineligibility due to doping although the prescribed anti-doping sanction has been served,[2] conditions imposed on permission to play outside the governing body's jurisdiction,[3] or where a player or other participant has been improperly discriminated against,[4] or where exclusion has been arbitrary or procedurally unfair.

1 *Hall v Victorian Football League* [1982] VicRp 6, [1982] VR 64, 58 FLR 180.
2 *British Olympic Association v World Anti-Doping Agency*, CAS 2011/A/2658, award dated 30 April 2012.
3 *Blackler v New Zealand Rugby Football League* [1968] NZLR 547.
4 *British Judo Association v Petty* [1981] ICR 660; *Campagnolo v Benalla and District Football League Inc* [2009] VSC 228, 11 June 2009; *Singh v Football Association, Football League and others* [2002] 1 SLJ p 87 *Martin v Professional Game Match Officials Ltd*, Employment Tribunal, April 13 2010; *Pistorius v International Association of Athletics Federations* CAS, 16 May 2008.

2.15   Further, the courts or arbitral tribunals are likely to be prepared to intervene where the question is essentially contractual[1] or possibly where a legitimate expectation of being able to compete or to be selected has arisen.[2] Governing bodies' decisions precluding others, for example journalists, from having access to particular events may also be the subject of challenge.[3]

1 *Hilton v National Ice Skating Association of the United Kingdom Ltd*, March 2009 QBD (2009) International Sports Law Review 2, SLR75–78.
2 *Jacob v Irish Amateur Rowing Union* [2008] IEHC 196, 10 June 2008, [2008] 4 IR 731.
3 *Rubython v FIA*, QB Gray J, 6 March 2003, [2003] EWHC 1355 (QB).

(g)   Challenge to the outcome of an event or an official's on-pitch decision

2.16   Just as the courts are reluctant to intervene when a player seeks to challenge a decision not to allow him or her to participate at a particular level, they are unlikely to allow a player to challenge the outcome of a particular event, or an official's decision during that event.[1] There may however be circumstances where challenges are possible, in the light of the rules governing the playing of the sport and the ability of the governing body to alter the result by reference to a failure to comply with those rules,[2] and it may also be possible to challenge the *consequences* which flow from a particular action of an official, as opposed to the action itself. Fraud by an official may in some circumstances form a basis for challenge.

1 *Conway v Irish Tug of War Association, Tug of War International Federation and others* [2011] IEHC 245, 7 June 2011; *Mendy v IABA* CAS Atlanta 96/006, award dated 1 August 1996, *Digest of CAS Awards 1986–1998*.
2 *Neykova v FISA and IOC* CAS Sydney 00/012, award dated 29 September 2000, *Digest of CAS Awards II 1998–2000*, p 674. An FA Rule K Interim Arbitral Tribunal considered the approach to take in respect to an application to suspend a three match ban against West Ham's Andy Carroll whilst the Club challenged the red card decision in *West Ham v The FA*, FA Rule K Arbitral Tribunal (Nicholas Stewart QC), 7 February 2014.

B   ACTIONS AFFECTING A CLASS OF INDIVIDUAL PARTICIPANTS

2.17   The second way in which the actions of sports governing bodies affect individual participants is when the sports governing body adopts rules that affect an entire class of individual participants, whether by requiring them to take particular steps, or to have particular qualifications, or by limiting their freedom of action. The lawfulness of the rule or rules themselves may be challenged.

(a) Player transfer rules

2.18   The first example of rules affecting all players are the transfer rules that control whether, when, and on what terms players can move from one club to another. These rules involve the supplementation (and in some respects circumvention) of national employment law by the operation of a registration system by the national governing body, in parallel to the national governing bodies in other states. Such systems preclude a player playing for a club unless he or she is registered to it, with the transfer of the registration being subject to conditions, in particular the payment of a fee to the club that currently holds the registration in return for releasing it. This provides clubs around the world with contractual stability so that they can build a team without fear that players will leave suddenly, and enables them to secure compensation for their development of players (aiding competitive balance and ensuring that clubs are not disincentivised from investing in youth development). However it also prevents players from moving when they want to do so, including at one time, but no longer, even when they were out of contract.

2.19   Sports governing bodies have had to adapt their transfer systems over the years as they have faced a number of successive challenges on the basis of restraint of trade, the EU free movement rules and competition law.[1] The challenges have not only been to the validity of the extent of restriction on movement at all, but also to the operation of transfer windows, ie periods outside which no transfers are allowed.[2]

1 *Eastham v Newcastle United and the FA* [1964] Ch 413; *Union Royal Belge des Sociétés de Football Association v Bosman* (C-415/93) [1995] ECR I-4292.
2 *Lehtonen v Fédération Royale Belge des Sociétés de Basketball* (C-176-96) [2000] ECR I–2681.

2.20   Notwithstanding broad agreement between football's governing bodies and the regulatory authorities on a fixed and compliant system,[1] there remains the possibility of further challenge to aspects of the system. FIFPro, the international football player's association, has brought a (pending) competition law challenge to the entire FIFA football transfer rule system.[2]

1 Agreement was reached between FIFA, UEFA and the European Commission, following the initiation of a competition investigation, on new transfer rules (the FIFA Regulations on the Status and Transfer of Players). See European Commission White Paper on Sport COM (2007) 391 Final and accompanying Staff Working Document SEC (2007) 935, and the statement to European Parliament by Viviane Reding, EU Commissioner, on the reform of the FIFA rules governing transfers [2001] 9(1) SATLJ 80; McGrath [2001] 9(2) SATLJ 109; Parker, Lane and Gibson [2001] 2 ISLR 156; Bennett [2001] 9(3) SATLJ 180.
2 See, 'FIFPro legal action against FIFA transfer system', 18 September 2015, (http://www.fifpro.org/en/news/fifpro-takes-legal-action-against-fifa-transfer-system).

(b) Foreign player and home grown player rules

2.21   Rules have also been imposed limiting the number of foreign players that a club can register, which impact on a player's ability to find a new employer as well as on the club's ability to choose whom to employ. Such rules have also developed over the years as they have faced a number of successive challenges in the courts on the basis of the EU free movement rules and competition law, and are now unlawful in respect of EU players[1] and players from countries with an equal treatment agreement with the EU.

1 *Union Royal Belge des Sociétés de Football Association v Bosman* [1995] ECR I-4292.

2.22   In contrast to foreign player rules, 'home grown player' rules requiring a specified proportion of players registered by a club to have been developed by clubs in the same association, do not discriminate directly on grounds of nationality because many home grown players come originally from abroad. Whereas direct discrimination on grounds of nationality cannot be justified, indirect discrimination may be.

(c) Salary caps

2.23   Sports governing bodies have sought to limit the amount that players can be paid, through the introduction of salary caps, in the hope of holding back spiralling costs and maintaining competitive balance.[1] Such caps can take many forms, from a hard cap (which cannot be departed from in any circumstances) on what any individual can be paid, through a cap on total squad salaries, to a soft cap which may be exceeded in limited circumstances or breach of which triggers pre-set financial consequences.

1 Salary caps are operated in the UK in rugby union, rugby league and basketball, and in European leagues in basketball and ice hockey. The salary cap in rugby was recently the subject of challenge, withdrawn before trial.

(d) Restrictions on taking part in other competitions

2.24   Sports governing bodies often attempt to preserve for themselves the sole ability to regulate the sport and to organise events. In order to prevent the development of rival organisations, they have sought to tie players in by prohibiting them from competing in other events, on pain of exclusion from 'official' events, and such rules have been the subject of challenge.[1]

1 *Greig v Insole (for the TCCB)* [1978] 1 WLR 302 (the court held in unreasonable restraint of trade the rules of the TCCB banning any player who wanted to compete under its auspices from taking part in competitions organised by any competing organisation, in that case Kerry Packer's cricket world series); see also *Wilson v British Darts Organisation Ltd* 95/NJ/1687 (Potts J); *FIA Formula One Championship* [2001] OJ C169/5. In October 2015, following a complaint by two Dutch ice speed skaters, Mark Tuitert and Niels Kerstholt, the European Commission announced that it had opened a formal antitrust investigation into International Skating Union (ISU) rules that permanently ban skaters from competitions such as the Winter Olympics and the ISU World and European Championships if they take part in events not approved by the ISU. The EU Commissioner in charge of competition policy said the Commission would investigate whether the ISU rules were being abused to enforce a monopoly over the organisation of sporting events or otherwise restrict competition because '*Athletes can only compete at the highest level for a limited number of years, so there must be good reasons for preventing them to take part in events.*' See European Commission Press Release, Antitrust: Commission opens formal investigation into International Skating Union's eligibility rules, Brussels, 5 October 2015 (http://europa.eu/rapid/press-release_IP-15-5771_en.htm).

2.25   Such practices may be more subtle than an express ban. The governing body may require that its permission is sought, or may require that players enter its competition by a certain time, or may prohibit a player playing in a rival event in the same time window or within a certain distance of an 'official event', or may require agreement in advance that if players reach a certain stage in a competition they will return the following year, or may accord greater status to its own matches for the purposes of a ranking system.[1] Such arrangements may well have a different aim, in the perceived interests of the sport, but nevertheless be criticised by players and rival organisations affected, as having the effect of excluding rival events.[2]

1 Some of which were discussed in *Hendry v World Professional Billiards and Snooker Association*, Lloyd J 5 October 2001, [2001] All ER (D) 71, [2002] 1 ISLR SLR-1.
2 The actions of the Asian Tour to prevent golfers playing on it from also playing on the OneAsia Tour were found to be in unreasonable restraint of trade in *Pilkadaris v Asian Tour (Tournament Players Division) Pte Ltd* [2012] SGHC 236 HC Sing, 27 November 2012.

(e)   Licensing systems and qualification criteria in general

2.26   As is clear from the challenges that have been brought by players when an individual decision affects them, players and other participants have often at the same time challenged the validity of the rules as a whole. Just as challenges can be brought to the validity of the doping rules across the board, so too challenges can be brought to the validity of licensing systems[1] and qualification criteria[2] governing access to participate in a sport or at a particular level.

1 See for example *Piau (Laurent) v Commission of the European Communities* (T-193/02) CFI 26 January 2005, [2005] ECR II-209 confirmed by the ECJ 23 February 2006 (C-171/05 P) [2006] ECR I-37.
2 See for example *London Welsh v Rugby Football Union, Newcastle Falcons intervening* (RFU Arbitration 29 June 2012, James Dingemans QC, Ian Mill QC and Tim Ward QC); *Park Promotion Ltd (t/a Pontypool Rugby Football Club) v Welsh Rugby Union Ltd* [2012] EWHC 1919 (QB), 11 July 2012.

C   FAILURE TO TAKE ACTION IN RELATION TO INDIVIDUAL PARTICIPANTS

2.27   The third way in which a sports governing body may affect individual participants is by *failing* to address a particular issue, or to address it adequately. Where personal injury to the player has resulted, challenges in the form of claims for damages have been brought.[1] A challenge could also be brought to require a governing body to act: a particular example of this is where a governing body suspends a participant pending a hearing, but fails to pursue disciplinary proceedings or to do so swiftly enough. An injunction may be available to require the governing body to convene a hearing.[2] Attempts have also been made to challenge the adequacy of disciplinary action against a rival participant, where this affects results, promotion or relegation.

1 A few cases have addressed the failure to deal with an issue in the rules: see, *Agar v Hyde* [2000] HCA 41, [2000] 201 CLR 552; *Watson v BBBC* [2000] EWCA Civ 2116; [2001] QB 1134; *Fox v Ministry of Defence* [2002] EWCA Civ 435; *In Re: National Football League Players' Concussion Injury Litigation No. 2*:12-md-02323 (E.D. Pa.).
2 Such an injunction was granted by the High Court to require British Gymnastics to proceed with disciplinary proceedings against a judge whom it had suspended but had not disciplined after discovering that he had been the subject of a sexual offence complaint in respect of alleged events 30 years before, outside the sport, which the police had not pursued at the time of the suspension.

D   ACTIONS AFFECTING SPECIFIC CLUBS

2.28   In team sports, the national associations or governing bodies are generally made up of the clubs, and there is generally (although not always) a contract between them on the basis of the rules of the association (or some of those rules). Action taken by a sports governing body against a specific club may be similar to action[1] taken against individual players and may be challenged, on the same bases as already discussed above,[2] by the club affected.[3] In addition, action taken by the sports governing body may also involve particular aspects of regulation specific to clubs that give rise to challenge. Further, there may be proceedings by members against the administrators of the governing body in respect of matters not directly connected with the administration of the sport.[4]

1 For example, the club or team was amongst those charged with misconduct on the pitch or track, see: *Football Association v Evra and Chelsea Football Club* (2009) International Sports Law Review 1, SLR1-9, *World Motor Sport Council v Renault, Briatore, Symonds* 21 September 2009; *European Rugby Cup v Richards, Brennan, Chapman and Harlequins* (2010) International Sports Law Review 1, SLR9-43, ERC Appeal Committee.

2 See for example *Enderby Town Football Club v FA* [1971] Ch 591, [1970] 3 WLR 1021; *St Johnstone Football Club Ltd v Scottish Football Association* 1965 SLT 171; *Anderlecht v UEFA* CAS 98/185, *Digest of CAS Awards II 1998–2000*, p 469.

3 In *Sheffield United v FAPL*, decision of FA Arbitration Panel dated 3 July 2007, [2007] ISLR-SLR 77. Sheffield challenged the FAPL disciplinary body's decision not to deduct points from West Ham United for admitted breaches of FAPL rules in the way that it secured the services in the 2006/2007 season of the Argentine internationals Carlos Tevez and Javier Mascerano without paying a transfer fee. A points deduction would have meant that West Ham, instead of Sheffield, would be relegated from the Premier League. Fulham were also allowed to join the claim as the decision not to deduct points affected their league placement and thus the money they would receive from central income. See also *Park Promotion Ltd (t/a Pontypool Rugby Football Club) v Welsh Rugby Union Ltd* [2012] EWHC 1919 (QB), 11 July 2012.

4 For example, in relation to the application of funds. See *Baker v Jones* [1954] 2 All ER 553. In *Re Crystal Palace Football Club Ltd* [2004] EWHC 2113 (Ch) it was held that the sale of a single share in the Football League by a company that ran a football club did not disentitle it to monetary awards accrued prior to the sale.

(a) Ban from competition on grounds of a club's ownership

2.29 Governing bodies may seek to prevent or restrict the common ownership of clubs participating in the same league or tournament.[1] They may also impose and apply fit and proper persons tests, controlling who may own a club.[2]

1 *AEK Athens and Slavia Prague v UEFA* CAS arbitration 98/200 interim decision 17 July 1998, final decision 20 August 1999, *Digest of CAS Awards II 1998–2000*, p 38 and in [2001] 1 ISLR 122.

2 A rule, the application of which is a subject of much debate in the context of football, following a series of acquisitions of clubs by owners abroad, and in the light of the sometimes complex corporate structures adopted, as in the case of Leeds United FC at the time of *Leeds Utd and Rotherham Utd v Football League*, decision of FA Arbitral Tribunal (Sir Phillip Otton, Peter Leaver QC, Peter Cadman) dated 1 May 2008. In 2013, Laurence Bassini, the former owner of Watford, was banned by a Football League FDC panel from holding a position of authority at a football club after being found guilty of breaches of Football League rules. In 2015, Massimo Cellino, the Chairman of Leeds United FC was banned twice by the Football League (on the second occasion subject to a stay during the appeal process) from being an owner or director of a football club, following tax evasion convictions in Italy.

(b) Refusal of permission to a club to play home matches abroad

2.30 Clubs affected have also challenged governing bodies' rules requiring their member clubs to play their home matches within the geographical boundaries of the country of the governing body.[1] Governing bodies in second countries have also sought to stop clubs playing matches there, pursuant to their involvement in a foreign league.[2]

1 *Excelsior Mouscron* decision, IP/99/965, dated 9 December 1999.

2 *Newport v Football Association of Wales* interlocutory hearing Jacob J [1995] 2 All ER 87, trial Blackburne J 12 April 1995.

(c) Refusal of permission to a club to move home stadium or to change name

2.31 Some governing bodies restrict the ability of member clubs to move home stadia within the relevant country, for example away from its original conurbation[1] or where to do so would adversely affect a neighbouring club.[2] Similarly, a governing body may have a rule that restricts a member club's choice to change its playing name.[3]

1 The homeless Wimbledon Football Club successfully challenged before an FA Arbitration Panel the Football League's refusal of its request to be allowed to establish a home ground in Milton Keynes. The club maintained that the League was acting in unreasonable restraint of trade, because the rationale for the ban was out of proportion to the damage to the club, and that the League had not approached its decision in the right way. The FA Arbitration Panel held (29 January 2002) that the League's decision was flawed on procedural grounds, and that the matter should be remitted to it for a new decision, which would have to be proportionate. The League referred the matter to an FA Commission to take a decision in its place. The FA Commission decided in May 2002 that the club's grounds for moving were sound and justified, and that it would not be appropriate for the League to restrain the club from moving.

2 In 2011, the Olympic Park Legacy Company undertook a tendering process for a lease of the Olympic Stadium after the 2012 Games. West Ham FC obtained permission from the FA Premier League to move ground, bid for the lease, and was successful. Tottenham Hotspur FC (which had also bid) and Leyton Orient FC (which had not) both objected to the way in which West Ham's bid had been made and accepted. Leyton also objected to the FAPL's granting of permission under the FAPL Rules to West Ham to move to a site so close to Leyton's ground, which would undercut its fan base. In *Leyton Orient v FAPL* FA Rule K arbitration, the club contended that the FAPL had acted in breach of its own rules, which provided that permission should not be given to move to a new site if it would adversely affect another club in the immediate vicinity of the new site. Leyton Orient withdrew its objection in 2014, after reaching a confidential settlement with the FA.

3 See *Hull City FC v The Football Association*, 23 February 2015, FA Rule K Arbitral Panel (Sir Stanley Burnton, Tim Kerr QC, Nicholas Stewart QC). The Council of The FA refused permission for the club to change its playing name from Hull City to Hull Tigers. The club challenged the decision on several grounds, but ultimately focussed on procedural challenges to the decision. The Arbitral Panel quashed the decision on grounds of bias/procedural fairness and held that the club was entitled to make a fresh application to be considered by the Council if it so chose.

(d) Promotion and relegation rules, and effect of points deductions

2.32 Clubs may be seriously affected by the application to them of the governing body's promotion and relegation rules, or by sanctions which affect promotion and relegation. Challenges may arise in circumstances where rule changes affect a particular club's prospects of staying in the top division, the most notable being reorganisations where the size of the top division is reduced,[1] where a club fails additional criteria for promotion set by the sports governing body which go beyond where the club finishes in the table,[2] and where relegation may be brought about by deductions of points as a result of a club's breach of the rules.[3]

1 *Park Promotion Ltd (t/a Pontypool Rugby Football Club) v Welsh Rugby Union Ltd* [2012] EWHC 1919 (QB), 11 July 2012. See also *Rotherham and English Second Division Rugby Ltd v English First Division Rugby Ltd, English Rugby Partnership Ltd and the RFU*, Ferris J 16 August 1999, [2000] 1 ISLR 33.

2 In *London Welsh v Rugby Football Union, Newcastle Falcons intervening* (RFU Arbitration 29 June 2012, James Dingemans QC, Ian Mill QC and Tim Ward QC), the club successfully challenged the lawfulness under EU and UK competition law of the RFU's decision to refuse it promotion to the Premiership on the grounds that it did not have 'primacy of tenure' at its ground).

3 *R v Eastern Counties Rugby Union, ex p Basildon Rugby Club*, 10 September 1987; *Sheffield United v FAPL* decision of FA Arbitration Panel of 3 July 2007 [2007] ISLR-SLR 77.

(e) Administration and the football creditors rule

2.33   Sports governing bodies may have rules imposing a points deduction upon a club going into administration and rules on the payment of creditors. The imposition of such points deductions have been subject to challenge.[1] Clubs[2] and HM Revenue & Customs[3] have repeatedly sought, but so far failed, to persuade the Courts to declare illegal the 'football creditors rule', which prioritises particular classes of creditors, such as players and other clubs, over other unsecured creditors when a football club becomes insolvent. However, in 2011 and then again in 2013 a Commons Select Committee demanded that The FA repeal it, and threatened legislative intervention if it failed to do so.

1 See for example *Leeds United 2007 Ltd v Football League Ltd* [2008] BCC 701, FA Rule K Arbitration, 1 May 2008.
2 *Exeter City v The Football Conference* [2004] EWHC 2304 (in some databases 831), [2004] 1 WLR 2910; *Fulham Football Club (1987) Ltd v Richards* [2011] EWCA Civ 855, [2012] Ch 333.
3 *Commissioners of Inland Revenue v Wimbledon* [2004] EWHC 1020 (ChD), [2004] EWCA Civ 65; *Revenue and Customs Commissioners v Portsmouth City Football Club Ltd (In Administration)* also known as: *Portsmouth City Football Club Ltd (In Administration), Re* [2010] EWHC 2013 (Ch), [2011] BCC 149, [2010] BPIR 1123; *Revenue and Customs Commissioners v Football League Ltd* [2012] EWHC 1372 (Ch).

E   ACTIONS AFFECTING ALL CLUBS

2.34   In the same way as a class of individual participants can be affected by a sports governing body's actions, a class of clubs may be affected. Again, the effects are often similar, but there are particular types of rules that especially affect clubs and that have been or are likely to be the subject of challenge.

(a) Collective selling, and restrictions on exploitation, of commercial rights

2.35   The collective selling by the sports governing body of the rights to broadcast matches may adversely affect particular clubs, although it helps others. The most successful clubs might be able to command a greater price for their home matches alone than their share of the income from the sale of all matches. Equally the individual sale of other commercial rights such as sponsorship, ticket and travel and corporate hospitality (especially in the context of tournaments) might be more lucrative for some clubs than collective sale. While in most contexts clubs have been content to maintain collective selling in the interests of the maintenance of the competition, some have sought to challenge the approach.[1] The governing body may also seek to impose other restrictions on the freedom of the club to exploit its rights, for example in relation to sponsorship or advertising.[2]

1 *Williams and Cardiff RFC v Pugh*, later known as *Williams and Cardiff RFC v WRU (IRB intervening)* [1999] Eu LR 195; *English First Division Rugby Complaint to the European Commission against the Rugby Football Union and the International Rugby Board* Case No IV/36.994 (March 1998); *Re an Agreement between the FA Premier League* [2000] EMLR 78, [1999] UKCLR 258 (Restrictive Practices Court July 1999).
2 A dispute arose in May 2002 between Arsenal and The FA, focusing on The FA's requirements that clubs playing home ties in The FA Cup give up the prime stadium advertising space to The FA's sponsors. In *Hendry v WPBSA*, [2001] All ER (D) 71, [2002] 1 ISLR SLR-1, [2002] 1 ISLR SLR-1, one of the rules upheld by the court was a rule restricting the number of logos that could be worn by a player: the rule was held to be necessary in the light of broadcasting restrictions.

(b)   Calendar issues and loyalty arrangements in side agreements

2.36   In many sports, a conflict arises in relation to when club and international matches are to be played, and this is often dealt with in the rules, or by a side agreement.[1] Some governing bodies have sought to impose loyalty arrangements in side agreements aimed at keeping clubs in their (and out of another organisation's) competitions for a defined period.[2]

1 See *Premier Rugby v RFU* [2006] EWHC 2068 (Comm).
2 *Williams and Cardiff RFC v Pugh*, later known as *Williams and Cardiff RFC v WRU (IRB intervening)* [1999] Eu LR 195.

(c)   Financial fair play rules

2.37   Sports governing bodies may set rules restricting the extent to which clubs may spend more than they earn in football revenue, which excludes non-commercial financial injections from owners that allow some clubs to outspend others, damaging competitive balance. These rules are regarded by some as controversial and are subject to various legal challenges, none of which has yet succeeded.[1]

1 UEFA's Financial Fair Play rules have been challenged in the Belgian Court of First Instance by Daniel Striani, an Italian national registered to work as a players' agent in Belgium. Mr Striani alleges that the rules violate EU competition law and infringe the fundamental freedoms of free movement of capital, workers and services. In June 2015, the Belgian Court made a preliminary reference to the Court of Justice of the EU and granted interim relief (in the form of a prohibition on UEFA extending its existing restrictions), however the reference was rejected and the injunction lifted. The challenge is ongoing. See also *QPR v The Football League* (FDC Arbitral Panel, ongoing).

(d)   Third party influence and investment in players

2.38   Sports governing bodies may impose rules that preclude a club from allowing a third party influence over its decisions. This has typically arisen where a player is registered by the club but the club has obligations to a third party, which has provided funding for the acquisition of the player in return for a right to a share in any future proceeds of the transfer of his registration,[1] as to whether, when or to what club the player is re-sold, or as to whether he plays.[2] Some sports governing bodies have gone further, and outlawed such forms of investment altogether. On 1 January 2015, FIFA introduced a ban (subject to transitional provisions) on all agreements entitling a third party to participate in compensation payable in relation to the future transfer of a player.[3]

1 Often referred to as 'economic rights' in contrast to the 'federative rights' held by the club in his registration.
2 The circumstances in which West Ham acquired Carlos Tevez's registration involved the investors acquiring third party influence over the club in breach of the FA Premier League's rules, and the club was fined in *FAPL v West Ham United* FAPL Disciplinary Commission, decision dated 27 April 2007. On the consequences and adequacy of this penalty, see *Sheffield United v FAPL* FAPL Rule S Arbitration; *Sheffield United v FAPL*, 13 July 2007 Smith J Comm Ct; *Sheffield United v West Ham* FA Rule K arbitration, 18 April 2008 and 18 September 2008; [2008] EWHC 2855 (Comm), [2009] 1 Lloyd's Rep. 167, [2008] 2 CLC 741, (2008) Sport and the Law Journal vol 16 iss 2 SLJR 4; *Fulham Football Club v West Ham United Football Club* FA Rule Arbitration 2011 International Sports Law Review 1, SLR1-7.
3 FIFA Circ no. 1464 (22 December 2014); FIFA Regulations on the Status and Transfer of Players, article 18ter, http://www.fpf.pt/Portals/0/Documentos/Centro%20Documentacao/FIFA/

regulationsonthestatusandtransfeofplayersapril2015e_neutral.pdf. The validity of arrangements where investors have an economic interest in the proceeds of the sale of the registration of a player, but no third party influence, was addressed in *Rio Football Services v Sevilla* [2010] EWHC 2446 (QB). See also *FA v Queen's Park Rangers FC (Faurlin)*, FA Disciplinary Hearing, February and May 2011.

(e)   Player release rules

2.39   Governing bodies often impose rules on clubs requiring them to release players for international duty, which clubs may perceive to be too onerous and therefore seek to overturn[1] or to disobey.[2]

1 In *Williams and Cardiff RFC v Pugh*, later known as *Williams and Cardiff RFC v WRU (IRB intervening)* [1999] Eu LR 195, the club also challenged rugby union's player release rules. The EFDR clubs did likewise in their complaint to the European Commission: *English First Division Rugby Complaint to the European Commission against the Rugby Football Union and the International Rugby Board* Case No IV/36.994 (March 1998), which settled without any decision. Toulon is currently seeking to challenge World Rugby's player release rules in the French Courts.

2 In *Welsh Rugby Union Ltd v Cardiff Blues* [2008] EWHC 3399 (QB) the WRU secured an injunction against the Region requiring it to comply with the Player Release rules.

F   ACTIONS AFFECTING OTHER SPORTS GOVERNING BODIES

2.40   The actions of one sports governing body may also affect other sports governing bodies. Disputes can arise between international associations and national associations in circumstances ranging from the international association's perception that the national association wrongly failed to charge or acquitted or treated too leniently a player charged with a doping or match fixing offence[1] or wrongly allowed its clubs to breach international rules,[2] to an international association's refusal to admit a national association to membership,[3] or a decision in relation to where an event should be held or what status it should be given,[4] or to the provision of a place in an international competition to a club from a particular country,[5] or to a decision on the eligibility of a player to play for the national association,[6] or to the number of places to be afforded to an NOC for the Olympics.[7]

1 *IAAF v UKA and Walker* IAAF Arbitral Award 20 August 2000 [2001] 4 ISLR 264 (arbitration proceedings, in which the IAAF challenged UKA's clearing of the athlete and which, before the award, gave rise to the *Walker v UKA and IAAF* litigation, Toulson J 3 July 2000, Hallett J 25 July 2000.

2 In 1998, the International Rugby Board brought disciplinary proceedings against the RFU and the WRU for failing to stop the EFDR clubs playing 'unofficial' friendlies against the then renegade Welsh clubs, Cardiff and Swansea.

3 *Reel v Holder (for IAAF)* [1979] 1 WLR 1252; affd [1981] 1 WLR 1226, CA (the Taiwanese athletics governing body obtained a declaration that the IAAF was not entitled to expel it from membership). A range of sports governing bodies from Gibraltar have challenged the refusal to admit them to membership of the corresponding international sports governing bodies. CAS has reached several decisions in favour of the Gibraltar Football Association, as a result of which Gibraltar was accepted as a UEFA member on 24 May 2013. CAS heard an appeal against FIFA's continued refusal to admit the association in May 2015.

4 The 2003 Rugby World Cup was originally granted to Australia and New Zealand together, with Australia as host Union and New Zealand as a sub-host. The tournament was subsequently granted to Australia alone, but the NZRFU ultimately did not challenge the decision. Following allegations that FIFA's decision to award the 2022 World Cup to Qatar was procured by bribery, unsuccessful bidders are reported to be considering legal action. A competition law challenge was brought to the ATP's decision as to the status of a Hamburg tennis event.

5 The Football League complained to the European Commission about UEFA's removal of a UEFA Cup place for the winner of the League Cup. The spot was restored before the matter progressed: see [1998] 6(1) SATLJ 36.

6 *Tonga National Rugby League v Rugby League International Federation* [2008] NSWSC 1173, Supreme Court of New South Wales, 27 October 2008.
7 The Italian Canoeing Federation and Olympic Committee, joined by their British equivalents, are challenging the International Canoeing Federation's decision as to the allocation of kayak places at the Rio Olympics. The successful federations and NOCs of France, Denmark and Russia, the places allocated to which the appellants seek to take, are joined as respondents.

2.41　　Disputes may arise between an international governing body with a specific narrow responsibility, and another governing body.[1] They may also arise between two national associations from different nations.[2] Disputes also arise between different sports governing bodies within a particular country.[3] Disputes between governing bodies are not confined to the playing and organisation of the sport, but extend to disputes in relation to commercial exploitation.[4]

1 *Dwain Chambers v British Olympic Association* [2008] EWHC 2028 (QB), (2008) Sport and Law Journal vol 16 iss 2 (2008) SLJR 4); CAS 2011/A/2658, *British Olympic Association v World Anti-Doping Agency*, 30 April 2012.
2 *Irish Football Association v Football Association of Ireland* CAS award dated 27 September 2010, (2011) International Sports Law Review 2, SLR151-162; *Fédération Luxembourgeoise de Boxe v British Board of Boxing Control* (2012 High Court, not decided, the FLB brought a competition law challenge alleging that the BBBC acted unlawfully to exclude it from the market for sanctioning bouts, by threatening to discipline those involved in an FLB bout in London between Hayes and Chisora, who were not licensed by the BBBC).
3 *R v Football Association Ltd, ex p Football League* [1993] 2 All ER 833, [1992] COD 52 (unsuccessful attempt by the Football League to challenge the decision to establish the Premier League); *Alwyn Treherne (for the Welsh Amateur Boxing Federation) v Amateur Boxing Association of England* [2002] EWCA Civ 381, [2002] All ER (D) 144 (Mar) (the WABF unsuccessfully challenged the ABAE's refusal to allow its clubs to affiliate with the ABAE); *Great Britain Rhythmic Gymnastics Group v British Amateur Gymnastics Association* (2012) International Sports Law Review 2, SLR23-30, (Association had unlawfully departed from the applicable Policy when it decided that the Group had not reached a sufficiently high standard to be entered for the 2012 Olympics).
4 For example, the dispute between the Celtic Unions and the Rugby Football Union as to the value that should be placed, for accounting purposes, on the element of the RFU's broadcasting contract with BSkyB relating to the Five Nations Championship, which was resolved by expert determination, as required by the terms of the Five Nations Accord.

G　ACTIONS AFFECTING COMMERCIAL PARTNERS

2.42　　Commercial partners are affected by the way sports governing bodies choose to deal with the commercial rights that they hold, in the interests of the sport. A number of challenges have arisen to the legality of those choices. In addition, sports governing bodies have to take steps to protect the exercise of the rights that they own, for example where third parties seek to take advantage of the goodwill generated by the sport without compensating the governing body with income for the continued development of the sport.[1] There will plainly also be straightforward contractual disputes as to the extent of the rights granted and failure to comply with specific contractual obligations.

1 For example, as in *PGA v Evans*, 25 January 1989 Vinelott J (unofficial corporate hospitality provider using Ryder Cup name).

(a)　Official endorsement of sports products

2.43　　For manufacturers of sports equipment, official endorsement by the governing body of the sport in a particular country provides an extremely useful advertising tool, suggesting as it does that the people who really know what the product has to do, have selected the particular manufacturer's product before those of others. The very usefulness of such an endorsement means that rival manufacturers are likely to be adversely affected, and to object,[1] particularly if the endorsement reflects no more than how much the 'official' manufacturer has been prepared to pay. On the other hand, it may be useful for the public to be informed by the sports governing body whether a particular product achieves a particular standard.

1 *Danish Tennis Federation* Case Nos IV/F–1/33.055 and 35.759, [1996] OJ C138/6, Commission press release IP/98/355 (tennis ball manufacturers adversely affected by the federation's choice of one manufacturer to be named as the official supplier of tennis balls, in that it suggested that the balls of other manufacturers were inadequate, complained to the European Commission which prohibited the practice and set stricter constraints on the degree of recognition that could be given by the sports governing body: the opportunity must be open to all manufacturers to obtain such recognition on the basis of objective criteria); *World Federation of the Sporting Goods Industry v FIFA and ISL*, Case No IV/F–1/35.266, complaint rejected by Commission decision letter dated December 2000 (football manufacturers challenged rule allowing use in official competitions only of 'FIFA-approved' footballs).

(b) Selected suppliers and approval of sports products

2.44   Equally manufacturers of sports equipment wish to be selected to supply sports products to governing bodies simply because such contracts are valuable. This is particularly the case where governing bodies seek to require or encourage their member clubs also to buy from that supplier. Selection processes have been the subject of challenge as anti-competitive.[1] Suppliers have also challenged the failure of sports governing bodies to approve equipment[2] for use in the sport.

1 *Danish Tennis Federation*, Case Nos IV/F–1/33.055 and 35.759, [1996] OJ C138/6, Commission press release IP/98/355.
2 See for example *BRV v FIA*, Case Comp/39732, 4 August 2011 Rejection Letter (the Commission refused to investigate an engine manufacturer's complaint that FIA rule excluding a particular type of engine part was anti-competitive); *McHugh v The Australian Jockey Club* [2012] FCA 1441 (Federal Court rejected a competition law challenge against the sports governing body's rules that excluded thoroughbreds bred by artificial insemination).

(c) Sponsorship, manufacturer's identification, advertising and official suppliers of other products or services

2.45   A large number of companies, unconnected with the sport itself, perceive a value in connecting themselves to it, whether through the sponsorship of events, leagues, clubs or individuals, or through their being identified as the manufacturer on sports equipment and clothing used by players, or through advertising of other products on players or at venues, or through being named as official suppliers of products ranging from timing equipment to soft drinks and of services such as payment methods. Sports governing bodies make dispositive choices that may be the subject of challenge, not only in how they allocate the contracts for the exploitation of the rights that they themselves hold, but also in the rules that they impose on other participants[1] in relation to such exploitation. Particular problems have arisen in the context of sponsorship of events by tobacco and alcohol producers,[2] and more recently internet betting operators.

1 Such as the steps taken by governing bodies to prohibit the use of equipment from a manufacturer other than the one sponsoring the national team, or restrict the advertising of other products in stadia or on a player's equipment or clothing. See *Adidas v Draper and others [representing the Grand Slams] and*

the International Tennis Federation [2006] EWHC 1318 (ChD) [2006] All ER (D) 30 and *National Football League/Adidas*, Court of Appeal of Paris, 29/2/2000, [2000] ECLR 10, p N.118/9.

2   In *Bacardi v Newcastle* a reference was obtained from the English courts [2001] Eu LR 45 in an action challenging the validity of the French Loi Evin which amongst other things restricts the broadcast on French TV of certain sports events taking place even outside France, where advertising of alcohol or tobacco is displayed at the event venue. However the European Court of Justice rejected the reference, [2003] ECR I-905, and the action was not pursued in England in the light of the similar proceedings in *European Commission (supported by the United Kingdom, intervening) v France; Bacardi France SAS v Télévision Française 1 SA (TF1) and others* (Cases C-262 and C429/02) [2004] ECR I-6569; [2005] All ER (EC) 157, in which the challenge to the French authorities' application of the Loi Evin was rejected.

(d)   Broadcasting and listed events

2.46   Coverage of premium sports events has been used by new platform broadcasters over recent years as a battering ram for new subscriptions. This has led to a massive increase in the sums of money that the governing bodies of such sports have been able to secure for the rights.[1] However the perceived value can only be realised by the grant of an exclusive contract for a sufficient period to allow the entitlement to be built upon and converted into increased revenue for the broadcaster.

1   See *Carlton Communications plc and Granada Media plc v Football League Ltd* [2002] EWHC 1650 [2002] All ER (D) 1, noted at (2003) SLJ vol 11 iss 1 p 182, which held that the broadcasters had not guaranteed the obligations of the subsidiary when they did not sign a formal guarantee. See also the ensuing *Football League v Edge Ellison* [2006] EWHC 1462 (Ch), [2006] All ER (D) 263 (professional negligence action by the League against its solicitors for alleged failure to warn the League of a lack of guarantee of OnDigital's obligations by its parents).

2.47   One consequence has been government initiatives to try and preserve some 'crown jewel' events for broadcast on terrestrial free to air television, by preventing them from being sold for broadcast on new platforms. The choices made as to what events are 'listed' in this way has been the subject of litigation.[1]

1   *FIFA v European Commission* (T-385/07) 17 February 2011 (GC) (Belgian listing); *FIFA v European Commission* (T-68/08) 17 February 2011 (GC) (UK listing); *UEFA v European Commission* (T-55/08) 17 February 2011 (GC) (UK listing); and the football bodies' appeal was rejected by the General Court in July 2013: Cases C-201/11 P, C-204/11 P and C-205/11 P *UEFA, FIFA v European Commission*. A purchaser of broadcasting rights may have sufficient interest to challenge a Commission decision on listing: *Commission of the European Communities v Infront WM AG* (C-125/06 P) ECJ 13 March 2008 [2008] ECR I-1451; [2008] 2 CMLR 28 on appeal from the CFI's decision [2005] ECR II-5897.

2.48   Governing bodies, and their commercial partners, have had to exercise vigilance to prevent attempts to circumvent the exclusivity of the arrangements by other broadcasters,[1] consumers[2] or third parties[3] and this has resulted in litigation.

1   *BBC v Talksport* [2001] FSR 53; *BBC v BSkyB* [1992] Ch 141; *England and Wales Cricket Board Ltd v Tixdaq Ltd* [2016] EWHC 575 (Ch).

2   The ability of sports rights holders effectively to prevent infringement of exclusive broadcast licences based on national territories was challenged in relation to the use of foreign decoder cards to watch in England, Premier League matches broadcast abroad in *Murphy v Media Protection Services Ltd* (C-429/08) and *Football Association Premier League Ltd v QC Leisure* (C-403/08) [2012] All ER (EC) 629, [2012] 1 CMLR 29; Advocate General's Opinion, [2011] ECDR 11; see also [2010] EuLR 391. The Court of Justice held amongst other things that national legislation making it illegal to import, sell or use foreign decoder cards infringed the freedom to provide services protected in Art 56 TFEU without justification and that prohibition in an exclusive licence agreement on the licensee supplying decoder cards for use outside their territory restricted cross-border competition contrary to Art 101 TFEU. The Court held that there was no need to protect the rights holders' territorial exclusivity

premium which was unreasonably high; that there was no copyright in the match itself to protect (although there might be in the surrounding programming); and that it would have been possible to use contractual obligations to prevent matches being shown on television when they were actually being played. Showing a programme in a pub would however be a 'communication to the public', which would require the copyright owner's authorisation. Following the preliminary rulings, the Divisional Court in *Murphy v Media Protection Services Ltd* [2012] EWHC 466 (Admin), [2012] 3 CMLR 2, allowed a publican's appeal by case stated, and quashed her convictions under the Copyright, Designs and Patents Act 1988 for using a foreign decoder card to screen football matches in her public house. In *Football Association Premier League Ltd v QC Leisure* [2012] EWHC 108 (Ch), [2012] 2 CMLR 16, the Chancery Division held that publicans who used a foreign decoder card prima facie infringed copyright in the broadcast of a match, but that section 72 of the Copyright, Designs and Patents Act 1988 afforded them a defence, since they had not charged for admission. The Court of Appeal affirmed this decision: *Football Association Premier League Ltd v QC Leisure* [2012] EWCA Civ 1708, [2013] Bus LR 866.

3 *Football Association Premier League Ltd v British Sky Broadcasting Ltd* [2013] EWHC 2058 (Ch), [2013] ECDR 14.

2.49 A wide range of disputes may arise in relation to sports governing bodies' approaches to broadcasting, including challenges to the length and terms of the arrangements granted,[1] to the validity of collective selling itself, to the validity of the bundling of rights to broadcast on different platforms,[2] and to the distribution of the proceeds.[3] Equally, disputes have arisen between governing bodies grouping together to sell rights collectively.[4] Disputes have also arisen as to the ownership of rights in the first place.[5] Governing bodies have had to be astute to ensure that television coverage does not damage the gate receipts of less successful clubs, taking steps which the broadcasters or regulators seek to challenge.[6] Furthermore, the exploitation of these commercial rights has given rise to straight contractual disputes as to the terms of the grant and as to payment.[7]

1 For example *Re an Agreement between the FA Premier League* [2000] EMLR 78, [1999] UKCLR 258 Restrictive Practices Court, July 1999 (consideration of the legality of the English FA Premier League's broadcasting arrangements with BSkyB and the BBC under the UK's predecessor competition legislation, see also [1999] 7(3) SATLJ 18); *Racecourse Association v OFT; BHB v OFT* [2005] CAT 29, [2005] All ER (D) 10.

2 See *British Sky Broadcasting Limited, Virgin Media, The Football Association Premier League Limited, British Telecommunications Plc v Office of Communications* Competition Appeal Tribunal, 8 August 2012 [2012] CAT 20 (non-confidential summary only), Ofcom's decision that Sky had to wholesale its core premium sports channels was overturned. The Tribunal's order has been set aside by the Court of Appeal, and remitted for further consideration: *British Telecommunications plc v Office of Communications and others* [2014] EWCA Civ 133, [2014] Bus LR 713. Previously in *British Sky Broadcasting Ltd v Office of Communications* Competition Appeal Tribunal 9 November 2010 [2010] CAT 29, [2011] Comp AR 3 it was held that where Sky had agreed to supply content wholesale to three parties, it was obliged also to supply it to a fourth.

3 For example the dispute in 2001 between the Professional Footballers' Association and the FA Premier League over the PFA's share of the rights fees derived from broadcasting of games in which its members played, and Cardiff RFC's challenge to the collective selling of rights by the WRU.

4 For example, in 1996 the Rugby Football Union sold BSkyB the rights to all its home games, including its home games in the Five Nations Championship (as it then was) without consulting the other Unions in the Championship. The remaining unions refused to play the RFU, and the RFU was forced to sign a September 1996 Accord that recognised the principle of central selling of such rights and sharing of the resulting revenues. Because the deal with BSkyB could not be avoided, the Accord included a requirement that the part of the £65m rights fee paid by BSkyB that was attributable to England's Five Nations matches be pooled by the RFU, the amount to be determined by a valuer if not agreed. In the event, the parties could not agree and an expert determination ensued, leading to a valuation decision in November 1999.

5 There remains an issue as to who or what owns what are commonly referred to as 'television rights' or 'broadcast rights'. In *Victoria Park Racing v Taylor* (1937) 58 CLR 479, it was held that these rights were the rights of the owner or controller of land to admit or to refuse to admit a broadcaster onto land in order to film an event.

6 Through 'blackout rules' under which matches cannot be broadcast at a time which would make it less likely that spectators would travel to and watch another live match. For example, a host of broadcasters complained to the European Commission (Case Nos IV/C2; 34.319, 33,734, 34.199, 33.145, 34.784, 34,790, 34,948, 35.001, 35.048) about UEFA's blackout rule which banned the broadcast of foreign matches in another country at the same time as that country played its own matches.

7 For example *Carlton and Granada v Football League Ltd* [2002] EWHC 1650 (Comm); *MTV v Formula One Management* Harman J 6 March 1998, Carnwath J 1 April 1998 (court refused to grant an interim injunction requiring the provision of the feed to the broadcaster because it had not been established to the court's satisfaction that a contractual entitlement had arisen); *Future Investments SA v Fédération Internationale de Football Association* [2010] EWHC 1019 (Ch), [2010] ILPr 34 (action against FIFA for causing loss by unlawful means in a broadcasting context).

(e)   Intellectual property

2.50   The increased commercialisation of sport has led to disputes over the use of the governing bodies' intellectual property rights, such as their rights in their lists of events and information about the events and those taking part in them,[1] their official trade marks,[2] their right not to have an unauthorised competition associated with them,[3] their domain names[4] and even the initials by which they are known.[5]

1 The Court of Justice held in *Football Dataco Ltd v Yahoo! UK Ltd* (C-604/10) [2012] 2 CMLR 24, [2012] ECDR 10, Advocate General's Opinion, [2012] ECDR 7 that a database within the meaning of the Directive 96/9 enjoys the protection laid down by the Directive if a national court determines that the selection or arrangement of the data in it amounts to an original expression of the creative freedom of its author. In *Football Dataco Ltd v Livescore Ltd* [2011] EWHC 2264 (Ch); *Football Dataco Ltd v Smoot Enterprises Ltd* [2011] EWHC 973 (Ch), [2011] 1 WLR 1978 and *Football Dataco Ltd v Sportradar GmbH* and *Football Dataco Ltd v Stan James Abingdon Ltd* [2012] EWHC 1185 (Ch), [2012] 3 CMLR 18, 8 May 2012 and on appeal [2013] EWCA Civ 27, it was held that a database right did subsist in the database containing facts and information about football matches. On 18 October 2012 the Court of Justice decided in *Football Dataco Ltd v Sportradar GmbH* (C-173/11) that the act of re-utilisation of data occurred at least where the utiliser intended people to receive it, so that the protection could not be sidestepped.

2 *Trebor Bassett Ltd v FA* [1997] FSR 211 (unsuccessful attempt to stop sweet manufacturer giving away cards bearing pictures of footballers wearing the England strip, including the 'Three Lions' symbol); *FAPL v Panini* [2002] EWHC 2779 ChD/, noted at (2003) 11(1) SLJ 180 (injunction granted to restrain use of Premier League lion logo in unofficial sticker collection); *Score Draw Ltd v Finch* [2007] EWHC 462 (Ch), [2007] All ER (D) 159 (once the badge had ceased to be used by the Brazilian football team, it had acquired significance as a badge connoting the former Brazilian football team and could no longer be said to denote the trade origin of anyone).

3 *Parish v World Series Cricket Pty Ltd* (1977) 16 ALR 172 (Australian Cricket Board granted injunction against World Series Cricket to restrain it from implying in advertising that its events were authorised by the Board).

4 There have been a number of cases involving the domain names of sports governing bodies, adjudicated upon by WIPO (see arbiter.wipo.int). See for example *ISL Marketting and FIFA v JY Chung*, 3 April 2000, Case D2000-0034; *UEFA v Alliance International Media* 25 April 2000, Case D2000-0153.

5 See the dispute over the right to use the initials 'WWF': *World Wide Fund for Nature v World Wrestling Federation Entertainment Inc* Jacob J, 1 October 2001 [2001] All ER (D) 50; on appeal [2002] EWCA Civ 196, 27 February 2002 [2002] All ER (D) 370; in resumed litigation [2006] EWHC 184 (Ch) 16 February 2006, [2006] All ER (D) 212 and 2 April 2007 [2008] 1 WLR 445.

(f)   Ticketing and the black or 'secondary' market

2.51   Governing bodies are often responsible for the issuing of tickets to matches that they organise, and the way in which they have chosen to do this has been the subject of examination by regulatory authorities,[1] and challenge from those excluded from the process, in particular those that wish to sell on the black, or as they would prefer to characterise it, 'secondary', ticket market.[2]

1 *Albertville* and *Barcelona*, Commission press release IP/92/593; *Atlanta*, 1996 Competition Report p 144 and *FIFA France 98* [2000] OJ L5/55, where the sports governing bodies' systems of ticket sales discriminated against supporters on the basis of nationality; *FIA Formula One Championship* [2001] OJ C169/5; *Italia 90 (Distribution of Package Tours)* [1992] OJ L326/31, Decision 92/521/EEC.

2 Governing bodies have secured many interim injunctions in the English courts to restrain 'secondary' market operators that have sold tickets alone or 'hospitality' along with a ticket, see for example *UEFA and EURO 2004 SA v Select Promotions and others* (Order of Patten J, 25 February 2004); *UEFA and EURO 2004 SA v Domino's Pizza* (Order of Lewison J, 8 April 2004) *UEFA and EURO 2004 SA v eBay International AG* (Order of Buckley J, 19 May 2004); *UEFA and EURO 2004 SA v BAC Travel Management and others* (Order of Richards J, 8 June 2004). On a number of occasions competition law defences were raised in the interim proceedings, but in each instance the action did not proceed once interim relief was obtained. There has therefore been no determination of validity of either the causes of action relied upon or the competition law defences.

(g)   Travel, accommodation and corporate hospitality

2.52   The grant of access to match tickets to package for resale with travel and accommodation arrangements, coupled with 'official' designation, is a major source of income for governing bodies organising sports events involving participants from abroad. Excluded travel providers have sought to challenge the selection of rivals and the exclusivity granted.[1] Governing bodies are often also in a position to sell the rights to provide a package of ticket and corporate hospitality at stadia where they have organised an event, and in order to extract maximum value they have tended to make exclusive appointments of businesses that they have designated as 'official' providers. In a number of cases, corporate hospitality providers have sought to challenge the selection of particular businesses as official hospitality providers, and the exclusivity of their appointment.[2] Governing bodies have also sought to enforce the exclusivity of appointments.[3]

1 For example the complaint that triggered the European Commission decision in *Italia 90 (Distribution of Package Tours)* [1992] OJ L326/31, Decision 92/521/EEC; the OFT's commencement of proceedings against the Rugby Football League, OFT Press Release 14/98, 26 March 1998 and the complaint to the European Commission in *Rugby World Cup 1999*.

2 For example *Hospitality Group v FA* 24 January 1996, Scott V-C in respect of Euro 96; *Hospitality Group v Australian Rugby Union* [1999] FCA 1136 (interlocutory), [2000] FCA 823 (first instance), [2001] FCA 1040, (2001) 110 FCR 157 (on appeal); the complaint to the OFT in respect of *Wimbledon*, OFT Press Release No 20/93, 23 March 1993, and the complaint to the European Commission in *Rugby World Cup 1999*.

3 For example, in *PGA v Evans* 25 January 1989, Vinelott J, in which the PGA and Keith Prowse obtained an interim injunction restraining a rival corporate hospitality provider from passing itself off as having any official connection with the Ryder Cup.

(h)   Arrangements with promoters and agents

2.53   Governing bodies often do not have all the resources to organise major events and so contract with the owners of stadia or racecourses and promoters, and employ sports agents, in order to put together an event and/or to develop a commercial programme for the event, giving rise to the potential for commercial disputes.[1] In other contexts the governing body may impose rules that make it difficult for promoters or agents to stage rival competitions or events.[2]

1 *R v Jockey Club, ex p RAM Racecourses* [1993] 2 All ER 225, DC (unsuccessful attempt to challenge the Jockey Club's allocation of race dates to racecourses); *Sepoong Engineering Construction Co v Formula One Management (formerly Formula One Administration Ltd)* [2000] 1 Lloyds Rep 602, [2000] All ER (D) 345 (dispute over the agreement that a Formula One grand prix should be staged at Sepoong's racecourse in Korea). The arrangements for the FIA Formula One World Championship

involve the governing body, Fédération Internationale de l'Automobile, contracting out exploitation of rights to various companies (for example FOM and FOA), which then organise the grands prix and sell on the commercial rights. In the context of football, FIFA licenses out the commercial exploitation of the World Cup (see *Rofa Sport Management v DHL International UK* [1989] 1 WLR 902); the World Cup 2002 was put in peril by the collapse of international sports agents ISL.

2 For example in the unresolved *ISI v International Rugby Board* case.

H   ACTIONS AFFECTING THE PUBLIC

2.54   The public, in the form of supporters, spectators and viewers, may be affected by the decisions of sports governing bodies. In the main, their interests have been pursued by decisions made by the regulatory authorities[1] or government,[2] although those decisions themselves may become the subject of litigation in the courts, either because the sports governing body itself challenges the decision, or because the administrative authority refers a matter to the courts.[3] Smaller groups within the public may however be, or perceive themselves to be, affected by particular matters, and seek to bring actions themselves.[4]

1 In particular the wider public interest has been protected by decisions of the competition authorities: for example *Albertville* and *Barcelona*, Commission press release IP/92/593; *Atlanta*, 1996 Competition Report p 144 and *France 98* [2000] OJ L5/55, where the sports governing bodies' systems of ticket sales discriminated against supporters on the basis of nationality; *FIA Formula One Championship* [2001] OJ C169/5; *Italia 90 (Distribution of Package Tours)* [1992] OJ L 326/31, Decision 92/521/EEC.

2 For example the listing of events by the Government as events which must be available on free to air television.

3 For example *Re an Agreement between the FA Premier League* [2000] EMLR 78, [1999] UKCLR 258 Restrictive Practices Court, July 1999 (consideration of the legality of the English FA Premier League's broadcasting arrangements with BSkyB and the BBC under the UK's predecessor competition legislation). In the context of taxation, HM Revenue & Customs has repeatedly sought, but so far failed, to persuade the courts to declare illegal the 'football creditors rule', which prioritises particular classes of creditors, such as players and other clubs, over other unsecured creditors when a football club becomes insolvent, including the taxpayers.

4 *Finnigan v New Zealand Rugby Football Union (Nos 1, 2 and 3)* [1985] 2 NZLR 159, 181, 190, NZ HC and CA (challenge to the decision by the NZRFU to send a team to South Africa); *Arnolt v Football Association* 2 February 1998 (unsuccessful action brought by a supporter against the FA for loss of the opportunity to use his season ticket to watch Premier League football as a result of the club's demotion following the docking of points); *MacDonald v FIFA and SFA* [1999] SCLR 59, [1999] 7(1) SATLJ 33 (unsuccessful claim by a fan against the governing bodies consequent upon the cancellation of an international fixture); *Tyrell v FA* (28 April 1997), Coward [1997] 5(2) SATLJ 5 (action against FA claiming damages for nervous shock caused by bad refereeing decision struck out); *Rubython v FIA*, QB [2003] EWHC 1355 (QB) [2003] All ER (D) 182 (no jurisdiction to grant a mandatory injunction requiring a motorsport governing body to issue press accreditation since it was domiciled in France and was not a public authority nor was it exercising public authority powers).

I   ACTIONS OF PARTICIPANTS AFFECTING OTHER PARTICIPANTS

2.55   The survey set out above does not address the situation where the actions of a participant (in other words, a person other than a sports governing body), such as an individual, a club or a promoter, affect another participant. In many instances, these disputes do not involve questions of the regulation of sport, but rather disputes between private parties that happen to arise in a sporting context. In some instances, however, disputes between participants may relate to the way that the sport is played under the rules,[1] or turn on, for example, the validity of a standard form contract for use between participants provided for in the rules of the governing body,[2] or be based on the rules of the sport as constituting a contract between two participants.[3]

Where this is not the case, and the governing body is not even involved to this extent, the possible factual scenarios in which disputes are brought to the courts or arbitral tribunals are numerous.

1 For example *Mercury Bay Boating Club Inc v San Diego Yacht Club and Royal Perth Yacht Club of Western Australia* 76 NY 2d 256 (Court of Appeals for New York 1990) (legal challenge by one competitor against another in relation to the eligibility to compete of a particular shape of yacht, there a catamaran).
2 *Watson v Prager* [1991] 1 WLR 726 (British Boxing Board of Control's standard form boxer-manager contract held in unreasonable restraint of trade); *Barry Silkman v Colchester United Football Club Ltd*, 15 June 2001 Morland J, in which it was held that the Football Association's rules on agents not being paid by clubs when they acted for the player were not incorporated into the contract between the club and the agent.
3 In *Sheffield United v West Ham* FA Rule K arbitration, Lord Griffiths, Sir Anthony Colman, Robert Englehart QC, West Ham had breached the FAPL rules in the way in which it had acquired two players. The FAPL rules expressly provided that they constituted a contract not only between the FAPL and each member, but between the members inter se.

CHAPTER 3

Identification of cause of action and respondent

3.1   After first assessing the facts in a given situation against the background of the historical review set out above, the second step in deciding whether to bring proceedings (whether in court or before an arbitral body) to challenge the actions of a sports governing body is to seek to fit the facts into a cause or causes of action against an appropriate respondent. Chapters 7 to 12 address the causes of action most commonly raised (although others may be relevant in specific factual circumstances). The identity of the appropriate respondent is obviously linked to the cause of action, although in some circumstances the situation may be complicated by other factors. The paragraphs below offer a brief guide as to how to approach the identification of a cause of action and respondent.

A   CAUSE OF ACTION

3.2   The identification of the appropriate cause (or causes) of action is best commenced by considering what it is that the governing body is regarded as a matter of fact to have done wrong. First, does the vice lie in the *application* to an individual or business of one of the sport's rules and regulations in a given instance, or in the *introduction* and maintenance of a particular rule or regulation? The complaint may be that a valid provision has been unlawfully applied, or that the very adoption of the provision was unlawful, or both. Secondly, is the complaint that the governing body has acted *contrary* to its express rules and regulations or a provision of the law of general application, or is the complaint rather that the process has been *unfair*, or that the decision is a *discretionary* one with which the claimant disagrees?

3.3   The distinctions are important because the discussion below reveals that in most instances a court or arbitral body will adopt a 'supervisory' approach to the review of the actions of sports governing bodies in the exercise of their regulatory functions,[1] at least insofar as those actions involve the sports governing body exercising a discretion, or making a decision involving an evaluation, based on its specialist knowledge and experience of the sport. In those circumstances the court or arbitral body examines the way in which the decision at issue was made and the legality of the arrangements against wider public policy considerations. They would not generally reopen the substantive merits of the matter or substitute their view for that of the sports governing body.

1 As opposed to when they are performing a purely commercial role. In such contexts normal principles apply.

3.4   This may not always be the case, however. First, even under a 'supervisory' approach, there are some grounds for review that have been described as 'hard-edged', in the sense that the court or tribunal will look at the substantive merits. This would be the case if, for example, the governing body had breached its own written rules and regulations, or if it had breached a separate legal provision of general application.[1] Secondly, there is an argument that where a private law sports governing body makes some forms of regulatory decision, for example that a participant has committed a breach of its rules or failed to satisfy a requirement of them, that decision amounts to no more than the *view*, of no more than *one of the parties*[2] to the contract constituted by the rules and regulations, as to the contractual position under those rules and regulations. Under this argument the decision, even where the governing body has exercised some degree of expert evaluation, is not dispositive and can create no issue estoppel. On this basis, the issue of whether there was in fact a breach of contract in the form of the breach of the rules by the participant would remain one for the court or arbitral body, which would have no obligation to defer to the expertise of the sports governing body. The precise bounds of this argument and its prospects of success are, however, uncertain.[3]

1 If the governing body is in a contractual relationship with the complainant on the basis of the rules and regulations, an obligation to comply with the rules arises as a matter of contract. However, a similar requirement arises in any event out of the governing body's monopoly control of its sport. The requirement to comply with the general law exists in any event.
2 This approach would only apply to decisions made by a governing body itself. Under this argument the approach would apply to the decisions of a governing body's disciplinary or regulatory tribunals unless and until they could be characterised as independent arbitral tribunals, in which case their decisions would only be reviewable on the narrow grounds available under the Arbitration Act 1996 (some of which can themselves be excluded or modified by agreement in the rules), subject to any right of appeal to a further arbitral body also provided for in the rules.
3 The argument is arguably precluded by the analysis of Richards J in *Bradley;* but see *Mullins v McFarlane (representing the Appeal Board of the Jockey Club) and the Jockey Club* [2006] EWHC 986 [2006] All ER (D) 66 at paras 37 to 39 and *McKeown v British Horseracing Authority* [2010] EWHC 508 (QB), at paras 32 to 37. It may be simplistic to conclude that the regulatory decisions of a sports governing body always fall to be measured against the same standards as would apply to the decisions of a public law body. The fact that the sports governing body is not a body whose decisions are susceptible to judicial review under CPR Pt 54 means that the precise standard of review may vary with circumstances.

3.5   The principal causes of action for a challenge to the actions of a sports governing body are the grounds for review[1] of such actions that arise as a result of the body's ability to control access to and regulate the sport. Those grounds for review are likely to be equivalent to those that the Administrative Court would apply to a body, the decisions of which are susceptible to judicial review under CPR Pt 54, although a sports governing body is not such a body. Those grounds relate (to varying degrees) to *how* a sports governing body takes a decision or adopts a rule or regulation, as opposed to its substance. In order to consider whether an action was taken in a way contrary to those principles, the claimant needs to have a copy of the rules and regulations of the governing body,[2] and should ask the governing body to give its reasons for its decision. While these grounds for review may in some circumstances apply to the adoption of a rule or regulation, their most obvious relevance is to specific mistreatment of a particular individual or business through the application of the rules or regulations to him, her or it. Broadly, the governing body cannot exercise its regulatory functions in a way:

(a)   that is in fact outside its powers as set out in its rules and regulations, or contrary to the general law; or

(b)   in a manner that is procedurally unfair or contrary to natural justice; or
(c)   that takes into account irrelevant considerations or fails to take into account relevant considerations; or
(d)   that has no factual basis; or
(e)   that is contrary to a legitimate expectation; or
(f)   that is unreasonable in the sense of being irrational, perverse, arbitrary or capricious.

As already referred to, and as described in more detail in the next chapter, the courts apply a varying degree of review to the different concepts: the question of whether the body has acted outside its rules and regulations or contrary to the general law is 'hard-edged', whereas at the other end of the spectrum the question of whether the action is irrational generally involves giving the sports governing body a substantial degree of latitude.

1   The possibility of any cause of action under the Human Rights Act 1998 also falls for consideration at this point.
2   Many sports governing bodies post their rules on their websites, although this is not yet the case for many of the smaller sports. In some instances what is posted on the website will not be complete, but will concentrate on the principal rules.

3.6   These grounds for review exist, and are enforceable by an action for a declaration (and possibly an injunction), whether or not there is a contract between governing body and claimant (at least where the requisite degree of control over the sport is established). Where a contract exists between the governing body and the claimant, it will be implicit in it that the decisions of the governing body are subject to the same grounds for review. Where such a contract exists on the terms of the rules and regulations (or some of them), a breach of them can be sued upon as a matter of contract. In such circumstances a cause of action in damages[1] may well arise. The situation is more complicated where there is a contract and the proposition is that the sports governing body has acted in a way contrary to one of the other grounds for review. It is possible, at least where a separate disciplinary tribunal of the sports governing body has reached the decision following a hearing, that the extent of the contractual obligation on the governing body is to provide a procedure reviewable by reference to the standard of review that exists absent a contract, and that there is no contractual obligation on the governing body that may give rise to a claim in damages that the decision will comply with that standard.[2] Where the action is that of the sports governing body itself, the argument that a cause of action in damages arises will be stronger, but may still not be made out.[3] Either way, where a contract can be shown to exist, the claimant will have additional arguments in comparison to the situation where it cannot be shown to exist.

1   Subject to the existence of a claim under the Human Rights Act 1998, the Competition Act 1998 or some other provision, or possibly an action in tort, a cause of action in damages only arises in contract. There is no general right to damages where the sports governing body has taken a decision that is simply reviewable on the grounds equivalent to those applied to public law bodies.
2   This flows from the analysis of Richards J in *Bradley*.
3   It might not be made out, for example, if on the proper construction of the contract, the only remedy agreed was the application of the disciplinary process contained in the rules. In *Sheffield United v West Ham* FA Rule K arbitration, Lord Griffiths, Sir Anthony Colman, Robert Englehart QC, 18 April 2008 interim award, it was held that on the proper construction of the FAPL rules, which expressly provided that they constituted a contract between each club, Sheffield was not confined to seeing West Ham disciplined for its breach of the rules in acquiring a player, but could sue West Ham for the damage it suffered in being relegated in place of West Ham if the acquisition of the player was the proximate cause of that relegation.

3.7   In the light of the above, after establishing what it is that the governing body has done wrong, the next step is to consider whether there is a contract between the individual or business affected and the governing body. Whether there is a contract, and if so its extent, will depend on all the circumstances, examined in the normal way. Such a contract may be contained in the rules, may be a separate written contract, or may arise orally, by conduct or even implicitly. It may be on the terms of the rules, or only some of them. It may impose additional requirements beyond the standard of behaviour required from all sports governing bodies by virtue of their role, which standard will be implicit in it. Where there is a specific contractual obligation, the courts will evaluate in the normal way whether the sports governing body has been in breach of it, and to this extent the exercise that they undertake is hard-edged, and may involve more than simply reviewing the way in which the decision was taken. Where there is no contract, resort can nevertheless be had to the grounds for review available irrespective of contract, albeit with the prospect of more limited relief.

3.8   In some contexts it may also be appropriate to give some consideration to whether the facts reveal the commission of a tort. The torts most often relied upon are breach of a duty of care in negligence,[1] and inducement to breach a contract.[2]

1 For example as in *Watson v BBBC* [2000] EWCA Civ 2116, [2001] QB 1134, where a duty of care was imposed on the governing body to ensure adequate medical assistance at the ringside.
2 On the basis that the decision or actions of the sports governing body disturb existing arrangements.

3.9   In addition to these grounds for review imposed on the basis of the governing body's control and regulation of the sport, and the possibility of an action in tort, both specific mistreatment of a particular individual or business and the introduction and maintenance of a rule that is unfair may be capable of challenge on the basis of the public policy principles contained in the restraint of trade doctrine,[1] the domestic and European competition law rules, and the European free movement rules. Although obviously the detailed constituents of the cause of action vary in each case, the trigger for the application of these principles is, very broadly:

(a)   whether the action significantly restricts the ability of the claimant (or of a class of persons) to earn a living where, and in the way that, he or she would wish to;

(b)   if it does, it is open to challenge unless the restriction has been imposed in pursuit of a legitimate aim in the interests of the sport and the restriction is proportionate.[2]

In this context too, therefore, the court does not strictly examine the merits of the underlying decision but rather how it was reached and whether it goes too far.

1 The doctrine covers decisions or actions as well as rules. It remains an open question whether the cause of action in restraint of trade is conceptually different to the cause of action based on the grounds for review arising out of the governing body's control of the sport: see para 35 of the judgment of Richards J in *Bradley*.
2 Proportionality is traditionally expressed in terms of whether a measure is the least restrictive available, and goes no further than is necessary to achieve a legitimate aim. This approach informs the formulation adopted by Lord Reed, in the context of the European Convention on Human Rights, in *Bank Mellat v HM Treasury (No. 2)* [2013] UKSC 38, [2014] AC 700: 'it is necessary to determine (1) whether the objective of the measure is sufficiently important to justify the limitation of a protected right, (2) whether the measure is rationally connected to the objective, (3) whether a less intrusive measure

could have been used without unacceptably compromising the achievement of the objective, and (4) whether, balancing the severity of the measure's effects on the rights of the persons to whom it applies against the importance of the objective, to the extent that the measure will contribute to its achievement, the former outweighs the latter' (para 74; Lord Reed dissented as to the outcome, but his formulation of the proportionality test commanded broad support (paras 20, 132, 166, 197)). When applying EU law, a court's approach to proportionality is context dependent: *R (Lumsdon and others) v Legal Services Board* [2015] UKSC 41, [2015] 3 WLR 121.

B   RESPONDENT

3.10   In most instances, the identity of the respondent will be plain. It will be the governing body that made the decision in the application of its rules and regulations, or adopted the particular rule or regulation. There are however three separate complications that may arise. First, where the vice is the introduction of a rule or regulation, it may be that the national sports governing body has been required to introduce it by the international governing body. Secondly, where the vice is the application of a rule or regulation, it may be that it has not in fact been applied by the sports governing body itself, but by a separate disciplinary or regulatory tribunal. Thirdly, the sports governing body may not itself have legal personality.

3.11   The national governing body of a sport is generally a member of the international governing body.[1] That membership is subject to the rules and regulations of the international governing body, which often require the national governing body to adopt particular rules and regulations, sometimes verbatim, and sometimes with a degree of discretion as to how the principles are to be implemented,[2] and generally provide the international body with a mechanism for enforcing its rules and regulations against its members. In such circumstances, it may be that the appropriate relief would best be sought against the international governing body, or both the national and the international governing bodies.[3] In other cases, a number of governing bodies may be responsible for different aspects of a single sport, and it will be important to identify which of them was responsible for the vice complained of.[4]

1   There are exceptions, such as the British Horseracing Authority, but the principle generally holds good.
2   An example is the FIFA Regulations on Intermediaries.
3   The optimum approach may vary with circumstances. In some cases it may be sufficient to seek relief against the national body, on the basis that it is irrelevant to the legality of its actions that it was forced so to act by the international body. While a finding that the national body had acted unlawfully might put it in an invidious position since it would have to obey the court's order putting it in breach of its obligations to the international body, it might be thought that that is a problem for the national body. Such an approach may lead the international body to intervene in proceedings, as in *Williams and Cardiff RFC v Pugh*, later known as *Williams and Cardiff RFC v WRU (IRB intervening)*, [1999] Eu LR 195, which involved a challenge to the legality of broadcasting central selling rules that the IRB required its members to introduce. In other cases it may be appropriate to target only the international governing body, for example in order to gain the support of the national governing body, which may itself oppose the new rule or regulation. Such a course may, however, run into jurisdictional difficulties if the international governing body is established abroad, and there is unlikely to be a direct contractual link between the claimant and the international governing body, unless the claimant is itself a national governing body (although there are exceptions, eg UEFA's role as the organiser of the Champions' League). The safest course may in some cases be to sue both national and international bodies, although this is likely to inflate costs.
4   In the context of football in England, for example, it would be necessary to assess whether the vice was the responsibility of The FA on the one hand, or The FA Premier League, Football League or Football Conference on the other. The FA may, for example, have caused the adoption of a particular rule or regulation by the leagues pursuant to the requirement that it approve their rules. The vice may also involve the cross over between leagues.

3.12   The second complication arises where the sports governing body has so arranged matters that a separate body is involved in making the decision in which the vice lies. It may be that that separate body's function only arises at the stage of an internal appeal against an essentially administrative decision of the sports governing body, or that the original decision itself is taken by it (for example with the sports governing body presenting one side of the case). It might be argued that unless and until the separate body satisfies the test[1] for an independent arbitral body,[2] it is in fact part of, and its decisions those of, the sports governing body itself, such that the governing body would be the appropriate respondent to a challenge to the validity of those decisions. In some circumstances this may be the case. It is however apparent from *Bradley v Jockey Club*[3] that it will not always be so. In that case Richards J examined the basis on which the courts should review the decision of the then governing body's Appeal Board to disqualify a former jockey for passing race information to punters. While it was common ground that the court could review the decision of the Appeal Board, it was in dispute whether the basis for that review was contractual or non-contractual and what the test to be applied was. The first instance disciplinary hearing had been before a Disciplinary Committee made up of three members of the Jockey Club and a legal assessor, which disqualified the jockey for eight years. An appeal lay to an Appeal Board made up of an independent legally qualified chairman and two members of the Jockey Club. The appeal was by way of review and not rehearing. The former jockey's appeal to the Appeal Board was for the most part rejected, but the disqualification period was reduced to five years. In court proceedings brought against the Jockey Club, the disqualified jockey invoked the courts' jurisdiction to exercise supervisory review over the sports governing body, alleging in particular that it owed an obligation in contract, and in any event, to impose no more than a proportionate sanction. He claimed that the five-year sanction imposed was disproportionate, and asked the court to substitute a proportionate sanction. Richards J first examined the non-contractual claim, holding that 'even in the absence of contract the court has a settled jurisdiction to grant declarations and injunctions in respect of decisions of domestic tribunals that affect a person's right to work'.[4] He endorsed the Jockey Club's acceptance that it could stand as the appropriate defendant to such a non-contractual challenge to the validity of the decision of the Appeal Board, although it contended that the Appeal Board was an independent body.[5] Richards J then addressed the test on such a challenge, holding that the court would apply essentially the same standards as would be applied by a court in public law proceedings to a body the decisions of which were susceptible to judicial review under CPR Pt 54.[6] Richards J then turned to the claim in contract, and the Jockey Club's contention that it itself owed no obligations to a participant who was the subject of a decision by the separate Appeal Board as to the quality of the decision or how it was taken beyond an obligation to make the appeal process available to that participant. Richards J held that there was a contract, but that its terms did not extend to any obligation on the Jockey Club to ensure that the decision of the separate Appeal Board was proportionate. He did this in part to reject an argument that the court could simply substitute its view of what was a proportionate sanction for that of the Appeal Board, but also on the basis that the Appeal Board was a separate body from the Jockey Club, and that its decisions were reviewable on the non-contractual basis that he had already held existed. Richards J however went on to hold that there might be an implied obligation on the Jockey Club that it would only apply a decision of the Appeal Board in so far as it was lawful, limiting the standard of review in contract to that which existed under the non-contractual claim. Applying these principles, Richards J concluded that the Appeal Board had not stepped outside the range of decisions as to sanction that was open to it in the exercise of its expertise. On appeal, the Court of Appeal endorsed Richards J's expression of the test for supervisory review,[7] and his conclusion on the proportionality of the sanction, but did not address the other issues.

1 In the context of sport, the test is set out in *Walkinshaw v Diniz* [2000] 2 All ER (Comm) 237 at 250e to 255j as summarised in Merkin, *Arbitration Law* (LLP, 2004), at para 3.6, and was recently applied in *England and Wales Cricket Board Ltd v Kaneria* [2013] EWHC 1074 (Comm) to determine that proceedings before an ECB disciplinary committee were arbitral proceedings, and therefore the Arbitration Act 1996 applied to them. There might be a sequence of arbitrations, with both the original body and the appeal body satisfying the test. See also *Baker v British Boxing Board of Control* [2015] EWHC 2469 (Ch).

2 And its decisions consequently only reviewable on the limited grounds set out in the Arbitration Act 1996.

3 [2004] EWHC 2164 (Richards J), [2004] All ER (D) 11, upheld [2005] EWCA Civ 1056, Before the Appeal Board it had been argued that the process failed to satisfy Art 6 ECHR, but the Appeal Board held that it was sufficiently independent and impartial and that in any event access to the courts cured any breach.

4 Op cit, para 35, citing *Nagle v Feilden* [1966] 2 QB 633; *Modahl v British Athletics Federation* [2001] EWCA Civ 1447, [2002] 1 WLR 1192.

5 Op cit, para 36. He stated that that acceptance was 'an obviously sensible position to adopt, since it is only through the Jockey Club's implementation of the Appeal Board's decision that an adverse effect on the claimant's livelihood arises, thus triggering the application of *Nagle v Feilden* and/or restraint of trade principles'.

6 Op cit, para 37 et seq. He described the test in these terms: 'That brings me to the nature of the court's supervisory jurisdiction over such a decision. The most important point, as it seems to me, is that it is *supervisory*. The function of the court is not to take the primary decision but to ensure that the primary decision-maker has operated within lawful limits. It is a review function, very similar to that of the court on judicial review. Indeed, given the difficulties that sometimes arise in drawing the precise boundary between the two, I would consider it surprising and unsatisfactory if a private law claim in relation to the decision of a domestic body required the court to adopt a materially different approach from a judicial review claim in relation to the decision of a public body. In each case the essential concern should be with the lawfulness of the decision taken: whether the procedure was fair, whether there was any error of law, whether any exercise of judgment or discretion fell within the limits open to the decision-maker, and so forth.'

7 At para 17; [2005] EWCA Civ 1056.

3.13   A number of points would appear to arise out of Richards J's analysis. In particular, first, it appears that the standard of, and grounds for, supervisory review that will be applied by the courts are the same irrespective of whether there is a contract. Secondly, care may have to be taken in the expression of the implied contractual obligations upon a sports governing body (as opposed to the express terms contained in the rules and regulations) to ensure that what is alleged does not seek to impose a greater obligation than that which would apply irrespective of contract. Thirdly, a claimant would be well advised to ensure that its claim is not articulated solely in terms of contract, but also in the alternative on the basis of the grounds for review that arise irrespective of contract as a function of the sports governing body's control and regulation of the sport. Fourthly, the extent to which a cause of action in damages arises when the grounds for review arise where there is a contract is a difficult question, affected by whether the decision is made by a separate disciplinary body, or the governing body itself. Fifthly, and most relevant to the subject matter of this section, where the decision is that of a separate disciplinary body, care should also be taken in the identification of the respondent to an action on the non-contractual basis, lest the governing body fail to adopt the 'obviously sensible' solution adopted by the Jockey Club of accepting that it should properly fulfil that role.[1] Absent some acceptance in pre-action correspondence that this is the position, it may be prudent to include the members of the relevant disciplinary body as defendants.

1 In *Sheffield United v FAPL*, decision of The FA Arbitral Tribunal dated 3 July 2007, [2007] ISLR-SLR 77, an FAPL rule Arbitration (Sir Philip Otton, David Pannick QC and Nick Randall) held that it was open to it, in an arbitration brought against the FAPL, to review the actions of the FAPL Disciplinary Commission notwithstanding an argument that it was independent from the FAPL itself. In *R (Mullins) v Appeal Board of the Jockey Club (Jockey Club as an interested party)* [2005] EWHC 2197 (Admin) and *Mullins v McFarlane (representing the Appeal Board of the Jockey Club) and the Jockey Club* [2006] EWHC 986 (QB) [2006] All ER (D) 66, the claimant first sought judicial review against the Appeal Board, then after the action was transferred to the QBD, took the precaution of suing the members of the Appeal Board as well as the Jockey Club itself. In *McKeown v British Horseracing Authority* [2010] EWHC 508 (QB), it appears that the transfer of regulatory functions from the Jockey Club to the BHA meant that no issue as to respondent arose. None at least was decided.

3.14   The third problematic situation is where the sports governing body, the decision of which is challenged, does not have legal personality. Although this is decreasingly the case, there remain for example a number of sports governing bodies that are unincorporated associations.[1] In these circumstances the sports governing body cannot be sued in its own right, and the action must be brought against its members.[2]

1 An example at national level is the Amateur Swimming Association, at international level World Rugby.

2 In 2006 in *ISI v International Rugby Board* proceedings were brought against rugby's international governing body, an unincorporated association. The early stages of the litigation, which settled before any judgment, related to the identity of the correct defendants to the action. ISI attempted to sue individuals who formed part of the executive of the IRB, in an attempt to avoid suing the national unions that were its members. In the event, the RFU was substituted as a representative defendant for the IRB. For the circumstances in which the officers or members of an unincorporated *club* may be liable, see *Harrison v West of Scotland Kart Club and RAC Motor Sport Association Limited* [2008] CSOH 33 (OH).

CHAPTER 4

Choice of forum for the challenge

4.1   Having analysed the facts and considered what causes of action are available, the third step is to consider whether the dispute arising on the facts and the law is best resolved, or falls necessarily to be resolved, in the courts or elsewhere.[1] The context (in other words not only the identity of the party affected, but also the nature, status and quality of the actions of the sports governing body or its independent tribunal) determines the route of challenge. It follows from the range of ways in which different individuals or businesses or groups of them can be affected, that sports governing bodies' actions can be characterised in a number of ways. They may for example be quasi-legislative, administrative, quasi-judicial or commercial. Sometimes the decision as to which route of challenge to follow is forced upon the claimant; sometimes it can be freely taken.

1 Under English law (and EU law), there is no body with general jurisdiction over challenges to the actions of sports governing bodies. However, first, the parties may have agreed through the rules to internal proceedings that form part of the ultimate decision-making of the sports governing body. They may also have agreed that any dispute, including a dispute as to the validity of a decision, falls to be reviewed by an arbitral body as opposed to the courts.

A   INTERNAL PROCEEDINGS AND INTERNAL DISPUTE RESOLUTION

4.2   In many instances, the actions of the sports governing body at issue involve a decision taken only after internal proceedings or an internal dispute resolution process. The choice to pursue those proceedings or that process arises at an earlier stage than the identification of a cause of action on the basis of which to challenge the decision. Internal proceedings arise most obviously in the context of disciplinary charges of doping, misconduct or other rule breaches. There may also be internal proceedings in the context of applications under the rules for a licence or permission to do something.[1] The internal proceedings may involve several stages, for example a first instance hearing and then an internal appeal process. As described above, the analysis in the *Bradley* case means that it may on occasion be a difficult question whether the relevant bodies are genuinely part of the sports governing body, such that their decisions remain those of the sports governing body. They may instead be independent bodies the decisions of which are reviewable on the same basis, or arbitral bodies whose awards are only subject to the review of the courts to the extent permitted by the Arbitration Act 1996 and the terms of the arbitration clause establishing them.[2] Depending on the rules, it may be that an appeal (whether to a further internal body or an arbitral body) can be made by the player or participant or by the sports governing body,[3] or even by another sports governing body.[4]

1 An example is Wimbledon FC's ultimately successful application to move to Milton Keynes. The rules of the Football League required it to obtain the permission of the Board of the Football League for the move. The Board refused. FA arbitration proceedings were brought challenging the decision on procedural and substantive grounds. An FA Arbitral Panel vacated the decision on procedural grounds, and remitted the matter to the League's Board. The League decided to ask an FA Commission to take the decision in its place. The Commission decided in favour of the club.

2 Under the Arbitration Act 1996 it is open to the parties in the arbitration agreement to exclude all but the 'mandatory provisions' of the Act. This means for example that it is possible to exclude the right to appeal on a point of law under s 69 of the Act. In the context of football, FA Rule K excludes that possibility (see, eg, *Sankofa and Charlton v The FA* [2007] EWHC 78 (Comm), whereas FAPL Rule S does not (see, eg, *Sheffield United v FAPL*, 13 July 2007 Smith J Comm Ct.

3 See *Korda v ITF* [1999] All ER (D) 337, CA (an independent Appeals Committee convened under the terms of the ITF Anti-Doping Programme upheld the finding of a doping offence, but found that 'exceptional circumstances' existed – namely the player's lack of knowledge of how the substance got into his body – that warranted waiver of any suspension. The ITF filed an appeal to the CAS against that decision. Lightman J granted the player a declaration that the ITF could not appeal its own decision to the CAS, but his decision was overturned by the Court of Appeal and the ITF was allowed to pursue its appeal).

4 See for example *IAAF v UKA and Walker* where the IAAF challenged UKA's acquittal of the athlete before the then IAAF Arbitral Panel [2001] 4 ISLR 264 and see [2000] 2 ISLR 41.

4.3   Equally, the rules may contemplate other disputes that can (or must) be referred to an internal dispute resolution process *after* an initial essentially administrative decision is taken by the executive. The mechanism for the internal resolution of disputes may be to refer the matter to another executive body, or to the governing body in a general meeting, or to a specially convened or standing commission, board, committee, or tribunal.[1] Again, as set out above, in some circumstances the appropriate characterisation of such bodies (as part of the governing body, an independent body, or an arbitral tribunal in its own right) may be a difficult question. There are as many systems for internal proceedings or for internal dispute resolution as there are sports governing bodies, and the concepts overlap.[2] Each system will take into account the particular history and circumstances of the sport to which it applies. What they will usually have in common however is that the decision they make is based on the substantive merits of the dispute, as opposed to the supervisory exercise undertaken by any court or arbitral body which is to review the way in which the decision is taken, and the legality of the arrangements in the wider context of public policy. The basis for the applicability of the internal proceedings (whether disciplinary or otherwise) or of any internal dispute resolution system is either the existence of some prior relationship between the sports governing body and the player or other affected participant, or the ability of the sports governing body to withhold access to the sport or a level of competition. Generally the player or participant is susceptible to the process, and equally entitled to rely upon it, because there is a contract to that effect arising out of membership or some other consensual agreement.[3] However, the player or other affected participant may be entitled to rely on a process set out in the rules of the sports governing body even in the absence of a contractual relationship, based simply on the fact that the body has made a decision in the course of its administration of the sport which affects the other party, for example because the other party has been refused membership or some sort of licence.[4] More difficult is the situation where it is the governing body that seeks to claim jurisdiction without any contractual basis.[5]

1 For example, the Football League's rules allow it to appoint a commission to decide an issue, or to ask The FA to appoint a commission to do so.
2 They may also overlap with the concept of external arbitration.
3 In *Bradley v Jockey Club* [2004] EWHC 2164 (Richards J), [2004] All ER (D) 11, upheld [2005] EWCA Civ 1056 the former jockey and the Jockey Club agreed that the rules of the governing body on the hearing of disciplinary proceedings would apply to his actions while a jockey, notwithstanding that he was no longer licensed.
4 The general grounds for review of a sports governing body's actions apply whether or not there is a contract. Another way of looking at it might be to say that a contractual term arises that any application will be dealt with in accordance with the rules.
5 Cf *Walker v UKA and IAAF* [2001] 4 ISLR 264. In that context it can be debatable whether jurisdiction strictly exists. In practice, however, such decisions of sports governing bodies can often be put into effect because even if the sports governing body cannot control the player by direct action in the courts, it can generally control access to the sport, through the organisation of competitions and its contracts with, or influence over, others involved in the sport.

4.4   In most contexts, the first stage of any challenge to the decision of a sports governing body is to fight through the internal disciplinary or regulatory proceedings, and to exhaust the appeal mechanisms provided for under the rules. Thereafter the resulting decision can be challenged elsewhere if appropriate, and if possible. It is generally better to pursue internal procedures first, because they are more likely to involve a decision that is (or at least ought to be) based on the substantive merits of the case. The governing body will be familiar with the sport. The 'prosecuting' executive of the governing body will often have to prove its case to a high standard of proof. As set out above, a court or arbitral tribunal exercising a supervisory function will in contrast often merely examine the way in which the decision is taken and the legality of the arrangements in the wider context of public policy; it will not look closely at the merits absent a breach of the rules. It will often be harder to show that the governing body has strayed outside the parameters set for it than to succeed on the underlying merits. In addition, the courts will generally expect the claimant to have exhausted all internal remedies.

4.5   However, in particular circumstances, the appropriate course may be to challenge the governing body's approach at an earlier stage,[1] particularly first where the sports governing body is asserting an exorbitant jurisdiction, the validity of which the player or other participant wishes to dispute, or secondly where the process is so procedurally unfair that there is little point in bowing to it.[2] In many instances it will be possible to take such points in front of the internal disciplinary (or dispute resolution) body involved.[3] Equally however, it may on occasion be felt that it is in the nature of such points that they are unlikely to find favour with the sports governing body's own creature and a challenger may think that his chances on the merits are worse if he takes jurisdictional points. If internal proceedings are continued in these circumstances, care must be taken not to submit to the very jurisdiction that it might be possible to challenge, or to waive any argument about procedural unfairness,[4] and in order to avoid doing this it may be necessary for the points to be taken, or at least reserved, before the internal body. Furthermore, if the internal proceedings are pursued, care must be taken by the player not to compound any injustice by his actions, which may preclude later complaint.[5] In these circumstances it may also be possible, and preferable, to bring court or arbitral proceedings before the matter is dealt with internally.[6]

1 See *Enderby Football Club v FA* [1971] Ch 591 at 606.
2 This was argued to be the case in *Stretford v The FA* [2007] EWCA Civ 238. Following the Court of Appeal's decision that any challenge to the legality of the FA's then disciplinary process fell to be pursued through Rule K arbitration, Mr Stretford commenced such an arbitration. The FA applied to the Chairman of the arbitral panel for a stay of the arbitration pending the hearing of the disciplinary proceedings against Mr Stretford. A stay was granted in *Stretford v FA (FA Rule K Arbitration)* Sir Martin Nourse, 5 December 2007, on the grounds that effective regulation was impeded by such challenges being made prior to disciplinary proceedings, that challenges based on procedural fairness were best assessed after the procedure impugned had taken place, and that the disciplinary proceedings might themselves resolve the complaints. The FA then pursued the disciplinary proceedings, and Mr Stretford duly raised in those proceedings his challenge to the legality of the process on the basis of Art 6 ECHR and common law appearance of bias. This challenge was rejected as a preliminary issue by the FA Regulatory Commission chaired by Nicholas Stewart QC, a decision upheld by the FA Appeal Board chaired by Peter Griffiths QC in *FA v Stretford (Disciplinary Proceedings)*, FA Appeal Board, 22 December 2008. Mr Stretford subsequently withdrew the Rule K arbitration.
3 This may depend on the rules in question, but as a general proposition it ought to be possible to take points going to the jurisdiction of, or the powers followed by, the internal body. If the points are well founded, the internal body is better off curing the problem as soon as possible, rather than seeing the matter go to court.
4 *Modahl v BAF*, 28 July 1997 CA, per Morritt LJ at 40G–42B of the shorthand writers' transcript (waiver of ability to allege appearance of bias); *UCI v A*, CAS 97/175, award dated 15 April 1998, *Digest of CAS Awards II 1998–2000*, pp 158, 166–67.
5 In *Bland v Sparkes* (1999) Times, 17 December, CA, it was held at p 9 of the Lexis transcript that Bland could not complain about the process 'when he refused to cooperate with the enquiry'. A lack of cooperation will probably not absolve governing bodies from affording natural justice, but may itself in fact be the cause of the problem.
6 *Enderby*, see note 1 above. The courts will not insist on futile internal proceedings being pursued. See *Stevenage Borough Football Club v Football League* (1996) 9 Admin LR 109 at 119C, CA. In *Collins v Lane*, 22 June 1999 CA, at p 12 of the shorthand writers' transcript, it was held that it would have been better for the claimant to have pursued his appeal, but that his failure to do so stemmed from the unlawfulness of the initial stages. He was therefore still entitled to relief.

B ATTEMPTS TO OUST THE JURISDICTION OF THE COURTS

4.6   Sports governing bodies cannot by their rules seek to oust the jurisdiction of the courts.[1] Nevertheless in the past many tried to do so,[2] and a few may still attempt this to a greater or lesser extent. A rule stating, for example, that the sports governing body's executive will have the final decision on a particular issue is invalid as contrary to public policy to the extent that it seeks to preclude recourse to the courts to challenge that decision on legal grounds. It is not possible to dress up the clause as one requiring the consent of the executive to any action being brought in the courts: that too is void.[3] Nor generally will it be possible to escape the jurisdiction of the English courts by claiming to be an international governing body not subject to English law or jurisdiction.

1 Except through a valid agreement to arbitrate.
2 *Baker v Jones (for British Amateur Weightlifters' Association)* [1954] 2 All ER 553 at 558. The governing body had power to act as the sole interpreter of rules and its decisions were expressed to be final. It was held that the parties could make an internal body the final arbiter on questions of fact, but could not make it the final arbiter on questions of law. The internal body could rule on such questions, but the court's jurisdiction to review matters of law could not be excluded.
3 *Enderby Town Football Club v Football Association* [1971] Ch 591 at 606.

C EXTERNAL ARBITRATION

4.7   The one exception to the rule that the jurisdiction of the courts cannot be ousted is that parties can contractually agree to refer disputes to arbitration. In the sports context, governing bodies often have a rule which provides for arbitration of future disputes arising between the governing body and a participant covered by the rules.[1] It is also open to the parties to reach an *ad hoc* agreement to arbitrate *after* the dispute has arisen. The type of arbitral tribunal provided for may be specific to the sport,[2] or may be a tribunal that specialises in sports arbitration more generally,[3] or may be one of the major commercial tribunals.[4] Whatever the form of the arbitration agreement, if the seat of the arbitration is in England, it will be governed by the Arbitration Act 1996.[5] Resort to external arbitration often occurs where a dispute has arisen in respect of a disciplinary or regulatory decision taken by the governing body (whether by its executive or after some sort of internal proceedings) or in respect of some other regulatory action such as the adoption of a rule, and the arbitral tribunal is substituted for the courts for the purposes of a challenge to that decision or action. The claim would then be based on the causes of action addressed in Chapters 7 to 12. In many contexts, however, the last appeal in internal disciplinary proceedings or in an internal dispute resolution system may take the form of reference to an external arbitration, whether brought by the player or participant or the sports governing body itself.[6] In those circumstances the arbitration may well address the substance of the issue and not be confined to supervisory review: the nature of the exercise will depend upon the rules. In some such contexts the reference to arbitration is not necessarily by the player or participant affected or the sports governing body, but may be by the international governing body in respect of a decision of the national governing body or its disciplinary or regulatory tribunals with which the international body disagrees.[7]

1 In many instances (eg, football) the international governing body insists upon such a clause. The same rule may also provide for arbitration between participants. See, eg, FA Rule K, which aims to ensure that all disputes between those involved in football under the FA rules are resolved through arbitration rather than the courts.

2 Again, such as the arbitration provided for under FA Rule K.

3 Such as the Court of Arbitration for Sport (CAS) based in Lausanne, or the National Anti-Doping Panel or Sport Resolutions (formerly the Sports Dispute Resolution Panel or SDRP), both based in London.

4 Such as the London Court of International Arbitration, ICC or UNCITRAL arbitration.

5 Under the 1996 Act resort may be had to the court amongst other things if the arbitration is improperly conducted or errs on a point of law. The court may also in some circumstances assist in the conduct of the arbitration, for example by the determination of preliminary points or the grant of interim relief.

6 See for example *Korda v ITF* [1999] All ER (D) 337, CA (an independent Appeals Committee convened under the terms of the ITF Anti-Doping Programme upheld the finding of a doping offence, but found that 'exceptional circumstances' existed – namely the player's lack of knowledge of how the substance got into his body – that warranted a waiver of any suspension. The ITF filed an appeal to the CAS against that decision. Lightman J granted the player a declaration that the ITF could not appeal its own decision to the CAS, but his decision was overturned by the Court of Appeal and the ITF was allowed to pursue its appeal to the CAS).

7 See for example *IAAF v UKA and Walker* IAAF Arbitral Award dated 20 August 2000 reported at [2001] 4 ISLR 264, see also [2000] 2 ISLR 41 (application of IAAF rules providing for independent arbitration of disputes between the IAAF and the national bodies which are its members, arising out of the national bodies' application of the doping rules to athletes from their countries). There are many other examples of such IAAF appeals: for some of them see [2001] 4 ISLR 254 et seq (*Sotomayor, Ottey, Walker, Christie, Cadogan*).

4.8　　　The test for whether arrangements establish an arbitration capable of taking the place of the courts was first set out in the context of sport in *Walkinshaw v Diniz*.[1] Broadly, the body established must be chosen by the parties, must be independent and impartial, and must decide the issue by reference to the law and the facts following a proper procedure, and it must be contemplated that the decision is binding. If the test is satisfied, then subject to any agreement for an arbitral appeal, the decisions of the arbitration can only be challenged before the courts on the limited grounds contained in the Arbitration Act 1996.[2] In *Kaneria* the High Court applied the *Walkinshaw* test to the England and Wales Cricket Board's appeal procedures and concluded that it satisfied the test. The Arbitration Act 1996 accordingly applied to it, and therefore the ECB's application pursuant to s 43 of the Act for a witness summons compelling an individual to give evidence at the hearing of Kaneria's appeal against his lifetime ban for match-fixing was granted.[3] The courts have subsequently adopted the same test in other sports, such as boxing.[4] Despite the relatively liberal approach that the English courts have applied to the disciplinary procedures of sports' governing bodies, a greater degree of scrutiny may be necessary in the future. In *Claudia Pechstein v The International Skating Union*,[5] the Munich Federal Appeal Court ruled that an arbitration clause between an athlete and a sports governing body that provided CAS with final jurisdiction was invalid under German and possibly European antitrust law. Key to the court's decision was the fact that CAS arbitrators are made up of a closed list appointed by a method that was perceived to favour the governing bodies in comparison to the athletes.[6] It is possible that litigants might seek to advance similar criticism of some national sports arbitral bodies. However, in June 2016 the German Federal Court ruled against Ms Pechstein[7] following the ISU's appeal, finding, amongst other things, that she voluntarily accepted the jurisdiction of CAS; the monopolistic situation of the ISU and its insistence that athletes accept an arbitration clause in favour of CAS does not constitute an abuse of a dominant position; CAS is a genuine arbitral tribunal; the advantages of having a uniform international sports jurisdiction, such as uniform standards and timely procedures stand not only for sports federations but also for athletes; and any possible predominance of federations is balanced by CAS procedural rules, the independence and neutrality of CAS arbitrators, who can be challenged and removed from a CAS panel if they are not independent from the parties and by the possibility given to any party affected by a CAS decision to file an appeal to the Swiss Federal Tribunal. Ms Pechstein has vowed to fight on to the Federal Constitutional Court, and, in any event, the fallout from the *Pechstein* case is likely to go away easily. FIFPro the powerful football players' union, has called on CAS and other sport stakeholders to work with player and athlete unions to ensure proper structural representation and absolute impartiality of its tribunals and administrations,[8] and CAS itself has issued a statement committing itself to continue to listen to and analyse the requests and suggestions of its users and ensure an efficient procedure and a fair trial for all its users.[9] There is likely to be further pressure on sports governing bodies to demonstrate their arbitral procedures are fair and transparent and that those appointed to arbitrate disputes between athletes and governing bodies are properly independent of the parties.

1 [2000] 2 All ER (Comm) 237 at 250e to 255j. Thomas J said the criteria to be applied in evaluating whether the rules amounted to an agreement to arbitrate were as follows:

'(1) The wording of the clause; "terminology, though a pointer, can be no more than that. It is necessary to examine the substance."

(2) The duty to apply the law; "the hallmark of the arbitration process is that it is a procedure to determine the legal rights and obligations of the parties judicially, with binding effect, which is enforceable in law, thus reflecting in private proceedings the roles of a civil court of law".

(3) The procedure adopted should be arbitral in nature. Thomas J adopted the analysis set out in Mustill & Boyd [*Commercial Arbitration*, 2nd edn at p 41], setting out the following attributes of arbitration:

    (i) The agreement pursuant to which the process is, or is to be, carried on ("the procedural agreement") must contemplate that the tribunal which carries on the process will make a decision which is binding on the parties to the procedural agreement.

    (ii) The procedural agreement must contemplate that the process will be carried on between those persons whose substantive rights are determined by the tribunal.

(iii)   The jurisdiction of the tribunal to carry on the process and to decide the rights of the parties must derive either from the consent of the parties…

(iv)   The tribunal must be chosen, either by the parties, or by a method to which they have consented.

(v)   The procedural agreement must contemplate that the tribunal will determine the rights of the parties in an impartial manner, with the tribunal owing an equal obligation of fairness towards both sides.

(vi)   The agreement of the parties to refer their disputes to the decision of the tribunal must be intended to be enforceable in law.

(vii)   The procedural agreement must contemplate a process whereby the tribunal will make a decision upon a dispute which is already formulated at the time when the tribunal is appointed.

(4)   Other factors characteristic of arbitration were that the parties were to have a proper opportunity of presenting their case; the tribunal should not receive unilateral communications from the parties and was required to disclose all communications with one party to the other party; the procedure was to be impartial; and there was proper and proportionate means for the receipt of evidence.

(5)   The composition of the tribunal is important, where lawyers compose it, it is an important indication that the process was intended to be arbitral.'

2   Which may themselves be further limited by agreement in the arbitration clause (as is the position in FA Rule K).

3   *England and Wales Cricket Board Ltd v Kaneria* [2013] EWHC 1074 (Comm).

4   *Bruce Baker v The British Boxing Board of Control* [2015] EWHC 2469 (Ch).

5   Pressemitteilung Zivilsachen, Oberlandesgericht München, 15 January 2015.

6   CAS operates a closed list from which the parties can select an arbitrator, and the people on that list are appointed by CAS's executive, ICAS. At the time of the decision in *Pechstein* the CAS code itself required that three fifths of arbitrators appointed were appointed following recommendations from sports governing bodies. Whilst that part of the Code has since been relaxed, the reforms CAS have made so far may be insufficient to answer the criticisms of the Munich Court. ICAS itself, which appoints the arbitrators, is still constituted overwhelmingly by members from sports governing bodies, those nominated by athletes' unions being very much in the minority. ICAS nominates the president of the CAS Appeals Arbitration Division who in turn has the power to nominate the president of each arbitral panel. At present the President of ICAS also happens to be the Vice-President of the International Olympic Committee, one of the most important international regulators. It has been suggested that this creates an inevitable conflict of interest, see for instance: *The Court of Arbitration for Sport after Pechstein: Reform or Revolution?* Antoine Duval, 17 November 2015, available at http://www.asser.nl/SportsLaw/Blog/post/the-court-of-arbitration-for-sport-after-pechstein-reform-or-revolution.

7   At the time of writing the full decision is not available, but a summary (in German) appears on the Court's website, here: http://juris.bundesgerichtshof.de/cgi-bin/rechtsprechung/document.py?Gericht=bgh&Art=pm&Datum=2016&Sort=3&nr=74892&pos=6&anz=103.

8   See, *Despite decision, Pechstein must trigger reform.* FIFPro statement, 7 June 2016: https://www.fifpro.org/en/news/despite-decision-pechstein-must-trigger-reform.

9   See, *Statement of CAS on the decision by the German Federal Tribunal in Claudia Pechstein v ISU*, 7 June 2016: http://www.tas-cas.org/fileadmin/user_upload/Media_Release_Pechstein_07.06.16_English.pdf.

4.9   A valid arbitration clause agreed between the parties and covering the dispute in question will be enforced by the courts, which will at the suit of a party[1] to the arbitration agreement almost always stay any action brought in the courts in breach of it.[2] If, however, the clause is for some reason invalid or inoperable,[3] or not binding on the claimant,[4] or does not cover the dispute,[5] a stay may be resisted. Equally, however, if a matter is not covered by an arbitration clause, the court may restrain arbitration proceedings.[6]

1   But in the absence of suit, a court is unlikely to take the point itself.

2   Under s 9 of the Arbitration Act 1996. See *Stretford v The FA* [2007] EWCA Civ 238; *Phoenix v FIA and FOM* [2002] EWHC 1028 (Ch).

3   In *Stretford v The FA*, it was argued unsuccessfully that FA Rule K was inoperable for the purposes of s 9 of the Arbitration Act 1996. The claimant contended that Rule K was in breach of Art 6 ECHR

because he had not unequivocally waived his right to go to court and the Rule K arbitral process did not satisfy Art 6. The Chancellor and then the Court of Appeal held that there had been an unequivocal waiver and Rule K was fully compliant with Art 6, notwithstanding that it was an unavoidable rule of a sports governing body. The court rejected a similar argument in *England and Wales Cricket Board Ltd v Kaneria* [2013] EWHC 1074 (Comm). Arguments may remain: it has been suggested in other unresolved and unreported litigation that even if the imposition of an arbitration clause complies with Art 6, it may nevertheless amount to an abuse of a dominant position in the form of making membership or a licence conditional on a separate, onerous, obligation. Such an argument faces the problem that a court would be unlikely to view arbitration as onerous, or the imposition of the rule as disproportionate.

4 Where a contract on the basis of the rules exists, then the position ought to be relatively straightforward: in *Stretford* it was also alleged that the arbitration clause contained in FA Rule K had not been properly incorporated into any contract between Mr Stretford and The FA, but the Chancellor and the Court of Appeal rejected this suggestion. In *Walker v UKA and IAAF* the athlete unsuccessfully disputed that the IAAF could appeal his acquittal by UKA of doping charges to the IAAF Arbitral Panel, because he claimed that there was no contract between him and the IAAF and no contractual submission by him to the jurisdiction of the IAAF Arbitral Panel (Toulson J 3 July 2000, Hallett J 25 July 2000, IAAF Arbitral Award 20 August 2000 reported at [2001] 4 ISLR 264, see also [2000] 2 ISLR 41. The issue of when an arbitration agreement applies to a non-party to the agreement, whose rights are derived from a party to the agreement, was discussed in *Phoenix v FIA and FOM* [2002] EWHC 1028 (Ch).

5 This will depend upon the construction of the arbitration clause. Arbitration clauses are generally expressed in very wide terms and are apt to cover just about any dispute or difference. However in some circumstances, an analysis of the rules may lead a court to conclude there is no submission to arbitration, and so it can decide the matter itself (and refuse an Arbitration Act 1996 stay where sought). In *Rangers Football Club Plc, Petitioner* [2012] CSOH 95; 2012 GWD 20-402, the SFA contended unsuccessfully that the Scottish courts had no jurisdiction to review its decision, on the basis of an arbitration agreement in favour of CAS. The Court of Session Outer House held that it had jurisdiction. Although the FIFA statutes required associations to provide the means for disputes to be resolved and to recognise CAS, and to provide for appeals to CAS in certain circumstances, they did not expressly require disputes between associations and member clubs to go to CAS, and the SFA provision did not require such disputes to be referred to arbitration before CAS. Furthermore, the SFA rules provided that the appellate tribunal's decision was final and binding and that there was no further right of appeal, which excluded any appeal to CAS. It is now clear that an arbitration clause will generally entitle a respondent to an Arbitration Act 1996, s 9 stay of a Companies Act 2006, s 994 unfair prejudice petition: *Fulham Football Club (1987) Ltd v Richards* [2011] EWCA Civ 855, [2012] Ch 333. In certain other jurisdictions, the courts' jurisdiction over competition law cannot be ousted: thus in *Sporting du Pays de Charleroi v FIFA* (C-243/06) [2006] OJ C212/11, the club's competition law claim was before the Belgian courts, as opposed to in arbitration. The position under English law is probably that competition law claims can be the subject of arbitration, although the regulatory authorities' jurisdiction cannot be excluded. A caveat is that in cases involving mandatory EU rules, there arguably must be the possibility of a reference to the European Court of Justice on points of law. On the face of it, arbitration under the 1996 Act might be thought to preclude such a reference (at least absent consent) since the arbitrators have no power to refer and the Act does not appear to contemplate the court making such relief in support of arbitration. However in *Eco Swiss China Time Ltd v Benetton International BV* (C-126/97) [1999] ECR I-3055, a mechanism was arguably found for ensuring that a reference could be made under a public policy provision that has an equivalent in the 1996 Act.

6 In *Sheffield United Football Club Ltd v West Ham United Football Club Plc* [2008] EWHC 2855 (Comm), [2009] 1 Lloyd's Rep 167, [2008] 2 CLC 741, (2008) Sport and Law Journal vol 16 iss 2 (2008) SLJR 4, the court granted Sheffield an anti-suit injunction restraining West Ham from seeking to raise before CAS a challenge to the decision of an FA Rule K arbitration.

4.10   As set out above (paras **4.8–4.9**), if there is a valid arbitration clause binding on the player or other participant and on which the governing body intends to rely, then the freedom of the player or other participant to choose a different route is very limited. However, where for whatever reason the player or other participant is able to opt for arbitration or another route, the advantages and disadvantages of arbitration in the specific context have to be weighed in order to make that choice. The principal advantage of arbitration is that the process is generally more flexible than litigation before the courts, or at least more flexible than litigation before the courts in the way that such litigation has traditionally been conducted. The arbitration panel will generally include experts on the particular sport who do not need to be brought up to speed on the background but who can instead proceed directly to the nub of the dispute. The arbitration panel will answer the question referred to it. In many instances, the issues that it will resolve will be the same or at least very similar to the issues that a court would have to resolve, but the parties do have the opportunity to narrow the issues. The arbitration panel may not be constrained by the same rules of evidence and procedure, and again it is open to the parties to agree to limit disclosure and to set constraints on the way that oral evidence and argument is presented. Arbitration may in particular instances represent a cheaper and quicker solution. It is theoretically possible to keep the result of an arbitration confidential.[1]

1 Though the desirability of this may need to be reappraised in the light of *Stretford v The FA* [2007] EWCA Civ 238 where The FA agreed to publication, with the result that even if Art 6 were applicable to Rule K arbitration, its requirements were fulfilled.

4.11   There are however significant drawbacks to arbitration. Arbitration can be less certain: the law and procedure applied by arbitration panels varies from body to body.[1] There may on occasion be a perception that the quality of decision making is lower. In addition, under the Arbitration Act 1996, the avenues for appeal of an arbitration decision are limited[2] and interim relief[3] or a reference to the European Court of Justice may well be harder to obtain. Conversely the choice to proceed by way of arbitration may also mean that there is a lack of finality, for example if the subject matter also falls under the jurisdiction of a regulatory authority,[4] or if a governing body respondent seeks at all costs to avoid complying with the arbitration's decision.[5] Because arbitration is consensual, it may be more difficult for the tribunal to allow interventions or to join parties, and it may not be possible to rely on the conclusions of the arbitral tribunal in another arbitration.[6] Arbitration panels may not have the same range of sanctions and final relief on offer as do the courts, and enforcement may involve resort to the courts in any event. Lastly, it may well no longer be the case that arbitration is cheaper and faster than going to court. The parties have to pay the arbitrator, whose fees may well exceed those to issue a court claim. The courts have become more and more prepared to join with the parties in fashioning a streamlined and efficient approach to the resolution of a particular dispute.

1 For example, the CAS Code of Sports-Related Arbitration provides: 'The Panel shall decide the dispute according to the applicable regulations and the rules of law chosen by the parties or, in the absence of such choice, according to the law of the country in which the federation, association or sports body which has issued the challenged decision is domiciled'. It is also possible to have the matter decided 'ex aequo et bono' and CAS will apply general principles of law. In relation to cases arising at the Olympic Games, CAS will apply Swiss principles of private international law to determine the applicable law.
2 See the Arbitration Act 1996; *Sheffield United v FAPL*, 13 July 2007 Smith J Comm Ct; *Stretford v The FA* [2007] EWCA Civ 238.
3 The circumstances in which the courts will grant interim relief under s 44 are quite narrow: see *Sankofa and Charlton v The FA*, 12 January 2007, Comm Ct Simon J; *Phoenix v FIA and FOM* [2002] EWHC 1028 (Ch). The arbitral body may or may not have jurisdiction to grant interim relief itself. FA Rule K.8 gives a tribunal jurisdiction to grant interim relief. CAS has jurisdiction to grant interim relief, but only once proceedings have begun: see Code, rule 37; applied for example in *Haga v FIM*, 2000/A/281, award dated 22 December 2000, *Digest of CAS Awards II 1998–2000*, pp 410, 412; *AEK Athens and Slavia Prague v UEFA* CAS arbitration 98/200 interim decision 17 July 1998, final decision 20 August 1999, *Digest of CAS Awards II 1998–2000*, p 35, and in [2001] 1 ISLR 122. It is however often open to a sports governing body to put the application of its decision on hold if a reference is made to arbitration under its rules:the IAAF's attempt to suspend the athlete pending an IAAF arbitration despite his acquittal of doping charges by UKA was criticised by Hallett J during submissions in *Walker v UKA and IAAF*, 25 July 2000, because the rule allowing this to be done was introduced after the events in question. The matter was compromised during the hearing. The IAAF decided to allow the athlete to compete pending the arbitration, but he chose not to do so.

4 CAS held that there was no breach of Arts 101 or 102 TFEU in UEFA's rule banning ownership of more than one club in the same competition, but this meant little to the European Commission, which proceeded to consider the matter unconstrained by CAS's determination. See, eg, *AEK Athens and Slavia Prague v UEFA* CAS arbitration 98/200 interim decision 17 July 1998, final decision 20 August 1999, *Digest of CAS Awards II 1998–2000*, p 35, and in [2001] 1 ISLR 122; Commission press release IP/99/965, 9 December 1999. The Commission eventually decided not to pursue ENIC's complaint: see Commission press release IP/02/942, 27 June 2002.

5 As in the long-running but unreported CAS litigation between the Gibraltar Football Association and UEFA. Gibraltar was eventually admitted to UEFA on 24 May 2013.

6 The principle of confidentiality of arbitrations means that an interested party cannot be joined without the consent of all: West Ham was refused permission in 2012 to intervene in *Leyton Orient v FAPL*. It also means that what has been decided in an earlier linked arbitration (*Sheffield Utd FC v West Ham FC*) is nevertheless inadmissible in a later one (*Fulham FC v West Ham FC*) addressed in 'Fulham Football Club v West Ham United Football Club' (2011) International Sports Law Review 1, SLR1-7.

D COURT

4.12 If arbitration is not forced upon, or opted for by the claimant, any challenge in legal proceedings will be before the courts. The action will be a private law one based on the causes of action addressed in Chapters 7 to 12. The remedies and procedure before the English courts are addressed in Chapters 13 and 14. The normal considerations apply in relation to the selection of the court in which to proceed. The particular form of the action initiated in the English courts will be determined by the quality of the sports governing body's actions, and its effects.

E ALTERNATIVE DISPUTE RESOLUTION OR MEDIATION

4.13 It may be possible in particular cases to resolve the dispute by way of an alternative dispute resolution process such as mediation. However, a difficulty which will often arise is that ADR works on the basis of compromise rather than a finding on a cause of action. Often, sports governing bodies are not in a position to compromise, because the dispute is not of the normal bilateral sort: rather, they are acting in vindication of the interests of all participants and of the public generally in the integrity of the sport: for example if the issue is whether a doping offence has been committed or a player has been improperly acquired.[1] Nevertheless, some disputes such as commercial disputes and personal injury actions[2] may be capable of mediation. There is an increased preparedness to follow this approach,[3] even in a regulatory context.

1 If a compromise were reached, there would be a significant risk that another party aggrieved by the way in which the settling complainant has been 'favourably' treated to the other party's perceived disadvantage, will itself complain.

2 In *Dean Ashton v Wright-Phillips, The FA, and Chelsea*, mediation was used to resolve the player's claim against The FA and the club, which was based on the Chelsea player whose tackle had injured him being on England international duty at the time.

3 CAS and Sport Resolutions both provide for mediation. Sport Resolutions states on its website that it has successfully resolved through mediation disputes over the termination of coaching contracts, deterioration in relationships within the board room or dressing room, issues arising from commercial contracts, rights and entitlements to govern sport and competitions, discrimination issues, and safeguarding children in sport issues.

F   ADMINISTRATIVE AUTHORITIES

4.14   In particular contexts, the actions of a sports governing body will be contrary to legal rules which are administered, under English domestic legislation or under EU legislation, by specified administrative authorities. The most obvious examples are the Competition and Markets Authority and the Competition Directorate of the European Commission. This jurisdiction often applies at the same time as a parallel jurisdiction in the English courts to enforce the same rules (or most of them) in private actions. An alternative to bringing costly court or arbitral proceedings may therefore be to complain to the administrative authorities, which have the power and obligation to bring an end to serious infringements of the rules. While this approach may cost less, and the arguments involved may be more readily accepted by the regulatory authorities than the courts, it has drawbacks. Once a complaint is made, the matter is effectively out of the control of the complainant. Although in many cases the authorities will not press ahead with a complaint if it is withdrawn or not actively pursued by the complainant, those authorities are able to continue an investigation if appropriate and in serious cases will do so. Equally, the basis of the resolution of any breach (for example by the acceptance of undertakings) is often outside the control or even significant influence of the complainant. The process will often take longer than court proceedings to produce a result, and the complainant cannot force the pace. If the breach of the competition rules involves an agreement to which the complainant is itself a party, there is a risk that the complainant could also expose itself to sanction. The parameters of the regulatory authorities' investigation cannot be confined quite as easily as the courts: there is a risk that practices that the complainant welcomed (for example collective selling of rights) might be put at risk as well as the particular application of which it complained (for example the sale of the rights to a competitor for too long a period and without a tender process). The last drawback is the corollary of the above: the Competition and Markets Authority may decide that a particular case does not warrant investigation, even if the legal analysis advanced by the complainant is correct.[1] Similarly, a complaint to the European Commission may prove fruitless as a result of the application of the concept of lack of 'Community interest'. The Commission is increasingly unwilling to look at complaints or notifications which it perceives to have little impact on international sport throughout the Community. Furthermore, the Commission is attempting to devolve the responsibility for the application of the competition rules onto the Member States.[2]

---

1 The OFT refused to investigate Ashley Cole's complaint in relation to the legality of the FAPL rules which prevented him even speaking to another club about future employment after the lawful conclusion of his current employment, a situation that cannot apply in other employment contexts.

2 See the European Commission – Press release, 'Antitrust: Commission opens formal investigation into International Skating Union's eligibility rules', Brussels, 5 October 2015 (http://europa.eu/rapid/press-release_IP-15-5771_en.htm) in which the Commission sought to set out the limits of its interest in intervening in sporting matters stating that generally disputes about sporting rules that raise issues related to governance of the sport, can usually be best handled by national courts rather than by the Commission. The Commission did however state that it would investigate rules that enforced a monopoly over the organisation of sporting events or otherwise restricted competition because 'Athletes can only compete at the highest level for a limited number of years, so there must be good reasons for preventing them to take part in events'.

CHAPTER 5

Public or private?

5.1   Sports governing bodies take a variety of forms on the spectrum between 'private' and 'public' bodies, and their decisions affect rights which range from the purely private, to rights which on any basis have many of the features of a public right. The governing body has responsibility (often sole responsibility) for regulating an area of public activity. It purports to act in the public interest. It is quite possible in many instances that if the governing body did not exist, it would have to be created by government. The governing body often has a particular expertise and experience in making the type of decision involved. Its decisions affect the rights of a range of individuals and businesses, often without there being a contractual relationship between them establishing the right or conferring jurisdiction on the governing body to make decisions affecting those individuals and/or businesses. Even where there is a nominal contractual relationship, arguably it is often not truly consensual or voluntary[1] but rather a constitutional arrangement of rules, regulations and codes of conduct that is deemed to apply to all those who participate in the sport. On the other hand, most governing bodies have their origins some time ago in individuals or groups of individuals forming an unincorporated association to run a sport in which they were involved. They remain characterised by having a membership of private persons (whether limited companies or individuals), and various committees drawn from their membership and acting in various areas. To the extent that they have modernised their structure, it has been in the direction of incorporation as private law companies. Their powers are not in the real sense of the word governmental, in that they are at least nominally predicated on a specific consensual or contractual arrangement. Arguably, the rights which their actions affect are also held through the consensus of those involved in the sport. If that consensus disappears, those involved are entitled to walk away and form their own new governing body, in competition with the original. Some sports governing bodies, such as those running leagues in sports where there is a separate regulatory body, have many of the characteristics of a commercial association of businesses.

1 *Per contra, Stretford v The FA* [2006] [2007] EWCA Civ 238. Both the Chancellor and the Court of Appeal were prepared to characterise the involvement of football agents in the sport under the terms of their FA licences (which included an obligation to comply with the FA's and FIFA's rules) as voluntary and consensual, although the agents had to have a licence in order to conduct their business (since clubs and players are only permitted to deal with agents who have such a licence).

5.2   This varying public element has had four consequences of significance to the bringing of a challenge to their actions. First, it has led to debate in the courts and in texts as to whether the decisions of sports governing bodies (or at least some of their decisions) are amenable to judicial review in the Administrative Court under CPR Pt 54 on the basis that their actions affect public rights. Secondly, it has raised the possibility of the application of the Human Rights Act 1998 to the decisions of sports governing bodies. Thirdly it has resulted in the extension to sports governing bodies of EU free movement obligations owed by the state and not by private bodies. Lastly, it has had a fundamental influence on the degree of review to which the courts are prepared to subject different types of decisions. This section looks at the first three consequences and the next section addresses the fourth, all in the context of a challenge to a sports governing body's actions.

A   PUBLIC OR PRIVATE FOR THE PURPOSES OF THE CHOICE OF PROCEDURE

(a)   The present position

5.3   On the current authorities, challenges under English law to the actions of sports governing bodies should be brought in private law proceedings (in the courts or by arbitration if appropriate) and not by way of judicial review. The English courts have consistently held,[1] most recently in *Mullins v Jockey Club*,[2] that the relationship between a governing body and its members or participants is a private law one (whether contractual or in any event based on the governing body's control of its sport) and that the rights affected are not capable of protection through judicial review before the Administrative Court under CPR Pt 54.

1   *Law v National Greyhound Racing Club Ltd* [1983] 1 WLR 1302; *R v Football Association of Wales, ex p Flint Town* [1991] COD 44; *R v Football Association, ex p Football League Ltd* [1993] 2 All ER 833; *R v Jockey Club, ex p Massingberd-Mundy* [1993] 2 All ER 207 and *R v Jockey Club, ex p Aga Khan* [1993] 1 WLR 909.

2   [2005] EWHC 2197 (Admin). Stanley Burnton J ordered the proceedings to be transferred to the QBD and continued as if begun by CPR Pt 8. In *Mullins v McFarlane (representing the Appeal Board of the Jockey Club) and the Jockey Club* [2006] EWHC 986 [2006] All ER (D) 66, Stanley Burnton J held that the challenge in private law failed.

(b)   Is there any exception?

5.4   As noted above, the basis for the courts' current approach lies chiefly in the fact that they have often felt able to identify a contractual relationship between a sports governing body and the relevant claimant, which has been regarded as precluding judicial review. There are two bases on which the existence of a contract precludes judicial review, and they have not been clearly distinguished in the authorities. First, a contractual relationship suggests that the rights affected are private law rights as opposed to public law rights. Secondly it means that there is an alternative remedy, which removes the need for a public law avenue for challenge. Although the existence of a contract is the most important factor, it is not the only one.[1] Each case must be assessed in the light of its own particular facts. It is therefore conceivable that a set of factual circumstances could arise where the sports governing body's decision affected rights in such a way that, even on the current state of the law, the court concluded that judicial review was available: for example if there were no contractual analysis upon which the court could fall back and a plainly injured party would be left without private law recourse.[2] Such a set of circumstances is however unlikely to arise in the light of two factors. First, it is now clear that sports governing bodies owe broadly the same obligations as a matter of private law as they would if their decisions were susceptible to public law review:[3] certainly it is more likely that a court would hold that the obligations were the same in both contexts than that a sports governing body was susceptible to judicial review. Secondly, the culmination of the *Modahl* litigation suggests that the courts are likely to be more ready than previously to find a contract between a governing body and a participant in the sport.[4]

1 See Fordham, *Judicial Review* (6th edn, Hart Publishing, 2012), Ch P34, and on availability of an alternative remedy, Ch P36; Wade and Forsyth, *Administrative Law* (11th edn, Oxford University Press, 2014) at pp 532–545; *R v Football Association, ex p Football League Ltd* [1993] 2 All ER 833; *R v Jockey Club, ex p RAM Racecourses* [1993] 2 All ER 225, DC. The generally applicable test is that in *R v City Panel on Take-overs and Mergers, ex p Datafin* [1987] QB 815.

2 But note *R v Lord Chancellor's Department, ex p Nangle* [1991] ICR 743 where Stuart-Smith LJ said *obiter* at 956 that 'the mere fact that someone has no private law remedy does not mean that they have a public law one'.

3 See in particular *Bradley v Jockey Club* [2004] EWHC 2164 (Richards J), [2004] All ER (D) 11, upheld [2005] EWCA Civ 1056. In neither *Bradley* nor *Mullins* did the lack of a contract between the Appeal Board and the claimant mean that the appropriate procedure was Pt 54.

4 In the light of *Modahl* and *Bradley*, the relevant terms of the contract may on occasion be uncertain. It is likely to be implicit in any contract found to exist between a member or participant and a sports governing body that, so far as its own actions are concerned, the sports governing body will be subject to the equivalent of the public law standard of review that would apply irrespective of the contract. But where a decision is taken by a separate regulatory or disciplinary body established by the sports governing body, the extent of the sports governing body's contractual obligations appear to be confined to (i) providing the procedure, and (ii) only applying and enforcing a decision in so far as it is lawful by the equivalent of the public law standard of review.

(c) The contrary view

5.5   In the first edition of *Sport: Law and Practice* edited by Lewis and Taylor, before the decision in *Mullins*, the view was advanced that short of the Supreme Court, the approach of the Court of Appeal in *Aga Khan* was likely to be followed in almost all circumstances, and that to seek to reopen the issue would be difficult. After the decision in *Mullins*, the prospects seem even worse, with Stanley Burnton J's rejection of the arguments there advanced. While it remains the position that a number of judges, commentators and practitioners have taken a contrary view to the Court of Appeal,[1] that the contrary view has found favour in other jurisdictions[2] and in analogous contexts (in particular the developments in the context of human rights),[3] each of these factors was found[4] insufficient to warrant a departure from *Aga Khan*.

1 The argument continues to be made in the texts and articles. See, for example, Michael J Beloff, 'Watching out for the googly: judicial review in the world of sport' (2009) 14(2) Judicial Review 136–141; Beloff, 'Pitch Pool Rink ... Court? Judicial Review in the Sporting World' [1989] PL 95 at 104; Pannick, 'Judicial Review of Sports Governing Bodies' [1997] JR 150; Beloff and Kerr [1996] JR 30. There remains the support given to the argument by Simon Brown J in *RAM Racecourses*. Furthermore, in *Stevenage Borough Football Club v Football League* (1996) Times, 1 August, Carnwath J appears to have preferred the proposition that sports governing bodies were public bodies.

2 For a comparative examination, see Eileen Kelly, 'Judicial review of sports bodies' decisions: comparable common law perspectives' (2011) 4 International Sports Law Review 71–75 (discussing *Mullins* and the differing Scots approach in *Wiles v Bothwell Castle Golf Club* 2005 SLT 785 (OH)). *Scotland*: in *Rangers Football Club plc, Petitioner* [2012] CSOH 95; 2012 GWD 20–402, the Scots' court quashed an SFA decision in judicial review proceedings. *Northern Ireland*: in litigation variously titled *Re Hubert's* and *Re Watson's Application for Leave to Appeal for Judicial Review* [2011] NIQB 66, [2012] NI 109, it was held that a club's application for Northern Irish judicial review of a decision of the Irish Football Association's Independent Arbitration Panel was excluded by an arbitration agreement excluding appeal to any court. *New Zealand*: *Finnigan v New Zealand Rugby Football Union*

[1985] 2 NZLR 159, 181 and 190; see also *New Zealand Trotting Conference v Ryan* [1990] 1 NZLR 143. Australia: *Forbes v New South Wales Trotting Club Ltd* (1979) 143 CLR 242; see also *Justice v South Australian Trotting Control Board* (1989) 50 FAR 613). *South Africa*: it was held in *National Horse Racing Authority of Southern Africa v Naidoo and Another* (AR254/08) [2009] ZAKZHC 6; 2010 (3) SA 182 (N) (23 February 2009) by a majority of the court that the review of a decision of a sports domestic disciplinary tribunal does not constitute public administrative action for the purpose of the South African Promotion of Administration Justice Act 2000. The decision is rather to be reviewed in accordance with the principles established in *Marlon v Durban Turf Club and Others* 1942 AD 112; *Jockey Club of South Africa and others v Feldman* 1942 AD 340, *Turner v Jockey Club of South Africa* 1974(3) SA 633 (A) and *Jockey Club of South Africa v Forbes* (1993) 1 SA 649. However in *Daniels and Others v WP Rugby and another* [2011] ZAWCHC 481, the court preferred the minority view in *Naidoo*, in reliance on amongst other things *Tifu Raiders Rugby Club v South African Rugby Union* [2006] (2) ALLSA 549 and held that the sports governing body was fulfilling a public function (see also *Louisvale Pirates v South African Football Association* [2012] ZAGPJHC 78). *Canada*: *Barrieau v US Trotting Association* (1986) 78 NBR (2d) 128, 198 APR 128. *Hong Kong*, where the conclusion that the decisions of sports governing bodies are not amenable to public law judicial review has been followed: *Hong Kong Rifle Association v Hong Kong Shooting Association* [2012] HKCU 1504. *India*: in *AC Muthiah v Board of Control for Cricket in India & Anr* [2011] INSC 436, the Supreme Court of India held that the BCCI is not a public body discharging public functions for the purposes of Indian law. *Kenya*: see *Kenya v Kenya Cricket Association*, 2006 (HC Kenya), discussed in Migai Akech, 'Kenya v Kenya Cricket Association: The Maurice Odumbe investigation and judicial review of the power of international sports organisations' (2008) 6(2) Entertainment & Sports Law Journal.

3   Reliance has been placed on the supposedly wider tests for the application of the Human Rights Act 1998, and under EU law. The same governing bodies that are supposedly not susceptible to judicial review are 'emanations of the state' for the purposes of EU law and could potentially be 'public authorities' for the purposes of the Human Rights Act 1998.

4   *R (Mullins) v Appeal Board of the Jockey Club (Jockey Club as an interested party)* [2005] EWHC 2197 (Admin), respectively at paras 32, 33 and 44.

(d)   Does it matter?

5.6   As mentioned above, it is now clear that sports governing bodies' decisions are broadly subject to the same standard of review as a matter of private law as they would be if their decisions were susceptible to public law review. This means that it is improbable that a claimant would be deprived of relief in private law proceedings that he or she would otherwise be able to obtain on judicial review. Such differences as do exist between private law proceedings and judicial review proceedings (in the latter case, a three-month limitation period, discretionary relief, less likelihood of interim relief, no automatic disclosure, no automatic cross examination, non-availability of damages) would seem to make judicial review a better option for the governing body and a worse option for the claimant. To that extent the inapplicability of judicial review proceedings might well matter to the sports governing body.[1]

1   Cf *Stevenage Borough Football Club v The Football League* Carnwath J (1996) Times, 1 August. In *Law v National Greyhound Racing Club Ltd* [1983] 1 WLR 1302, the governing body argued unsuccessfully that any challenge to its decision should have been brought by way of judicial review.

B   THE HUMAN RIGHTS ACT 1998

5.7   The Human Rights Act 1998 introduced mechanisms for the enforcement in the English courts of the rights protected by the European Convention on Human Rights. In the context of a challenge to a sports governing body's actions, the Act may conceivably provide a new cause of action, does provide a comparative argument, and in one instance at least has 'horizontal effect'.

(a)   Possible new cause of action against a sports governing body

5.8   Under s 6 of the Act, 'public authorities' must act in accordance with the Convention rights. The intention behind the legislation is to constrain state action, not to impose obligations on private persons, or indeed on public bodies for 'private acts'. If public authorities act contrary to the Convention rights protected, in pursuit of a public function, the claimant may be entitled to an injunction and damages.[1] Prior to *Mullins*, it had been suggested that sports governing bodies might in some cases fall within the definition of a public authority, such that their regulatory actions would be public rather than private acts. This would make them directly bound to act in accordance with the Convention rights, affording a claimant a new cause of action if they failed to do so. However as part of his analysis as to why Pt 54 judicial review was not available to the claimant, Stanley Burnton J also rejected the proposition that the Jockey Club or the Appeal Board constituted public authorities for the purposes of the Act.[2]

1 The difficulty in obtaining damages in the absence of a contract means that such relief for a breach of the Act may well be pursued by claimants. Diane Modahl is reported to have considered such an attack following the failure of her damages action based in contract.
2 *R (Mullins) v Appeal Board of the Jockey Club (Jockey Club as an interested party)* [2005] EWHC 2197 (Admin).

(b)   As a comparative argument

5.9   The courts must interpret legislation so far as possible in accordance with the Convention rights, taking into account the decisions of the European Court of Human Rights. When the courts come to review decisions of sports governing bodies, they will also have in mind the standards that would be required from a public authority in an analogous situation. It is possible that even if a sports governing body is not a public authority for these purposes, these factors may affect the basis on which its decisions are assessed by the courts. It is after all the position, as set out above, that the standard of review to which sports governing bodies are subjected is the equivalent of the public law standard. Claimants can seek to rely on the position under the Convention in order to inform the debate about the extent of common law protection.

(c)   Horizontal effect of Article 6

5.10   In the context of at least one right, the right to the public determination of civil rights and obligations within a reasonable time before an independent and impartial tribunal protected by Article 6, the courts must however go further even where the sports governing body is not a public authority. The courts themselves are public authorities, and are consequently obliged to ensure that Article 6 is complied with. If a process before a sports governing body involves the determination of civil rights and obligations in a way that does not satisfy Article 6, the court must step in: this is known as Article 6 having horizontal effect.[1] Separately, an attempt has been made to complain to the European Court of Human Rights that a signatory state failed to prevent the adoption and implementation of sports rules that infringed rights.[2]

1 See para 33 of the Court of Appeal's judgment in *Stretford v The FA* [2007] EWCA Civ 238, which records that it was common ground that the Court as a public authority had to give effect to Art 6. In *Bradley v Jockey Club* [2003] ISLR-SLR 71, it was argued before the Appeal Board that the process failed to satisfy Art 6 ECHR, but the Appeal Board held that it was sufficiently independent and impartial and that in any event access to the courts cured any breach. It was again common ground that Art 6 applied.

2 The footballer Adrian Mutu sought to challenge the legality of the FIFA compensation rules by making a complaint to the European Court of Human Rights that they infringed his right to work, following the Swiss Federal Court's upholding of CAS's rejection of his case.

(d) Waiver

5.11   It is open to parties to waive their rights, or at least some of them, under the Convention. In *Stretford v The FA*, it was held that the FA's rule K arbitration clause constituted a valid waiver of the agent's Art 6 rights.[1]

1 See paragraphs 33 to 68 of the Court of Appeal's judgment in *Stretford v The FA* [2007] EWCA Civ 238.

(e) The content of the rights

5.12   The possibility of relying upon the Convention and the Act in the ways set out above is only useful to the extent that the substantive rights protected under the Convention and engaged on the facts afford a greater degree of protection than already exists under the common law or other provisions. It appears likely that the most important rights will be the right to a fair trial under Art 6,[1] the right to privacy under Art 8,[2] the right to property (and to work) under Art 1 of the First Protocol,[3] and (in combination with another right) the right not to be discriminated against under Art 14. In individual circumstances other rights may be engaged.[4]

1 Article 6 protects due process in the determination of civil rights and obligations: everyone is entitled to a fair and public hearing within a reasonable time by an independent and impartial tribunal. If sports governing bodies' actions are regarded as something more than 'private acts', their internal disciplinary proceedings could be held to be caught. This would mean that challenges could be made to the validity of decisions taken after such proceedings on the basis (for example) that the disciplinary body was not impartial or independent, or that it took too long to resolve a particular matter.

2 In the context, for example, of drugs testing or rules against inappropriate sexual relationships. A challenge based on Art 8 to the validity of UK Athletics' rules against sexual relationships between coach and athlete, even where both were consenting adults, failed (in unreported arbitral proceedings) on the basis amongst others that the provisions were necessary and proportionate.

3 In the context, for example, of rules depriving clubs of the ability to sell commercial rights other than collectively, or depriving clubs of a place in a higher division.

4 Roy Keane reportedly considered reliance on the protection of freedom of expression (Art 10) as precluding the FA from proceeding against him in respect of his admission in his autobiography of deliberately setting out to injure Alf-Inge Haaland in revenge for a perceived sleight three years previously.

C THE EXTENSION TO SPORTS GOVERNING BODIES OF EU FREE MOVEMENT LAW

5.13   Many EU law obligations, such as the free movement rules,[1] are ostensibly owed only by Member States and their emanations, and not by private bodies. It now appears however that the majority of sports governing bodies will generally be regarded as fulfilling a role which subjects them to at least the free movement rules (as well as the competition rules), on the grounds that their rules are aimed at collectively regulating employment and the provision of services in a particular sector.[2] An action can be brought in the English courts on this basis.[3]

1 The competition rules do not fall into the category of rules applicable only against the state because they apply between private parties. Sports governing bodies are subject to the competition rules.
2 See *Union Royal Belge des Sociétés de Football Association v Bosman* (C-415/93) [1995] ECR I-4921, paras 69–87 (free movement rules held to apply to national football associations, and their transfer systems were struck down as an unjustifiable restriction on freedom of movement); *Walrave and Koch v Association Union Cycliste Internationale* (36/74) [1974] ECR 1405, paras 12–25 (governing body held subject to the free movement rules, but its provision limiting the composition of national teams to citizens of the nation in question was not a restriction on free movement); *Donà v Mantero* (13/76) [1976] ECR 1333 at 1341 (governing body again caught, but rule confining place in a national team to nationals upheld); *Lehtonen v Fédération Royale Belge des Société de Basketball* (C-176/96) [2000] ECR I-2681 (governing body subject to the free movement rules, but transfer windows held capable of justification); *Deliège v Ligue Francophone de Judo* (C-51/96) [2000] ECR I-2549 (governing body subject to free movement rules but selection criteria for national representation not a restriction on free movement); *Deutscher Handballbund v Kolpak* (C-438/00) [2003] ECR I-4135 (governing body precluded from applying a foreign player restriction in relation to players from a country with an equal treatment agreement with the EU who were already in the EU); *Cañas v Commission* (T-508/09) General Court, order of 26 March 2012 (challenge to Commission Decision not to pursue an investigation into the tennis player's complaint that the anti-doping rules to which he had been subject breached the competition and free movement rules, failed because he no longer had an interest in the complaint. An appeal to the Court of Justice failed (C-269/12 P)); *F91 Diddeleng v Commission* (T-341/10), General Court 16 April 2012; European Commission White Paper on Sport COM (2007) 391 Final and accompanying Staff Working Document SEC (2007) 935.
3 See *Wilander and Novacek v Tobin and Jude* [1997] 2 Lloyd's Law Rep 296, CA (in the event, permission to amend to add the competition and free movement arguments was denied because on the facts a restraint of trade argument, which raised similar questions of proportionality, had already been struck out); *Edwards v British Athletics Federation and the International Amateur Athletics Federation* [1998] 2 CMLR 363, [1997] Eu LR 721 (BAF and the IAAF obliged to respect the free movement rules).

5.14   The difference between the courts' approach to the availability of judicial review and the applicability of the free movement rules raises a theoretical problem for the practitioner, since a free movement argument would normally be run as an illegality point in judicial review proceedings. In practice, however, the argument can be run in private proceedings[1] and in view of the courts' reluctance to see form triumph over substance, it is unlikely that any procedural point would succeed.

1 As in *Wilander, Edwards,* and *Williams and Cardiff v WRU*, the point can equally be taken in response to an argument that a foreign law precludes compliance with a contractual obligation, as in *Bacardi v Newcastle* [2001] Eu LR 45 in which Bacardi sued Newcastle for failing to show advertisements at a match which was to be broadcast on French television. Newcastle defended on the basis that the French Loi Evin precluded the adverts being shown, and Bacardi responded by challenging the validity of the Loi Evin under the free movement rules. The European Court of Justice rejected the reference made by Gray J. The Loi Evin was subsequently challenged unsuccessfully in *European Commission (supported by the United Kingdom, intervening) v France; Bacardi France SAS v Télévision Française 1 SA (TF1) and others* [2004] 3 CMLR 2.

CHAPTER 6

The varying degrees of review

A JUDICIAL RELUCTANCE TO INTERVENE

6.1   In many instances, the expertise and experience of a particular sports governing body makes it best placed to decide how to regulate its own sport and to determine issues arising in the course of its administration of the sport. In addition, many of the decisions taken have a quasi-public or regulatory element to them. In these circumstances, English judges have consistently expressed reluctance to intervene in the regulatory decisions of sports governing bodies. More recently, this reluctance has been expressed as a reflection of the proposition that the actions of sports governing bodies are subject to the equivalent of the public law standard of review,[1] under which a court will not substitute its view for that of the public body: it is an expression of the constraint on the circumstances in which the grounds for review can be invoked. Its origins[2] are however older than the cases in which that proposition became established, and lay in the belief that, save in cases of clear breach of obligations (or rank injustice), an association governing an essentially non-commercial activity should be allowed to get on with it without being subjected to time-consuming and costly complaints to the courts about what it was doing. The principle continues on occasion to be articulated as almost an independent proposition,[3] although there have been recent moderations of it.[4] Either way, this principle affords the practitioner representing a sports governing body a useful tool, and poses a problem for those representing the player or club challenging the actions of the governing body.

1 *Bradley v Jockey Club* [2004] EWHC 2164 (QB, Richards J), [2004] All ER (D) 11 and [2005] EWCA Civ 1056, at paras 43 to 47 of Richards J's judgment and para 20 of the Court of Appeal's judgment. At para 43, Richards J said that the court's role was not 'to stand in the shoes of the primary decision-maker', but to evaluate whether the primary decision-maker's decision 'falls outside the range of reasonable responses to the question of where a fair balance lies'. See also *Sheffield United v FAPL*, decision of FA Arbitral Tribunal dated 3 July 2007 [2007] ISLR-SLR 77 (the FAPL rule S Arbitration (Sir Philip Otton, David Pannick QC and Nick Randall) held that although it would itself have deducted points from West Ham as the appropriate sanction for the club's actions, the Disciplinary Commission's decision to fine did not fall outside the range of decisions legitimately open to it.
2 For earlier cases, see *McInnes v Onslow-Fane* [1978] 1 WLR 1520 at 1535F–H; *Calvin v Carr* [1980] AC 574 at 597; and *Cowley v Heatley* (1986) Times, 24 July (Browne-Wilkinson V-C: 'sport would be better served if there was not running litigation at repeated intervals by people seeking to challenge the decisions of the regulating bodies').

3 For example, *Flaherty v NGRC* [2005] EWCA Civ 1117 [2005] All ER (D) 70A, in which Scott Baker
LJ stated at para 21: 'Sports regulating bodies ordinarily have unrivalled and practical knowledge of
the particular sport that they are required to regulate. They cannot be expected to act in every detail as
if they are a court of law. Provided they act lawfully and within the ambit of their powers, the courts
should allow them to get on with the job they are required to do...' Cf Evans-Lombe J's approach in
the same case at first instance, *Flaherty v NGRC* [2004] EWHC 2838 (Ch), paras 104 to 105, in which
he decided that judicial reluctance to intervene was an aspect of the application of the equivalent of the
public law test, and that if that test were satisfied, the court should intervene.

4 In *McKeown v British Horseracing Authority* [2010] EWHC 508 (QB), Stadlen J reiterated the
importance of the court not seeking to second guess the expert and experienced decision maker but
stressed that this does not mean that the court should show 'unthinkingly servile obeisance'.

B THE CONTEXTS IN WHICH THE PRINCIPLE HAS BEEN APPLIED

6.2   The English courts have been slow to intervene in the governing body's
formulation of its rules,[1] in its exercise of its discretion to grant licences under the
rules,[2] in its decisions as to selection or national representation,[3] and in its application
of its rules, for example as to doping or access to the sport.[4] The principle extends
beyond reluctance to near certain refusal to intervene in the context of challenges to
the on-field decisions of referees or umpires applying the 'laws of the game'.[5]

1 *Gasser v Stinson*, 15 June 1988 Scott J, at p 40 of the shorthand writers' transcript.

2 *McInnes v Onslow-Fane* [1978] 1 WLR 1520 at 1535F–H; *Park Promotion Ltd (t/a Pontypool Rugby
Football Club) v Welsh Rugby Union Ltd* [2012] EWHC 1919 (QB).

3 *Cowley v Heatley* (1986) Times, 24 July; *Couch v British Swimming*, 29 June 2012, Appeal Committee
of British Swimming, (2012) International Sports Law Review 2012, 3, SLR37-39 (it was not for the
Committee to second guess the selector's decision if it fell within the range allowed by the selection
criteria); *Jacob v Irish Amateur Rowing Union* [2008] IEHC 196, [2008] 4 IR 731 (court held that it
should not intervene in a selection or de-selection decision in the absence of bad faith by the governing
body or an egregious injustice to the rower).

4 *Bradley v Jockey Club* [2004] EWHC 2164 (QB), para 80, upheld [2005] EWCA Civ 1056; *Flaherty v
NGRC* [2005] EWCA Civ 1117, [2005] All ER (D) 70A; *Mullins v McFarlane and the Jockey Club*
[2006] EWHC 986 (QB), [2006] All ER (D) 66 at paras 37 to 39.

5 Such decisions are a fortiori examples of where the court is worse placed than the decision maker to
reach a conclusion. It is also integral to the authority of the referee or umpire, to certainty of results and
to fairness to players, that the courts and arbitral bodies (and indeed the sports governing body itself)
should not intervene in this context. See *Mendy v IABA* CAS (1996) Atlanta Arbitration 006, *Digest of
CAS Awards 1986–1998*, p 413.

C LIMITATIONS ON THE PRINCIPLE

6.3   Even where it applies, however, this principle does not today mean that
an English court or arbitration will never interfere: the principle of self-regulation
is given its rein, but the courts will still exercise a supervisory jurisdiction over
the activities of the governing body, and will intervene if the governing body steps
outside the boundaries set for it by the quasi-public law test.[1] The governing body
will be afforded a margin of appreciation, or latitude, in its decision-making but
will still be held to account if it goes too far. As developments in public law make
that quasi-public law test more intrusive, the level of judicial reluctance to intervene
should decline.[2]

1 But note that the court retains a discretion whether to grant relief, even where for example it has
determined that there has been a breach of natural justice. See the debate in *Stinnato v Auckland Boxing
Association* [1978] 1 NZLR 1 at 28 and 12 (the majority refused relief even though the boxer had been
afforded no opportunity to be heard on his application for a licence). See also *Mullins v McFarlane and
the Jockey Club* [2006] EWHC 986 (QB) [2006] All ER (D) 66 (in relation to the discretionary nature
of the grant of a declaration).

2 In *Flaherty v NGRC* [2004] EWHC 2838 (Ch), paras 104-5 Evans-Lombe J approached judicial reluctance to intervene as an aspect of the application of the quasi-public law test, concluding that the court should intervene if the test were satisfied. This was arguably in contrast to the Court of Appeal, which overturned his decision in [2005] EWCA Civ 1117 [2005] All ER (D) 70A.

6.4   Further, the extent of the margin of appreciation, or latitude, will vary from context to context. It will be at its widest where rules confer a discretion on the governing body, and where there may be a range of permissible alternatives open to the governing body. By contrast, there may often be only one correct answer where an obligation under the rules is to be interpreted, and no margin will apply. The courts will intervene on a point of law, applying a 'hard edged' test. The supervisory roles of the courts cannot be excluded, however: the rules cannot for example require the sports governing body's consent to any litigation.[1] Further, while the principle applies at the interim stage, the court is then only attempting to ascertain whether an arguable case exists and this may therefore mitigate the effect of the principle.[2]

1 See *St Johnstone Football Club v Scottish Football Association* 1965 SLT 171 at 175.
2 See *Williams and Cardiff RFC v Pugh*, 23 July 1997 Popplewell J at p 5 et seq of the shorthand writers' transcript.

6.5   The principle does not (or ought not to) extend to the situation where the decision of the governing body is taken in the context of purely private law actions, such as the grant of contractual rights to a commercial partner[1] or a personal injury claim.[2] It should be confined to situations where the decisions of the sports governing body are made pursuant to its regulatory role. Just as an English court will not express reluctance to intervene in the private law activities of a public body, so too it should be prepared to intervene in the non-regulatory actions of a sports governing body. In that context, the courts have an original jurisdiction, as opposed to a supervisory one, and the normal mechanisms will apply.

1 Just as the normal private law rules apply when a public body is caught by them: *R v Lord Chancellor, ex p Hibbit and Saunders* ('the shorthandwriters' case') DivC, (1993) Times, 12 March.
2 See *Watson v BBBC* [2000] EWCA Civ 2116, [2001] QB 1134, where a duty of care was imposed on the governing body to ensure adequate medical assistance at the ringside.

6.6   Further, the increased commercialisation of sport has removed one of the underpinnings of judicial reluctance to intervene.[1] It is no longer appropriate to base judicial reluctance to intervene on anything other than the margin of appreciation, or latitude, that should be afforded to a specialist body making a decision within the boundaries of the regulatory function entrusted to it.

1 In *Jones v WRU* (1997) Times, 6 March, Ebsworth J distanced himself from the view that 'the processes of the law have no place in sport', on the grounds that 'sport today is big business' and that it would be 'naïve to pretend that the modern world of sport can be conducted as it used to be not very many years ago.'

6.7   Lastly, there is an argument of uncertain validity that where a private law sports governing body makes some forms of regulatory decision, for example that a participant has committed a breach of its rules or failed to satisfy a requirement of them, that decision amounts to no more than the *view*, of no more than *one of the parties* to the contract constituted by the rules and regulations, as to whether there has been a breach of contract by the participant, and it remains the role of the court or arbitrator to determine whether there has been such a breach free of any obligation to defer to the expertise of the sports governing body.

D DOES THE PRINCIPLE APPLY IN THE CONTEXT OF RESTRAINT OF TRADE?

6.8   An open issue, addressed in Chapter 10, is whether the restraint exhibited by the courts in applying the grounds for review of fairness and reasonableness to the actions of sports governing bodies is or should be extended by the courts into their application of the private law restraint of trade doctrine. Carnwath J has advanced an argument obiter[1] that it should, and that the courts should apply the public law test when considering the justifiability or reasonableness of a restraint, reversing the burden of proof and elevating the standard to be satisfied by a challenger. On the other hand, the test that has been applied by the courts has in the past been the normal test under the doctrine, and there are a number of arguments (discussed below in Chapter 7) why this should continue to be the case.

1 *Stevenage Borough Football Club v Football League Ltd*, Carnwath J, (1996) Times 1 August, and 9 Admin LR 109, CA. At least 'interest' in, if not necessarily support for, Carnwath J's approach was expressed by Richards J in *Bradley* at para 35.

E SHOULD SPECIALIST ARBITRAL BODIES BE SO RELUCTANT?

6.9   Arbitral bodies will prima facie apply the same reluctance to intervene as an English court.[1] The principle may however be tempered in the context of arbitrations. The applicable rules,[2] or the agreement of the parties,[3] may confer an original jurisdiction on the arbitral body to review the merits of the case without restraint, for example if it is the last stage of appeal. Equally, they may specify a supervisory jurisdiction. It has been held by CAS that the principle of judicial restraint does not apply with quite the same force where a specialist arbitral tribunal is established under the rules of the governing body.[4]

1 See for example in the context of an English arbitration, *Sheffield United v FAPL*, award dated 3 July 2007 [2007] ISLR-SLR 77.
2 The questions to be answered by arbitral tribunals to which disputes are referred will often be specifically defined in the rules. Thus in *IAAF v UKA and Walker* [2001] 4 ISLR 264, the question for the IAAF's independent arbitral panel was wide: whether the UKA's disciplinary body 'had misdirected itself' or 'reached an erroneous conclusion'. In other contexts, the question(s) may be narrower.
3 The CAS rules allow the parties to agree a full review on the merits. In addition, it claims for itself on appeals 'full power to review the facts and the law', which power it has exercised often to conduct *de novo* rehearings. See CAS Code of Sports-Related Arbitration, rule 57.
4 *Watt v Australian Cycling Federation* CAS 96/153, *Digest of CAS Awards 1986–1998*, a challenge to a selection decision. At paras 7–10, the Tribunal noted the courts' reticence to intervene in such matters, but said that the arbitration agreement indicated that the parties wanted the tribunal to scrutinise the decision, in the sense of enquiring into whether it was reached fairly and with such regard (if any) as was properly owed to the appellant's interests. The arbitrators went on to overturn the selection decision.

F RELUCTANCE TO INTERVENE UNDER EUROPEAN LAW

6.10   Under EU law, sport is only subject to the free movement and competition law rules to the extent that it involves an economic activity. Up until 2006, this led to the European Commission applying the concept of a 'sporting exception' under which rules or actions of a purely sporting nature were not susceptible to review under either the free movement or the competition rules.[1] Economic rules or actions, or those not obviously purely sporting, were reviewable. The position was changed by the European Court of Justice's decision in *Meca-Medina*.[2] In that case two swimmers challenged the legality of a two-year ban imposed by FINA for a positive finding of nandrolone on the basis that it infringed European free movement and competition law. In August 2002, the European Commission rejected the challenge on the ground that anti-doping rules are necessary for the protection of the integrity of the sport and therefore fell within a 'sporting exception' to European law. The CFI upheld the Commission's decision. The Court of Justice however overturned the CFI's decision, rejecting the argument that there is any such 'sporting exception' taking rules of the sport itself outside competition law. The Court of Justice held that a sport's rules must be assessed in the light of competition law and are just as much subject to the requirement that they be justifiable as any other rule of an association governing access to an occupation. On the facts, however, the Court of Justice concluded that the ban was in all the circumstances proportionate.

1 *Walrave and Koch v Union Cycliste Internationale* (36/74) [1974] ECR 1405, para 4 (rule requiring support riders to come from the same country upheld as a rule of a purely sporting nature); *Donà v Mantero* (13/76) [1976] ECR 1333 at 1340 (rule confining place in a national team to nationals upheld as a rule of purely sporting nature); *Union Royale Belge v Bosman* (C-415/93) [1995] ECR I-4921 at paras 69–87 (transfer rules outside the sporting exception and court will strike them down to the extent that they are incompatible with the free movement rules); *Jyri Lehtonen v Fédération Royal Belge des Sociétés de Basketball* (C-176/96) [2000] ECR I–2681 (transfer window subject to review but in the event not contrary to free movement rules); *Deliège v Ligue Belge de Judo ASBL* (C-51/96) [2000] ECR I–2549 (confining participation in international event to those selected by national federations not contrary to the free movement rules as a rule of purely sporting nature). The European Commission (and for that matter the OFT) would not investigate the actions of a sports governing body which were related to the underlying sporting activity itself. Rules which were inherent in the sport or necessary for its organisation, and their application, would not be examined. The clearest example of such rules were the rules of the game itself (eg the offside rule or rules about the safety requirements on racing cars). But the principle was extended to rules which related to how sport is organised, such as the rule that representative teams from one country can only field players from that country, or the rule that a club must play in a particular country (*Excelsior Mouscron*, Commission press release IP/99/965, dated 9 December 1999) or rules which define the number of club teams from each country that can participate in an international club competition, or rules on how individuals are selected for representative sides.

2 *Meca-Medina v Commission*, Commission press release IP/02/1211, Court of First Instance (T-313/02) [2004] ECR II-3291, [2004] 3 CMLR 1314 and European Court of Justice (C-519/04P) [2006] ECR I-6991, [2006] ISLR SLR-175, [2006] All ER (EC) 1057.

6.11   The demise of the 'sporting exception' does not however mean that judicial, or regulatory, reluctance to intervene has no role under EU law. The analysis in *Meca-Medina* was that although sports' rules fell to be reviewed against the EU free movement and competition law provisions, they would survive that review if they were necessary to the organisation of the sport and pursued a legitimate aim proportionately. Part of that exercise includes affording an expert body a margin of appreciation in its evaluation of what the sport requires.[1]

1 That margin of appreciation will however vary depending upon the extent to which the decision is genuinely in relation to the sport, as opposed to the purely commercial exploitation of it. In *London Welsh v Rugby Football Union, Newcastle Falcons intervening*, RFU Arbitration 29 June 2012, James Dingemans QC, Ian Mill QC and Tim Ward QC, the club challenged the lawfulness under EU and UK competition law of the RFU's decision to refuse it promotion to the Premiership on the grounds that it did not have 'primacy of tenure' at its ground. The club contended hat the aims pursued were in fact only commercial ones not inherent in the sport, and that therefore the margin of appreciation to be afforded to the RFU was considerably less. The tribunal decided that the rules and their application were hybrids, but that they had a sufficient sporting aim to engage the wider margin of appreciation under *Meca-Medina*. However, on the evidence the rules and their application went further than necessary, whatever test was applied.

CHAPTER 7

Grounds for review arising out of control of the sport

A   THE EXTENT OF AND BASIS FOR THE GROUNDS FOR REVIEW

(a)   Two broad propositions

7.1   Sports governing bodies' regulatory actions are reviewed by the courts on grounds that arise out of the control exercised over the sport by those bodies, independently of any other cause of action. The Court of Appeal's approval of Richards J's decision in *Bradley v Jockey Club*,[1] and the cases that have followed,[2] indicate that two broad propositions now summarise the extent of and basis for these grounds for review (albeit possibly subject to qualification in some circumstances).

1 *Bradley v Jockey Club* [2004] EWHC 2164 QB, 1 October 2004 Richards J, [2004] All ER (D) 11; upheld on appeal [2005] EWCA Civ 1056, 12 June 2005, Lord Phillips MR, Buxton LJ, Scott Baker LJ, [2006] L.L.R. 1, (2005) Times, 14 July.

2 In particular *Flaherty v National Greyhound Racing Club* [2004] EWHC 2838 Ch, 8 December 2004, Evans-Lombe J; on appeal [2005] EWCA Civ 1117 CA, 14 September 2005, Sir Mark Potter, Scott Baker LJ, Sir Peter Gibson, (2005) Times, 5 October, [2005] All ER (D) 70A; *R (Mullins) v Appeal Board of the Jockey Club (Jockey Club as an interested party)* [2005] EWHC 2197 Admin, 17 October 2005 Stanley Burnton J and *Mullins v McFarlane (representing the Appeal Board of the Jockey Club) and the Jockey Club* [2006] EWHC 986, 5 May 2006, Stanley Burnton J, [2006] All ER (D) 66; *Fallon v Horseracing Regulatory Authority* [2006] EWHC 1898 QB, 28 Jul 2006 Davis J, [2006] All ER (D) 427; *Sheffield United v FAPL*, FAPL Arbitration, award dated 3 July 2007, [2007] ISLR-SLR 77; *Stretford v FA*, FA Rule K Arbitration, Sir Martin Nourse, 5 December 2007; and *Stretford v The FA* [2006] EWHC 479 Ch, 17 March 2006, Morritt C [2006] All ER (D) 275 and on appeal [2007] EWCA Civ 238, 21 March 2007, Clarke MR, Waller and Sedley LJJ (see para 7.26); *Dwain Chambers v British*

Olympic Association [2008] EWHC 2028 QB, 9, 17 and 18 July 2008 Mackay J, and also at (2008) Sport and Law Journal Vol 16 iss 2 (2008) SLJR 4; *McKeown v British Horseracing Authority* [2010] EWHC 508 QB, 12 March 2010 Stadlen J; *Park Promotion Ltd (t/a Pontypool Rugby Football Club) v Welsh Rugby Union Ltd* [2012] EWHC 1919 QB, 11 July 2012 Sir Raymond Jack.

7.2   The first proposition is that, although sports governing bodies are not public bodies for the purposes of judicial review, their control over a sport[1] means that their regulatory actions (or the actions of their separate disciplinary bodies), especially those actions that affect a person's right to work, are subject to a supervisory standard and grounds for review equivalent to those applied to public bodies, with the court or tribunal giving considerable deference to the expert decision-maker where appropriate. Sports governing bodies are required, in all their decision-making pursuant to the regulatory functions contained in their rules, to act lawfully (which includes, in this context, acting in accordance with those rules), fairly in a procedural sense (and in accordance with natural justice), on the basis of only relevant considerations, on a sound basis in fact, in accordance with legitimate expectations, and rationally (as opposed to perversely, arbitrarily, or capriciously).

1 The term 'sports governing bodies' does not here include bodies without regulatory powers and which instead simply represent a single interest within a sport. See *Towcester Racecourse v The Racecourse Association Ltd* [2002] EWHC 2141 Ch, 17 October 2002, Patten J.

7.3   The second proposition is that these grounds for review are the same, both (1) where there is a contract between the sports governing body and the claimant (in which case the grounds are likely to be implicit in that contract and enforceable by an action for breach); and (2) where there is no contract between the sports governing body and the claimant (in which case they are enforceable by an action for a declaration). There may therefore be two causes of action, contractual and non-contractual. Where a contract does not exist, the only relief available is a declaration, and possibly an injunction.

7.4   Where a contract does exist, the relief available for its breach will depend on the terms of the contract, to be construed in all the circumstances. In the absence of a clear exclusion clause, damages will generally be available for breach of express terms. Further, even if an express term is not breached, it is likely to be implicit in any contract arising on the basis of the rules of a sports governing body that the governing body's regulatory actions (and the actions of its separate disciplinary bodies) are subject to the supervisory standard of review described above. That does not mean that it will always also be implied that the sports governing body owes an obligation in contract, sounding in damages, that its actions (or at least those of its separate disciplinary bodies) will take a particular form or meet a particular standard. Instead, the supervisory nature of the grounds of review described above has two consequences. First, a court or arbitral tribunal will not step into the shoes of a sports governing body: it will not regard an implied contractual obligation as breached simply because it would not itself have reached the same conclusion. Rather the extent of the implied contractual term is likely to be that the discretionary action is subject to the court's assessment of whether the governing body (or separate disciplinary body) stepped outside the parameters of what was reasonably open to it in the exercise of its discretion, with the court giving considerable deference to the experience and expertise of the governing body/disciplinary body. Secondly, and consequently, a court or arbitral tribunal will not always approach a discretionary action (at least of a separate disciplinary body) in a contractual context on the basis that if that action falls foul of one of the grounds for review, this will sound in damages against the sports governing body. In other words, the fact of a contract ought not to alter the basis on which a sports governing body's action (or the action of its separate disciplinary body) is reviewed, and may not in every case lead to greater remedies.

7.5   The two basic propositions are subject to at least the following caveats:

(a)   First, they have developed gradually, over some time, and different courts and arbitral tribunals have applied different reasoning in support of them. Courts and arbitral tribunals have in the past required sports governing bodies to act lawfully, fairly, and in a non-arbitrary way, but in some contexts have set relatively restrictive criteria as to when these requirements arise and as to their extent. Under those past criteria, not all sports governing bodies were caught in all contexts, and the content of the requirements was not necessarily the same as in the case of a public body. These authorities may still provide useful arguments for those seeking to limit the applicability or the extent of the grounds for review of the actions of a particular sports governing body to a particular claimant in a specific context reflected in those cases, although perhaps decreasingly so as the development of the law continues.

(b)   Secondly, the position on the recent authorities, and in principle, as to the situation where a contract arises is complex. For example, it remains the case that a breach of express rules (where they constitute a contract) will sound in damages, and it is possible that in some contexts a sports governing body's actions (or the actions of its separate disciplinary body) that offend other grounds for review may also give rise to an action in damages against the sports governing body (again where a contract arises).

The analysis below therefore starts off by examining the ways in which the historically-applied criteria are restrictive[1] and then addresses the developments in the law on the authorities and in principle.[2]

1 See paras **7.6–7.10**.
2 See paras **7.11–7.46**.

(b) The need for there to be monopoly power and an effect on the claimant's ability to earn a living

7.6   The historical basis for the courts to exercise a supervisory jurisdiction over sports governing bodies, at least in the absence of a contract, was (and to a significant extent still is) the existence of monopoly power in the hands of the governing body that has an effect on the ability of the claimant to earn a living (and thus restrains him in his trade). If a claimant could not establish that the governing body in question fell into that category or that its decision had that consequence, the grounds for review did not arise. The starting point for the modern law is the Court of Appeal's decision in *Nagle v Feilden*.[1] In that case the Jockey Club refused to issue a trainer's licence to Florence Nagle because she was woman. On the Jockey Club's application to strike out her challenge to its decision, the Court of Appeal held that although there was no contractual relationship between the parties, an arbitrary or capricious decision or one taken by the Jockey Club in a procedurally unfair manner would be subject to review in an action for a declaration.[2] The Court of Appeal held that the refusal to issue a licence to a trainer just because she was a woman was indeed arbitrary and capricious. The basis for the requirements on the Jockey Club was that:

> 'When ... authorities exercise a predominant power over the exercise of a trade or profession, the Courts may have jurisdiction to see that it is not abused.'[3]

Applying this reasoning, a claimant was required to show (absent a contract) that the governing body controlled the sport completely and that its decision prevented the claimant earning a living. The grounds for review would not apply where for example the claimant was an amateur, or where the sports governing body did not hold monopoly power. The courts however relatively quickly relaxed this criterion to the extent that it was sufficient to show significant control over a significant part of a sport rather than monopoly power,[4] and a significant impact on the claimant rather than a complete prevention from earning a living.[5] However (subject to recent developments discussed below) where there is no contract and no impact at all on the claimant's ability to earn a living, the grounds for review analogous to the public law standard arguably would not arise.[6] It would arguably not be enough that the claimant is affected in an important aspect of his life.[7] As discussed below,[8] there is authority for the proposition that an effect on the right to work must be shown in Mackay J's judgment in *Dwain Chambers*. However also as discussed below,[9] in *Mullins*, Stanley Burnton J expressed a provisional, *obiter* view that the court's discretion to grant a declaration was not limited to cases involving an impact on the claimant's right to work or the imposition of a financial penalty.[10] The issue whether the court's discretion ran more widely than simply in cases affecting a claimant's right to work did not arise in *Bradley*, since the decision did indeed affect the claimant's right to work.[11]

1 [1966] 2 QB 633.
2 Per Lord Denning MR at 645 and 646 to 647.
3 Per Lord Denning at 647. See also at 646, and per Danckwerts LJ at 650 and per Salmon LJ at 654–655. See also Scott J's description in *Watson v Prager* [1991] 1 WLR 726 at 746–747 of the basis for the decision in *Nagle v Feilden* and Carnwath J's description in *Stevenage Borough Football Club v Football League* (1996) Times, 1 August. In *Stinnato v Auckland Boxing Association* [1978] 1 NZLR 1, intervention was put firmly on the basis of restraint of trade through the exercise of monopoly power. See also *Gasser v Stinson*, 15 June 1988 Scott J; and *Newport Association FC Ltd v Football Association of Wales Ltd* (Jacob J on the interlocutory application) [1995] 3 All ER 87, [1995] 1 WLR 1217.
4 *Fisher v National Greyhound Racing Club*, 31 July 1985 CA, per Oliver LJ at p 6 of the Lexis transcript; *Pett v Greyhound Racing Association* [1969] 1 QB 125 per Lord Denning MR at 128 where he noted that the governing body did not have monopoly power but exercised important control over a large part of the industry.
5 *Fisher v National Greyhound Racing Club*, 31 July 1985 CA, per Oliver LJ at p 6 of the Lexis transcript (the fact that the claimant greyhound-owner had only one dog and could not be deprived of his entire living as a result of a refusal of a licence was no bar to the application of the grounds for review).
6 *R v British Basketball Association, ex p Mickan*, 17 March 1981 CA, at p 4 of the Lexis transcript (in holding that the governing body did not owe an obligation not to act capriciously towards two top amateur players, the Court of Appeal concluded that 'the legal rules imposing duties upon bodies which exercise a monopoly over the opportunities of persons to earn their living do not extend to arrangements for amateur participation in games or other forms of recreation'); *Lovell v Pembroke County Cricket Club*, [2003] ISLR iss 2 SLR 38 Neuberger J, 1 May 2002 at para 37 (absent a contract, an amateur player cannot invoke the grounds for review).
7 *Currie v Barton* CA (1988) Times, 12 February, per Nicholls LJ at p 9 of the Lexis transcript.
8 See paras **7.31–7.32**.
9 See paras 37 to 39 of *Dwain Chambers v British Olympic Association* [2008] EWHC 2028 QB, 9, 17 and 18 July 2008 Mackay J.
10 See paras **7.23–7.24**. See paras 38 to 39 of the second *Mullins* decision, *Mullins v McFarlane (representing the Appeal Board of the Jockey Club) and the Jockey Club* [2006] EWHC 986, 5 May 2006, Stanley Burnton J, [2006] L.L.R. 437, [2006] All ER (D) 66.
11 See paras **7.15–7.21**. See para 35 of Richards J's decision in *Bradley v Jockey Club* [2004] EWHC 2164 QB, 1 October 2004 Richards J, [2004] All ER (D) 11.

7.7   Where on the other hand a contractual relationship existed between the claimant and the sports governing body, it appeared to be implicit in that relationship that the sports governing body had a contractual obligation to take decisions that were lawful, fair and non-arbitrary.[1] In a contractual situation, it did not appear to be necessary to show monopoly power or an effect on the claimant's ability to earn a living in order to establish and enforce such requirements.[2] Nor, at least where there was monopoly power, would any attempt in the rules to detract from the right to be treated in this way be enforceable.[3]

1 *Lee v Showman's Guild* [1952] 2 QB 329; *Enderby Town Football Club v Football Association* [1971] Ch 591 at 605C–607A, [1970] 3 WLR 1021 at 1025–1026; *Calvin v Carr* [1980] AC 574, [1979] 2 All ER 440; *R v Jockey Club, ex p Aga Khan* [1993] 1 WLR 909 at 916 per Lord Bingham MR and at 933 per Hoffmann LJ.
2 *Collins v Lane*, 22 June 1999 CA (rules of natural justice applied to an amateur shooting club); *Lovell v Pembroke County Cricket Club*, [2003] ISLR iss 2 SLR 38 Neuberger J, 1 May 2002 at paras 37–49 (absent a contract, an amateur player cannot invoke the grounds for review, but a contract did arise).
3 In *Nagle v Feilden* (cited in para **7.6** above) at 647, Lord Denning doubted that natural justice could be excluded by contract and in *Enderby Town* (cited above) at 606, he stated that the contract contained in rules of a sports governing body (which he regarded as a fictional one in any event) could not displace the rules of natural justice. For a slightly different approach, turning on the particular facts, see *Towcester Racecourse* (cited in para **7.2** above).

(c) Application, expectation and forfeiture

7.8   The second historical restriction on the grounds for review of the actions of sports governing bodies related to the varying extent of the requirements if they arose, depending upon the circumstances. In *McInnes v Onslow-Fane*,[1] the British Board of Boxing Control refused the claimant's application for a boxing manager's licence. Again there was no contractual relationship between the parties. Megarry V-C held that a duty to act fairly and in accordance with natural justice arose, based on the analysis involving monopoly power and effect on the ability to earn a living in *Nagle v Feilden*.[2] The intensity of the duty, however, and precisely what would be required under it, varied depending upon whether the case could be described as an 'application' case, an 'expectation' case, or a 'forfeiture' case. Forfeiture cases involved the situation where something is to be taken away, and in that context the claimant was entitled to have proper notice of the arguments being made for removing his licence, an opportunity to make representations orally, and a decision taken without caprice or bias. In that instance there was arguably a pre-existing contractual arrangement. In application cases on the other hand (where there was no pre-existing contractual relationship), the right was confined to having a decision made honestly and without caprice or bias. Expectation cases involved applications for something by a person who has some entitlement to expect that it will be granted.[3] Megarry V-C did not define the ambit of the obligation in that instance. He stated that the courts should be slow to allow the obligation to be fair to be used to bring before the courts honest decisions of bodies exercising jurisdiction over sporting activities.[4] He held that since the case before him was an application case, the claimant had no right to know why he was refused a licence or any opportunity to present his case. On the basis of this authority, therefore, the extent of the grounds for review of the sports governing body's actions would in many instances be limited. However, as discussed below,[5] in *Bradley* Richards J arguably did not contemplate a different test dependent upon Megarry V-C's categories. That said, it may be that those categories would now simply reflect the varying extent to which the court would be prepared to intervene in varying circumstances.

1 [1978] 1 WLR 1520.
2 [1978] 1 WLR 1520 at 1528.
3 For expectation cases, see *Fisher v National Greyhound Racing Club*, 31 July 1985 CA, per Oliver LJ at p 8 and Purchas LJ at p 16 of the Lexis transcript; *Cowley v Heatley* (1986) Times, 24 July, Browne-Wilkinson V-C.
4 [1978] 1 WLR 1520 at 1535 F–H.
5 See paras **7.15–7.21**. See paras 35 and 38 of Richards J's decision in *Bradley*.

(d)   No obligation to accept a claimant as a member

7.9   The decisions in both *Nagle v Feilden* and *Onslow-Fane* reflect the traditional approach of English law that a private law sports governing body cannot be forced to accept as a member someone with whom it has no pre-existing contractual relationship[1] (although in neither case was the claimant seeking to become a member as such). Under the traditional approach, sports governing bodies can sometimes be constrained to act fairly in their decision-making, but the court will not force them to admit a club or person as a member, because to do that would be to force them into a contract.

1 *Lee v Showmen's Guild* (cited at para **7.7** above) per Denning LJ at 342; *Faramus v Film Artistes' Association* [1964] AC 925 at 941 to 942 per Lord Evershed.

(e)   Attempts to make sports governing bodies subject to judicial review

7.10   There have been a number of unsuccessful attempts to seek the public law remedy of judicial review of the actions of sports governing bodies. These culminated most recently in the *Mullins* decision,[1] in which Stanley Burnton J rejected the proposition that the developments in the law as to what constitutes a public authority for the purposes of the Human Rights Act 1998 meant that sports governing bodies fell to be regarded as public bodies, the decisions of which were amenable to judicial review by the Administrative Court under CPR Pt 54. The *Mullins* decision has laid to rest for the present the argument that a sports governing body's decisions are amenable to public law judicial review in the English courts.

1 *R (Mullins) v Appeal Board of the Jockey Club (Jockey Club as an interested party)* [2005] EWHC 2197 Admin, 17 October 2005 Stanley Burnton J.

(f)   Development of a less restrictive approach as to when the grounds for review arise and as to their extent

7.11   From 1996 there were signs that the English courts might be prepared to adopt a less restrictive approach both to the circumstances in which sports governing bodies would be held to be subject to the requirements to act lawfully, fairly and rationally, and in relation to the content of those requirements. In *Stevenage v Football League*[1] (a case in which there was no contract and the challenge was based on restraint of trade), Carnwath J held that the exercise of discretion by bodies such as The Football League, which exercise regulatory power in the public interest, fell to be reviewed by reference to the same tests as are applied to bodies subject to judicial review. He then went on, however,[2] to follow the approach in *McInnes v Onslow-Fane*, which arguably does not impose the same tests. In *Jones v WRU*,[3] Ebsworth J (later supported by the Court of Appeal[4]) concluded that it was arguable for the purposes of interim relief that the WRU was required as a matter of natural justice to allow a player appealing against his sending off not only to have an oral hearing, but also to be represented (although not necessarily by a lawyer), to question witnesses, and to comment on the video-tape recording of the incident as the disciplinary body watched it.[5] She stressed the greater financial significance of sports governing bodies' decisions today,[6] and doubted the validity in modern circumstances of the courts' traditional reluctance to intervene.[7] She went on to suspend the ban imposed on the player until after the trial of the action.[8] The WRU changed its rules to meet Ebsworth J's concerns.

1 *Stevenage Borough Football Club v Football League Ltd*, Carnwath J, (1996) Times, 1 August.
2 At p 25 of the New Law Online transcript. See (1996) Times 9 August and (1997) 9 Admin LR 109 for the judgment on appeal.
3 27 February 1997 Ebsworth J, (1997) Times, 6 March.
4 19 December 1997 CA, (1998) Times, 6 January (albeit still in the context of interim relief).
5 At p 9 of the Lexis transcript of Ebsworth J's judgment.
6 At pp 2 and 9 of the Lexis transcript.
7 At p 9 of the Lexis transcript.
8 At p 10 of the Lexis transcript.

7.12   In *Wilander and Novacek v Tobin and Jude*,[1] two tennis players challenged the validity of rule 53 of the ITF Anti-Doping Programme, under which tennis players found to have committed a doping offence were to be banned. Lord Woolf MR concluded[2] that even if the ITF's disciplinary body were not judicially reviewable it was still subject to the same requirements that it act lawfully, fairly and rationally, and expressly added the public law concepts that a sports governing body must not fail to take into account relevant considerations, must not take into account irrelevant considerations, and must have a sound basis in fact for its decisions:

> 'Assuming, but not deciding, that the appeals committee is not subject to judicial review because it is not a public body, this does not mean that it escapes the supervision of the High Court. The proceedings out of which this appeal arises are part of that supervision. The Appeals Committee's jurisdiction over the plaintiffs arises out of a contract. That contract has an implied requirement that the procedure provided for in rule 53 is to be conducted fairly (*Lee v Showmen's Guild* [1952] 2 QB 329 and *Conteh v Onslow-Fane* (1975) Times, 26 June, CA). If the Appeals Committee does not act fairly or if it misdirects itself in law and fails to take into account relevant considerations or takes into account irrelevant considerations, the High Court can intervene. It can also intervene if there is no evidential basis for its decision.'

While it is true that the facts of this case satisfied the criteria in the earlier cases (it involved the contractually binding rules of a governing body with monopoly power, and a decision that affected the claimant's livelihood by withdrawing something that he already had), Lord Woolf MR chose to express the standard of review to which the governing body (or its appeals committee) was subject in a much broader way, as being directly equivalent to the standard that applied in public law. It is to be noted that Lord Woolf's expression of what was implicit in the contract was that the sports governing body's actions would be subject to that degree of review. He did not state expressly that it had obligations sounding in damages to act in a particular way.

1 [1997] 2 Lloyd's Rep 293. For other stages of the litigation, see 19 March 1996 Lightman J, (1996) Times, 8 April CA and [1997] 1 Lloyd's Rep 195, Lightman J.
2 [1997] 2 Lloyd's Rep 293 at 300, col 1.

7.13   Lord Woolf MR also considered the courts' supervisory jurisdiction over sports governing bodies in *Modahl v British Athletic Federation*.[1] In that case Diane Modahl, having been banned for a doping violation by an internal BAF tribunal but subsequently exonerated by a BAF appeal tribunal, sued the BAF for damages for breach of the implied contractual duty in its anti-doping programme to apply that programme fairly, including avoiding manning its internal tribunals with biased members. When the BAF's application to strike out came before the Court of Appeal, Lord Woolf MR held[2] that the normal judicial review standard of fairness applied to the review of private body disciplinary decisions:

> 'Mr Pollock suggested that Mr Pannick was in error in seeking to rely on what he referred to as an administrative law approach in the different field of contract. There are distinctions between an action which is brought for breach of contract and proceedings for judicial review but Mr Pollock is wrong in suggesting that the approach of the Courts in public law on applications for judicial review have no relevance in domestic disciplinary proceedings of this sort. The question of whether a complaint about the conduct of a disciplinary committee gives rise to a remedy in public law or in private law is often difficult to determine. However, the complaint in both cases would be based on an allegation of unfairness. While in some situations public and private law principles can differ, I can see no reason why there should be any difference as to what constitutes unfairness or why the standard of fairness required by an implied term should differ from that required of the same tribunal under public law ... Indeed in areas such as this, the approach of the Courts should be to assimilate the applicable principles. There would however remain the procedural differences and differences as to the remedies which are available.'

Lord Woolf here expressly stated that different 'remedies' might be available for breach of the implied term, raising the possibility of a cause of action in damages, which were what Diane Modahl sought.

1 The *Modahl* case went before the High Court and the Court of Appeal twice, first on the strike out application Popplewell J 28 June 1996 and CA 28 July 1997, and then on the substantive hearing Douglas Brown J 14 December 2000, [2000] All ER (D) 2274 and CA [2001] EWCA Civ 1447, [2002] 1 WLR 1192, [2001] All ER (D) 181) 8 October 2001. The case went to the House of Lords on the strike out appeal: 22 July 1999 (1999) Times 23 July.
2 CA 28 July 1997, at pp 20F–21G of the shorthand writers' transcript.

7.14   In the House of Lords, the issue as to standard of review did not arise. At the substantive hearing, Douglas Brown J investigated the content of the putative implied term (which he held could not exist as no contract existed) on the basis of the content of public law grounds for review.[1] When the matter came before the Court of Appeal on the second occasion, it was held (by the majority) that there was indeed a contract between the athlete and the BAF. In so holding the court may have displayed a greater preparedness to infer an implied contract out of the circumstances of a governing body/member relationship than it had displayed previously, but it limited the extent of the terms that would be implied into that contract, and consequently the availability of damages. Latham LJ, having found that a contract arose, stated:[2]

> 'The remaining question is what was the ambit of the obligations undertaken by the Respondent? ... In one sense, the obligations can be easily stated. First the Respondent undertook to carry out the disciplinary procedures in accordance with the rules. Second, it undertook to carry them out fairly. Both these obligations are accepted by

the Respondent even in the absence of contract. It is the ambit of the second which is the subject of debate... It does not seem to me that the nature or extent of the obligation to act fairly depends upon the existence or otherwise of a contract. In other words the answer to the question whether or not the respondent did act fairly should be the same whether or not a contract exists. I can see no justification for implying into the contract any further or different obligation from that which would be considered the appropriate test in considering the exercise of the Courts' supervisory jurisdiction whether or not the proceedings were fair.'

Jonathan Parker LJ (who doubted the existence of a contract, but as he was in the minority addressed the issue on the basis that there was one) stated:[3]

'In the first place, the notion of the body which has the obligation to set up a disciplinary tribunal being in some way contractually responsible for the manner in which that tribunal, once set up, conducts the proceedings seems to me to be something of a contradiction in terms, since it is inherent in the process itself that the tribunal should so far as practicable be free from influence by the body which sets it up ... In the second place, it seems to me in any event that it is reasonable to assume that no such body, properly advised, would voluntarily assume contractual responsibility for matters outside its control ... In those circumstances, it seems to me that any implied contractual obligation on the part of the BAF relating to the disciplinary process should be limited to the setting up of the disciplinary committee, and should not extend to the exercise by the disciplinary committee of its functions once it had been set up...'.

Mance LJ stated:[4]

'I note, in relation to any independent appeal panel, that the rules provide that one of the three members should not even be appointed by the defendant and that one, although nominated by the defendant, should be a barrister or solicitor. Whilst the fair conduct of appeal proceedings by the independent appeal panel was no doubt a condition of both parties' willingness to be bound by their outcome, I would see little attraction, and some incongruity, in holding the defendant contractually responsible in damages for failure by properly appointed members of an expressly 'independent' appeal panel to behave fairly. Such a failure might abort the proceedings and be potentially unfortunate for whichever side had lost below, but I do not see why, without more, the defendant should be treated as having contracted that it would not occur ... Whilst the disciplinary committee is under the rules more closely linked in composition to the defendant, it is inherent in the claimant's own case, as well as in the defendant's, that the disciplinary committee was intended under the rules to fulfil an independent adjudicatory role. On that basis, which I accept, I again see no reason for treating the defendant as answerable for all aspects of a disciplinary committee's behaviour, as if its members were acting as employees or agents ... In these circumstances, I would regard any implied obligation on the part of the defendant under its rules as extending, at most, to an obligation to act in good faith and take due care to appoint persons who so far as it knew or (probably) had reason to believe were appropriate persons to sit on the relevant disciplinary committee.'

1 See, for example, p 12 of the shorthand writers' transcript (citing *Lloyd v McMahon* [1987] 1 AC 65 for the ambit of the requirement to apply a fair process).
2 [2002] 1 WLR 1192 at 1209, paras 52 to 54 (and also per Latham LJ at para 61, that the term relates to the process as a whole, not each individual stage of it, and at 66–67, doubting that even if apparent bias were established, there was cause of action in damages if overall there was a fair result, because there was no actual bias).
3 [2002] 1 WLR 1192 at paras 85–88.
4 [2002] 1 WLR 1192 at paras 120–122.

(g)   The test under Bradley v Jockey Club

7.15   It is against this background that the more recent analysis of the test is to be viewed. The first, and leading, authority is *Bradley v Jockey Club*.[1] The former jockey Graham Bradley had been a witness at the trial of one of his friends, another jockey, alleged to have been involved in drug smuggling. His friend had received sums of money from another defendant, and the prosecution alleged that this was connected to drug smuggling. Bradley gave evidence that such sums had been paid for information in relation to races, and under cross-examination was led into saying that he too had received gifts, such as nights out, from the other defendant. He was charged by the Jockey Club with passing information to a punter, which was contrary to the Rules of Racing. The first instance disciplinary hearing was before a Disciplinary Committee made up of three members of the Jockey Club and a legal assessor.[2] It rejected the former jockey's arguments as to why he was not in breach, and disqualified him for eight years, with the result that he could not go onto racecourses or other Jockey Club licensed premises for that period, which meant that he could not conduct his new business as a bloodstock agent. This very long disqualification was imposed notwithstanding that the sanctions imposed in all other cases of the offence had been measured in weeks or at most months, and at a time when the Jockey Club was under pressure in the media to clean up racing. Graham Bradley appealed to an Appeal Board made up of an independent legally qualified chairman and two members of the Jockey Club.[3] The appeal was by way of review and not rehearing.[4] The Appeal Board first rejected the jockey's argument that the Jockey Club's disciplinary system lacked independence and impartiality and so was in breach of Art 6 of the European Convention on Human Rights. The former jockey's appeal on liability was then substantially refused, but a disqualification of five years was substituted for the eight imposed by the Disciplinary Committee.[5] That sanction was challenged before the courts. It was alleged that the Jockey Club fell under an obligation, both as an implied term of the contract and irrespective of contract, to impose a sanction that was proportionate, and that the role of the court was to identify in place of the Appeal Board, a sanction that the court regarded as proportionate.[6] The Jockey Club accepted[7] that the court could review the decision of the Appeal Board. What was in dispute was whether the basis for that review was contractual or non-contractual and what the test to be applied was.

1   *Bradley v Jockey Club* [2004] EWHC 2164 QB, 1 October 2004 Richards J, [2004] All ER (D) 11; upheld on appeal [2005] EWCA Civ 1056, 12 June 2005, Lord Phillips MR, Buxton LJ, Scott Baker LJ, (2005) Times, 14 July. For the Court of Appeal's earlier decisions, see [2005] EWCA Civ 245, 16 February 2005 (Court of Appeal's grant of permission to appeal) and [2005] EWCA Civ 851, 28 June 2005 (Buxton LJ's refusal of permission to add a breach of Art 6 ECHR complaint). For the Jockey Club Appeal Board decisions, see [2003] ISLR-SLR 71.
2   See the judgment of Richards J, para 11.
3   At para 17. The legal qualified chairman was the former High Court Judge, Sir Edward Cazalet.
4   At para 19.
5   At para 27.
6   At paras 29 to 32. Damages were not sought.
7   At para 2.

7.16   Richards J first examined the non-contractual claim, holding that:[1]

'Even in the absence of contract the court has a settled jurisdiction to grant declarations and injunctions in respect of decisions of domestic tribunals that affect a person's right to work. That applies both to 'application' cases such as *Nagle v Feilden* itself and to 'expulsion' or 'forfeiture' cases in which a person is deprived of a status previously enjoyed, though in the latter category of case it is likely in practice that a contractual relationship will also have been established.'

He endorsed the Jockey Club's acceptance that it could stand as the appropriate defendant to such a non-contractual challenge to the validity of the decision of the Appeal Board, even though it contended that the Appeal Board was a separate and independent body.[2] Richards J then addressed the test on such a challenge, holding that the court would apply essentially the same standards as would be applied by a court in public law proceedings to a body whose decisions were susceptible to judicial review under CPR Pt 54.[3] He described the test in these terms:

'That brings me to the nature of the court's supervisory jurisdiction over such a decision. The most important point, as it seems to me, is that it is *supervisory*. The function of the court is not to take the primary decision but to ensure that the primary decision-maker has operated within lawful limits. It is a review function, very similar to that of the court on judicial review. Indeed, given the difficulties that sometimes arise in drawing the precise boundary between the two, I would consider it surprising and unsatisfactory if a private law claim in relation to the decision of a domestic body required the court to adopt a materially different approach from a judicial review claim in relation to the decision of a public body. In each case the essential concern should be with the lawfulness of the decision taken: whether the procedure was fair, whether there was any error of law, whether any exercise of judgment or discretion fell within the limits open to the decision-maker, and so forth.'

Having cited passages from the leading cases in support of the supervisory nature of review, he went on to explain what it meant in the context of the case before him:[4]

'... the issue in the present case is not one of procedural fairness but concerns the proportionality of the penalty imposed. To my mind, however, that underlines the importance of recognising that the court's role is supervisory rather than that of a primary decision-maker. The test of proportionality requires the striking of a balance between competing considerations. The application of the test in the context of penalty will not necessarily produce just one right answer: there is no single "correct" decision. Different decision-makers may come up with different answers, all of them reached in an entirely proper application of the test. In the context of the European Convention on Human Rights it is recognised that, in determining whether an interference with fundamental rights is justified and, in particular, whether it is proportionate, the decision-maker has a discretionary area of judgment or margin of discretion. The decision is unlawful only if it falls outside the limits of that discretionary area of judgment. Another way of expressing it is that the decision is unlawful only if it falls outside the range of reasonable responses to the question of where a fair balance lies between the conflicting interests. The same essential approach must apply in a non-ECHR context such as the present. It is for the primary decision-maker to strike the balance in determining whether the penalty is proportionate. The court's role, in the exercise of its supervisory jurisdiction, is to determine whether the decision reached falls within the limits of the decision-maker's discretionary area of judgment. If it does, the penalty is lawful; if it does not, the penalty is unlawful. It is *not* the role of the court to stand in the shoes of the primary decision-maker, strike the balance for itself and determine on that basis what it considers the right penalty should be.'

---

1 *Bradley* per Richards J, at para 35.
2 At para 36. He stated that that acceptance was 'an obviously sensible position to adopt, since it is only through the Jockey Club's implementation of the Appeal Board's decision that an adverse effect on the claimant's livelihood arises, thus triggering the application of *Nagle v Feilden* and/or restraint of trade principles'.
3 At para 37 et seq.
4 At paras 43 and 44.

7.17   Richards J then turned to the claim in contract, and the Jockey Club's contentions that there was no contract but if there were, the Jockey Club itself owed only an obligation to make the appeal process available to a participant, and owed no obligations to the participant as to the quality of the decision by the separate Appeal Board or how it was taken. Richards J concluded that in the normal course a jockey under licence would be in a contractual relationship with the Jockey Club,[1] but in the case before him Graham Bradley was no longer under licence. Nevertheless, a contract arose because the former jockey had been offered a choice between being dealt with as if he were licensed, or under the warning off provisions, and chose the former.[2] Richards J then dealt with the terms of that contractual relationship. He was not confronted with a claim for damages, as had the courts in *Modahl*, but he did have to deal with an argument advanced by the former jockey that the existence of a contract in some way imposed a contractual obligation on the Jockey Club that the sanction imposed on him had to be proportionate, which fell to be enforced by the court assessing what it viewed to be proportionate in place of the governing body and making a declaration to that effect.[3] Richards J rejected this argument on two bases. First, he held that the Appeal Board was a separate body from the Jockey Club. Its decisions were reviewable on the non-contractual basis that he had already held existed, and there was no basis for the implication of a term that the Jockey Club should be contractually responsible for its actions.[4] Secondly, he took the view[5] that there was no room for implication into the contract of a different standard of review to that which he had held existed in any event on that non-contractual basis: the court could only assess whether the decision was lawful, and could not make a declaration as to what it considered to be a proportionate sanction.[6] If Richards J had stopped there, it would be difficult to see how any argument could survive that there was a cause of action in damages against a sports governing body in respect of the decision of a separate disciplinary body convened under the sports governing body's rules. However Richards J went on to hold that what *could* be implied into the contract in the circumstances of the case were (a) an obligation on the Jockey Club to give effect to the decision of the Appeal Board and no more than that decision; and (b) an obligation on the Jockey Club that it would only apply a decision of the Appeal Board in so far as it was lawful.[7] In Richards J's words:

> 'It may be necessary to imply a term that the Jockey Club would give effect to the Appeal Board's decision, or would not implement any penalty or sanction beyond that decided on by the Appeal Board. In my judgment, however, there is no basis for implying any material obligation on the Jockey Club going beyond that. The non-contractual route provides a satisfactory basis for any challenge to the lawfulness of the Appeal Board's decision. Alternatively, if reliance on the non-contractual route is considered unsatisfactory, the contractual analysis could be extended so as to imply a term that the Jockey Club would give effect to the *lawful* decision of the Appeal Board, or would not implement any penalty or sanction beyond that *lawfully* decided on by the Appeal Board. That would provide the basis for a contractual claim against the Jockey Club, but one under which the Appeal Board's decision would be assessed by the court in the same way as I have held to be appropriate in the non-contractual context. In either event the court is limited to the supervisory function of reviewing the lawfulness of the Appeal Board's decision and it is not for the court to substitute its own judgment or decision for that of the Appeal Board.'

1 *Bradley* per Richards J, paras 51–53.
2 At paras 55–56.
3 At paras 56 and 61.
4 At paras 59–62.

5 At paras 61 and 75.
6 The distinction may on occasion be a fine one, for obvious reasons.
7 At para 62.

7.18   *Bradley* is therefore authority that where a disciplinary body created by, but separate from, the sports governing body takes a decision: (a) that decision is reviewable on a non-contractual basis by reference to the same grounds for review as the Administrative Court would apply to the decisions of a public law body, entitling the claimant to a declaration and possibly an injunction; (b) as well as the members of that separate disciplinary body, the sports governing body can be a respondent to that non-contractual claim, as it enforces the decision;[1] (c) where a contract arises between the sports governing body and the claimant, no term can be implied into it that imports a greater standard of review; but (d) there may be a claim in contract against the sports governing body if it enforces a decision not reached by the separate disciplinary body, or if the sports governing body enforces a decision reached by the separate disciplinary body in breach of that standard of review.[2] Although Richards J did not so state (and there was no claim for damages before him), it would appear that if the governing body acted in this way, it would be in breach of contract, and that would in the normal course sound in damages. However, in addition to his making no express statement as to the availability of damages, Richards J's statement of the existence of the second implied term was arguably equivocal.[3] In addition such a result would arguably go further than what had been contemplated in the cases on which he relied (*Singer, Modahl*, and *Colgan*). Furthermore, the proposition that there should be the same standard of review irrespective of implied contractual obligation raises the argument that the remedies available should also be the same. In other words, the implied term would be confined to one that contemplates the same standard of review *and the same consequences* as would arise irrespective of contract, consequently excluding damages.[4]

1 But a cautious practitioner would be well advised to seek relief against the members of the separate disciplinary body as well.
2 And a cautious practitioner will plead the case on both the non-contractual and the contractual bases, taking care correctly to express the implied term so as not to allege too much.
3 'Alternatively, *if* the reliance on the non-contractual route is considered unsatisfactory, the contractual analysis *could* be extended…' [emphasis added].
4 Breach of an express term would, however, be another matter.

7.19   The implications of Richards J's analysis for the position where the action challenged is *not* that of a separate body have not been conclusively established. It would appear that what flows from Richards J's analysis is that where a sports governing body *itself* acts, then: (a) that action is reviewable on a non-contractual basis by reference to the same grounds for review as the Administrative Court would apply to the decisions of a public law body, entitling the claimant to a declaration and possibly an injunction; (b) the sports governing body would be the respondent; (c) where a contract arises between the sports governing body and the claimant, no term can be implied into it that imports a greater standard of review; but (d) there may be a claim in contract, if the sports governing body enforces an action that is in breach of that standard of review.[1] Again, if there is a breach of contract, the normal consequence would be that damages would be available. Where the sports governing body itself acts, it is responsible for its own actions. However, the argument described above (that if there is to be the same standard of review irrespective of the implied contractual obligation, the *remedies* available should also be the same), could still be made.[2] In any event, it would therefore appear that where the action is that of the sports governing body itself, the prospects of damages ought to be stronger.

1 And a cautious practitioner will plead the case on both bases, taking care correctly to express the implied term so as not to allege too much.
2 Again, breach of an express term would, however, be another matter.

7.20   Applying these principles, Richards J concluded[1] that the Appeal Board had not stepped outside the range of decisions on sanctions that were open to it in the exercise of its expertise. In so doing, he refused to entertain new evidence, on the basis that the question for him was whether the Appeal Board had stepped outside the range of decisions open to it on the basis of the information before it,[2] and accepted the argument that the Appeal Board had legitimately distinguished Graham Bradley's case from those of jockeys who had been subjected to much shorter bans for the same offence.[3] Lastly, Richards J stated that if he had had to reach the decision himself, he would have reached the same conclusion as the Appeal Board.[4]

1 *Bradley* per Richards J, at paras 106–116.
2 At para 84.
3 At para 100.
4 At para 117.

7.21   On appeal, Lord Phillips MR fully endorsed, and set out 'key' passages of, Richards J's expression of the test for supervisory review,[1] in a way that confers on his analysis the imprimatur of Court of Appeal authority:

> 'Richards J dealt at length with the role of the court in a case such as this and conducted a careful analysis of the relevant authorities. I would commend the entirety of his analysis and, as his judgment is accessible on the website through the neutral citation number, I propose only to cite the key passages…
>
> I have cited the relevant passages from the judgment of Richards J because I am satisfied that they correctly state the law and do so with a clarity that I could not hope to better.'

While the passages set out related to the test on a non-contractual claim, it is arguable that the Master of the Rolls was also approving Richards J's analysis of the position where a contract arises, and his approach to a case where the decision was made by a separate disciplinary body, although neither he nor any other member of the Court of Appeal addressed these issues separately. Lord Phillips MR also endorsed Richards J's conclusion on the proportionality of the sanction.[2]

1 [2005] EWCA Civ 1056 CA, [2006] LLR 1, 12 June 2005 Lord Phillips MR, Buxton LJ, Scott Baker LJ, (2005) Times, 14 July, at paras 17–18. See also Buxton LJ at para 28.
2 At para 25.

(h)   The cases following Bradley v Jockey Club

7.22   Shortly after Richards J's decision in *Bradley*, Evans-Lombe J in *Flaherty v NGRC*[1] set aside a decision finding a greyhound owner guilty of administering a drug to the greyhound on the basis that the decision was affected by apparent bias and was undermined by the fact that the chief executive of the NGRC appeared to have interfered in the deliberations of the tribunal by retiring with them when they considered their decision. Evans-Lombe J held that there was a contract between the NGRC and those governed by its rules.[2] He rejected an argument that the decision was one which a tribunal properly instructing themselves as to the facts and the law could not reasonably have reached, plainly based on public law standards,[3] before addressing whether the proceedings had been fairly conducted or had rather been tainted by apparent bias and the actions of the chief executive. He held, again on the basis of public law standards, that they had been so tainted as to render them unfair.[4] The governing body appealed and the Court of Appeal overturned Evans-Lombe J's decision. Scott Baker LJ held that Evans-Lombe J had sought to apply the *correct* test but had erred in its application.[5] There was no appearance of bias in the approach and connections of one member of the disciplinary body, and the actions of the chief executive in retiring with the disciplinary body, although not good practice, had not given rise to an appearance of bias either. Further, any defects in the procedure did not affect the fact that there had been a fair result overall. Scott Baker LJ repeated the exhortation of many judges that sporting bodies should be given as free a hand as possible, consistent with the fundamental requirements of fairness, to run their own disciplinary processes without the interference of the courts.[6]

1 *Flaherty v National Greyhound Racing Club* [2004] EWHC 2838 Ch D (8 December 2004, Evans-Lombe J).
2 At para 3, in reliance on *Law v National Greyhound Racing Club* [1983] 3 All ER 300, [1983] 1 WLR 1302, CA.
3 At paras 43–44.
4 At para 62. The test that he applied was the public law test examined in *Re Medicaments and Related Class of Goods* [2001] 1 WLR 700; *Porter v Magill* [2002] 2 AC 357.
5 [2005] EWCA Civ 1117 CA, 14 September 2005, Sir Mark Potter, Scott Baker LJ, Sir Peter Gibson; (2005) Times, October 5, [2005] All ER (D) 70A, in particular Scott Baker LJ at paras 77 to 81, relying in particular on *Modahl v BAF* [2001] EWCA Civ 1447, [2002] 1 WLR 1192, [2001] All ER (D) 181, 8 October 2001 per Latham LJ at para 61 and Mance LJ at para 115.
6 *Flaherty* at paras 19 to 21.

7.23   In *Mullins*, a horse trained by the claimant was stripped of victory in a major race after morphine was found in the sample taken from it after the race. It was common ground that the morphine originated in contaminated food and that no blame attached, but under the applicable rules the presence of the drug was sufficient to lead to disqualification. The trainer unsuccessfully challenged the decision of the Disciplinary Committee before a Jockey Club Appeal Board. The trainer then sought from the courts a declaration that the Appeal Board's decision was unlawful on the bases that the Appeal Board had misconstrued the applicable rules and had acted capriciously and arbitrarily (or irrationally). The trainer commenced proceedings for judicial review in the Administrative Court under CPR Pt 54, but Stanley Burnton J ordered that the case continue as if begun under CPR Pt 8.[1] When the matter returned before him in private law form,[2] he addressed the scope and nature of the jurisdiction he was being asked to exercise, stating:[3]

'The first issue raised by Mr Mullins' claim is as to the scope and nature of the jurisdiction of the Court on a challenge to a decision such as that of the Appeal Board of the Jockey Club, a domestic disciplinary tribunal of a private organisation that is the governing body of a sport. Mr Kerr QC submitted that the Court will interfere with a decision of a body such as the Appeal Board of the Jockey Club if that decision is arbitrary or capricious or is based on a misinterpretation of the applicable rules of the sporting body in question ...

Mr Warby QC on behalf of the Jockey Club accepted that this Court has a supervisory jurisdiction over tribunals such as the Appeal Board, irrespective of the existence of a contract between the claimant and the tribunal or the body appointing it. However, he submitted that the jurisdiction of the Court is more restricted than Mr Kerr suggested: it is limited to cases of restraint of trade (or the claimant's "right to work") and those where the tribunal has acted unfairly. He relied upon the judgment of Richards J in *Bradley v*

The Jockey Club [2004] EWHC 2164, a judgment commended by the Court of Appeal on appeal at [2005] EWCA Civ 1056. Mr Warby submitted that the present case was not one affecting Mr Mullins' right to work; it was not a case in which a penalty had been imposed, because the disqualification of a competitor is not a penalty for this purpose; it was not contended that the hearing before the Appeal Board had not been fair; and that accordingly this was not a case in which the Court could, or should, interfere. Mr Warby's submissions led to discussion of the correct interpretation of Paragraph 14 of Appendix J to the Rules of Racing, i.e., whether it treated disqualification as a penalty.

... in my judgment, I can decide the present claim on the assumption that Mr Kerr's submissions correctly represent the law. My provisional view is that there is no jurisdictional (in the narrow sense of the word) boundary to the power of the Court to grant declaratory relief in this context: the jurisdiction of the Court under CPR Part 40.20 to grant declaratory relief in unrestricted. The restrictions on the power are discretionary. The discretion will be exercised having regard to the respect and caution appropriate when considering the decision of an impartial qualified tribunal whose knowledge and experience of the subject matter in question is likely to exceed those of the Court. But the power to grant declaratory relief will not necessarily be excluded because, for example, the decision under challenge does not involve payment of a financial penalty. The importance of the challenged decision to the parties is an important factor, and I do not think that the extent or the exercise of the jurisdiction is to be determined (although it may be influenced) by the correct interpretation of Paragraph 14 of Appendix J.'

1 *R (Mullins) v Appeal Board of the Jockey Club (Jockey Club as an interested party)* [2005] EWHC 2197 Admin, 17 October 2005 Stanley Burnton J.
2 *Mullins v McFarlane (representing the Appeal Board of the Jockey Club) and the Jockey Club* [2006] EWHC 986, 5 May 2006 Stanley Burnton J, [2006] All ER (D) 66. After the action was transferred to the QB, the claimant took the precaution of suing the members of the Appeal Board as well as the Jockey Club itself, in the light of Richards J's decision in *Bradley*.
3 At paras 37 to 39 of his second judgment.

7.24   Two points arise. First, while Stanley Burnton J contemplated a wide discretionary jurisdiction to grant a declaration, which might arguably be said to encompass the possibility of such relief in situations outside the supervisory standard and grounds for review set out in *Bradley*, he expressly stated that the jurisdiction fell to be exercised showing deference to the decision of the expert decision-maker. In their context, his conclusions are consistent with *Bradley* (as they were required to be, given the Court of Appeal's endorsement of the approach in *Bradley*). Secondly, he rejected, albeit *obiter* and on an expressly 'provisional' basis, the Jockey Club's argument that the grounds for review only arose where a claimant's right to work was affected. Stanley Burnton J went on to hold that the challenge in private law failed, because the Appeal Board had neither misconstrued the rules nor acted capriciously or arbitrarily, both grounds for review contemplated in the test set out in *Bradley*.[1]

1 At paras 48, 52 and 56 of his second judgment.

7.25   In a further horseracing case against the Jockey Club's immediate regulatory successor, *Fallon v Horseracing Regulatory Authority*,[1] the jockey's licence was suspended when he was charged with a criminal offence, pending trial. When he challenged the interim suspension before the courts, Davis J held that in circumstances where a member of a professional body is charged with a grave and complex criminal offence, a disciplinary tribunal is not always obliged, if asked, to hear evidence and receive submissions from that member as to the alleged weaknesses of the charges brought. Davis J based his approach firmly on *Bradley* and *Flaherty*:[2]

> 'It is well established that a decision of a body such as the HRA cannot be challenged by judicial review proceedings. But it is equally well established that the High Court retains a supervisory jurisdiction over such decisions, and the approach to be adopted is essentially that which the Administrative Court would adopt in public law cases.'

And later:[3]

> 'I turn then to the issue as to whether the sanction of prohibition of Mr Fallon from riding in races in Great Britain was disproportionate. Clearly for this purpose I must apply the approach laid down in the cases of *Bradley* and *Flaherty*. Mr Pannick fairly accepts that and he fairly accepts that there is a generous margin of appreciation here. At the same time he submits, and I agree, that the court must not show unthinkingly servile obeisance to such a decision of an expert tribunal. If the court decides that a particular sanction is disproportionate and unjustified then it should not shrink from saying so.'

1 *Fallon v Horseracing Regulatory Authority* [2006] EWHC 1898 QB, 28 July 2006 Davis J, [2006] All ER (D) 427.
2 At paras 12 to 14.
3 At para 53.

7.26   In the *Stretford v FA* litigation, on the hearing of The FA's application for an Arbitration Act 1996 stay of court proceedings challenging the legality of The FA's disciplinary process, the Court of Appeal proceeded on the basis that the *Bradley* approach was applicable.[1] It was also taken to be the correct approach by Simon J in *Sankofa and Charlton v The FA*.[2] In *Adidas v Draper and others*,[3] Morritt C rejected an argument that the *Bradley* supervisory approach in domestic law precluded, even by analogy, the competition law challenge in that case, which he held fell to be assessed by the principles expounded by the European courts. However, the Chancellor did not cast doubt on the appropriateness of the approach in the domestic context.

1 *Stretford v The FA* [2007] EWCA Civ 238, 21 March 2007 Clarke MR, Waller and Sedley LJJ, at para 49 of the Master of the Rolls' judgment. In *Stretford v FA (FA Rule K Arbitration)* Sir Martin Nourse, 5 December 2007, it was held that the principles in *Bradley*, *Flaherty* and *Sheffield v FAPL* governed the substance of Mr Stretford's challenge in the arbitration to the legality of The FA's then disciplinary process.
2 *Sankofa and Charlton v The FA* [2007] (12 January 2007, Comm Ct, Simon J).
3 *Adidas v Draper and others [representing the Grand Slams] and the International Tennis Federation* [2006] EWHC 1318 (ChD, Sir Andrew Morritt C, 7 June 2006) [2006] All ER (D) 30.

7.27   The nature and scope of the grounds for review fell for examination by an FAPL Rule S Arbitration Panel in *Sheffield United v FAPL*.[1] The club challenged the FAPL disciplinary body's decision[2] that West Ham United should only pay a fine for its admitted breaches of FAPL rules in the way that it secured the services in the 2006/2007 season of the Argentine internationals Carlos Tevez and Javier Mascherano without paying a transfer fee. A points deduction would have meant that West Ham, instead of Sheffield United, would be relegated from the Premier League. The disciplinary body had acknowledged that in the normal course a points deduction would be imposed for conduct of this type, but gave seven reasons why in this instance it chose to depart from the norm. Relying on the non-contractual claim and the implied terms identified in *Bradley*, Sheffield United challenged the decision on the basis that the disciplinary body had ignored relevant considerations (the need to restore competitive balance) and taken into account irrelevant considerations (in the form of most of the seven reasons relied upon) and that the decision was irrational and disproportionate. The FAPL contended that it was not the appropriate respondent to such an action, that it was not open to a club that was not the subject of the disciplinary proceedings to seek review of the disciplinary body's decision on the grounds relied upon, and that in any event the disciplinary body had not acted in such a way as to trigger one of the grounds for review.

1 *Sheffield United v FAPL*, award dated 3 July 2007 [2007] ISLR-SLR 77.
2 27 April 2007.

7.28   The FAPL Rule S Arbitration Panel held[1] that, in accordance with the principles set out in *Bradley*, the non-contractual claim could be brought against the governing body even if the decision-maker was its separate disciplinary body:

> 'Despite the FAPL's reliance elsewhere on a submission that the Disciplinary Commission is an independent body, the FAPL is an appropriate defendant to a claim seeking a declaration that the Disciplinary Commission acted unreasonably. This seems to this Tribunal to be an obviously sensible approach ...
>
> It is clear from *Bradley* that although the decisions of sports bodies are not subject to judicial review, the High Court will entertain a challenge on principles analogous to judicial review, whether on a contractual or non-contractual basis. That is so even if the sports body is independent, as was the case in relation to the Jockey Club disciplinary decision in issue in Bradley.'

The Arbitration Panel therefore concluded that it was unnecessary to examine whether Sheffield United had a contractual cause of action on the basis of the *Bradley* implied terms, or whether the independence of the disciplinary body meant that its decision could not be challenged on that basis.[2]

1 At paras 23 to 25.
2 At paras 29.

7.29   The FAPL Rule S Arbitration Panel went on to hold[1] that it was open to Sheffield United to mount a challenge on the basis of the *Bradley* grounds for review even though, first, it was not a party to the disciplinary proceedings, and secondly, the challenge was not based on a breach of the rules by the governing body. The Panel decided the question of standing on the basis of principles analogous to those that apply before the Administrative Court, but stressed that its decision was an exceptional one based on the particular circumstances of Sheffield United and the FAPL, where the 'decision directly and vitally [affected] the fundamental interests of [Sheffield United] as a member of the FAPL'. This took into account the fact that part at least of the purpose underlying the need to enforce the rules of a league such as the FAPL is to vindicate the interest of other clubs (in competition with the offending club) in a fair and equal competition by removing advantages gained in breach of the rules, as well as punishing the offending club.

1 At paras 27 to 28.

7.30   On the substance of the challenge, the Arbitration Panel went so far as to state that had it sat in place of the disciplinary body, it would have deducted points.[1] It went on to conclude, however, applying the approach in *Bradley*, that the decision only to fine did not fall outside the range of decisions reasonably open to the disciplinary body.[2] The club subsequently unsuccessfully attempted to challenge the Arbitration Panel's decision under s 69 of the Arbitration Act 1996 on the basis that the arbitrators had applied the wrong test by concentrating on rationality and not addressing whether relevant considerations had been ignored and irrelevant ones taken into account.[3] This case illustrates the supervisory, and often limited nature of the review on offer: the club innocent of any wrongdoing was demoted, whereas the club guilty of serious breaches of the rules (meriting in the view of the Arbitration Panel a points deduction and consequent demotion in place of Sheffield United) escaped that fate on the basis of the margin of appreciation to be afforded to sports governing bodies (and their tribunals, if separate) by a court or arbitral tribunal exercising only supervisory review.

1 At para 36.
2 At paras 37 to 39.
3 *Sheffield United v FAPL*, 13 July 2007 Comm Ct Smith J.

7.31   In *Dwain Chambers v British Olympic Association,*[1] Mackay J applied the approach in *Bradley* to the evaluation of the legality of the British Olympic Association's then bylaw under which any athlete who had been convicted of doping was thereafter ineligible for selection for the British Olympic team. The bylaw was challenged as being in unreasonable restraint of trade, in breach of the competition law rules, and irrational. The application was for an interim injunction, but since it would dispose of the claim, a high degree of assurance was required. Mackay J quoted Richards J's analysis in *Bradley*, emphasising in particular paras 34 and 35 dealing with how the jurisdiction arises where a person's right to work is affected. Mackay J then went on to ask himself two questions: first, whether the case before him was one where the athlete's 'right to work' was significantly restricted[2] and secondly whether the by law was in any event proportionate in the sense that it fell within the range of actions reasonably open to the BOA in pursuit of its aims.[3] On the first question he concluded that the athlete would face an uphill struggle at trial, since the Olympics were a quadrennial amateur event with no prize money and the athlete had very limited prospects of securing a medal (which might lead to indirect benefits).[4] On the second question, he asked:[5]

> '...Does the byelaw, when subjected to the intensity of review described in *Bradley*, go further than is reasonable or necessary to achieve the legitimate aims of the BOA?'

He concluded that there was no evidence to demonstrate that the bylaw was disproportionate to the needs pursued through it by the BOA.[6]

1 *Dwain Chambers v British Olympic Association* [2008] EWHC 2028 (QB), Mackay J, 9, 17 and 18 July 2008.
2 At para 41 and following.
3 At para 48 and following.
4 Mackay J declined to discard *Currie v Barton* (1988) Times, 12 February (see para **9.6** note 6), and *Gasser v Stinson* 15 June 1988, Scott J (see para **10.13**), which set a high standard for when a sportsman was restrained in his trade or had his right to work affected. Mackay J was not prepared to regard any effect adverse to the athlete as being sufficient.
5 At para 48.
6 At para 54. He also held that the competition law argument was insufficiently separately developed to warrant separate analysis, and that he doubted that *Meca- Medina v Commission* (C-519/04P) [2006] European Court of Justice, 18 July 2006 [2006] ECR I-6991; [2006] ISLR SLR-175; [2006] All ER (EC) 1057, imposed a significantly different test.

7.32   Two points arise, in particular, from *Chambers*. First, Mackay J was in no doubt that the *Bradley* basis and standard of review applied beyond disciplinary decisions of a separate disciplinary body, to the sports governing body's own regulatory and policy decisions.[1] Secondly, Mackay J was in equally no doubt that the *Bradley* basis and standard of review only applied where there was a significant effect on the right to work or restraint of trade, and that that requirement should not be taken lightly.

1 Indeed, Richards J's observations in *Bradley* as to the appropriate *"discretionary area of judgment"* have been cited in judicial review cases outside the sport context. See eg *R (McVey) v Secretary of State for Health* [2010] EWHC 437 (Admin) 5 March 2010, LTL 11 March 2010, [2010] Med LR 204 at paragraphs 74, 95 per Silber J; *R (Westech College) v Secretary of State for the Home Department* [2011] EWHC 1484 (Admin) at paragraphs 28, 29(e) per Silber J.

7.33   The approach in *Bradley*, *Flaherty* and *Fallon* was followed and developed by Stadlen J in *McKeown v British Horseracing Authority,*[1] the regulatory successor in turn of the Horseracing Regulatory Authority. The jockey challenged the decisions of the BHA's disciplinary panel and appeal panel that he had breached the rules of racing by deliberately failing to ride horses on their merits and by conspiring with a trainer to provide inside information to gamblers. He contended, first, that the conclusion that he had not ridden horses on their merits was irrational, ie, no reasonable panel could have reached it. Secondly, he contended that it was not possible to conclude that a jockey was guilty of a corrupt practice when the only evidence was that information had been obtained by gamblers who had subsequently bet on the basis of it. Thirdly, he contended that each panel had been tainted with the appearance of bias. Lastly, before the appeal panel he had attempted, but had not been allowed, to raise new factual arguments that he had not made before the disciplinary panel, pointing to the trainer alone being responsible. He contended that the appeal panel's approach in denying him this opportunity was unlawful. Before addressing those arguments, Stadlen J described the legal principles governing the court's jurisdiction:[2]

'21. In *Fallon v Horseracing Regulatory Authority* [2006] EWHC 2030 (QB), a case in which a well-known jockey challenged a decision of the defendant's predecessor as the body responsible for regulating horse racing, Davis J held that 'it is well established that a decision of a body such as the HRA cannot be challenged by judicial review proceedings. But it is equally well established that the High Court retains a supervisory jurisdiction over such decisions, and the approach to be adopted is essentially that which the Administrative Court would adopt in public law cases.' (Para 12.)

22. The correct approach to be adopted by the court in the exercise of this supervisory jurisdiction was laid down by the Court of Appeal in the two cases of *Bradley v Jockey Club* [2005] EWCA Civ 1056 ... and *Flaherty v The National Greyhound Racing Club Limited* [2005] EWCA Civ 117...'.

Stadlen J noted Richards J's identification of the non-contractual cause of action as arising where the decision of a domestic tribunal affects a person's right to work,[3] his explanation of the strictly supervisory nature of the cause of action,[4] and his analysis of what that means when reviewing the lawfulness of a sanction. Stadlen J then turned to the fact that Mr McKeown's challenge was to findings of liability as opposed to sanction. He held that Richards J's analysis in *Bradley* therefore did not apply directly, but continued:[5]

'32 ... However by parity of reasoning, in my judgment it follows that in so far as the challenge is to findings of fact made by the Disciplinary Panel and upheld by the Appeal Board, the role of this court in adjudicating on that challenge is not to stand in the shoes of the primary decision-maker and determine what it considers the right findings of fact should be. Just as the application of the test of proportionality as to penalty will not necessary produce just one right answer, so it may be that different tribunals honestly doing their best may reach different findings of fact on the basis of the same evidence. Just as in an application for judicial review of a decision based on findings of fact, the question for the court is not whether had it been the primary decision-maker it would have reached the same or different findings of fact but rather whether the findings of fact actually reached took into account all relevant and excluded all irrelevant considerations and whether they were perverse

33. In *Bradley* Richards J emphasised as a reason reinforcing the importance of the court limiting itself to a supervisory role the fact that the Appeal Board in that case included members who were knowledgeable about the racing industry. The relevance of that factor in that case was that they were better placed than the court to decide on the importance of the Rules in questions and the precise weight to be attached to breaches of those Rules when reaching a view on a proportionate penalty. It does not, however in my judgment, follow that the importance and relevance of that factor is confined to cases where the challenge is one to the proportionality of a penalty. There may be all sorts of factual issues in the context of liability where members of a disciplinary tribunal or Appeal Board who are knowledgeable about the racing industry are better placed than the court to make findings of fact. Obvious examples are where a finding of fact depends wholly or in part on interpreting video evidence of a race in which a jockey's motives and efforts are impugned or on assessing the plausibility of explanations given by a jockey for his conduct of a race or by a gambler for his decision to place a bet.'

Stadlen J then reiterated the importance of the court not seeking to second-guess the expert and experienced decision maker, as described in *Flaherty* and in the cases cited in it.[6] However he then went on to stress that the fact that such a 'generous margin of appreciation' must be afforded does not mean that the court should show 'unthinkingly servile obeisance' to the decision maker.[7] The preparedness to intervene may be different when the issue involves findings of fact, as opposed to the exercise of a pure discretion:

'In relation to a finding of fact, it is submitted that the court should interfere only if, allowing for the special expertise of the tribunal and the fact that it saw and heard the witness or (in this case) video evidence, the court is nevertheless satisfied that no reasonable tribunal could have made the finding on the evidence before it. I did not understand Mr Winter to challenge this submission as materially incorrect and I accept it. It emphasises a number of important points: (1) The function of the court is not to make findings of fact but to decide whether it is satisfied that no reasonable tribunal could have made a finding of fact made by the sporting tribunal on the evidence before it; (2) In considering whether it is so satisfied the court should allow for the special expertise of the tribunal and the fact that it saw and heard the witnesses and/or as in this case video evidence; (3) The fact that the tribunal had special expertise does not, however, prevent the court from carefully examining the evidence before the tribunal and concluding in an appropriate case that, notwithstanding the special expertise of the tribunal, the evidence before it was such that no reasonable tribunal could have made the findings of fact which were in fact made; (4) The importance of the court not showing unthinkingly servile obeisance to the decision of an expert sporting tribunal is particularly important where, as here, the decision under challenge affects a person's livelihood.'[8]

1 *McKeown v British Horseracing Authority* [2010] EWHC 508 (QB), 12 March 2010.
2 At 20 and 21 of his main judgment.
3 At para 24 of his main judgment.
4 At paras 25 to 31 of his main judgment.

5 At para 32 and following of his main judgment.
6 At paras 35 and 36 of his main judgment.
7 At para 37 of his main judgment.
8 At paras 35 and 36 of his main judgment.

7.34   Applying the legal principles to the facts,[1] Stadlen J held that it was not perverse or unreasonable for the panels, in their expertise and experience and based on their assessment of the evidence (including video evidence) to conclude that the jockey had not ridden the horses on their merits. The panels were also entitled to reach the conclusion, again based on their expertise and experience, that the only plausible explanation for the jockey's behaviour was that he was involved in a betting conspiracy. That conclusion was not based on the mere passing of information, but also on the additional finding that the jockey had known to what end the information was being put, and that was just as much corrupt as taking a bribe.[2] The panels had not put the evidence of the bets that had been made before their assessment of the video evidence.[3] The requirements of apparent bias had not been made out.[4] As to the arguments of fact that the jockey had not been permitted to advance before the appeal panel, the argument that one of the horses had lost two shoes, indicating the trainer's guilt, would not have made a difference if it had been made.[5] The second argument on the other hand, that the trainer had lied and was not credible, might have made a difference, and procedural fairness required that it be remitted to the disciplinary panel. In a second judgment of the same day,[6] Stadlen J rejected arguments made as to why he should not remit. On that remission, the disciplinary panel rejected the jockey's arguments.[7]

1 In paras 38 to 255 of his main judgment ([2010] EWHC 508 (QB)), Stadlen J undertook a detailed analysis of the facts in order to reach his conclusions that the panels' findings on the facts fell within the range reasonably open to them.
2 At paras 278 to 322 of his main judgment.
3 At paras 256 to 277 of his main judgment.
4 At paras 323 to 352 of his main judgment.
5 At paras 353 to 386 of his main judgment.
6 The second, subsidiary judgment is also referenced [2010] EWHC 508 (QB) and dated 12 March 2010.
7 On the basis that there was other sufficient evidence that led to the same conclusion as had originally been reached, namely that the jockey was at least also the source of the information: see *British Horseracing Authority Disciplinary Panel: decision on penalty reconsideration of Dean McKeown* (2010) International Sports Law Review 3/4, SLR157–158.

7.35   *McKeown* confirms that *Bradley* review applies to the decisions of a sports governing body's disciplinary and appeal panels both as to liability and as to sanction. Further, Stadlen J's reasoning recognises that *Bradley* review can apply to non-disciplinary decisions of the sports governing body. He emphasised that the jurisdiction covers 'application' as well as 'expulsion' or 'forfeiture' cases.[1] There is a wide range of decisions, including 'application' decisions such as the grant of a licence, and forfeiture decisions such as the reorganisation of a league structure, that affect participants just as much as disciplinary decisions. It is right that such decisions should be subject to the same supervisory review. *McKeown* did not address whether the supervisory jurisdiction applies at all where the right to work is not affected[2] or whether the standard of review varies depending upon which of the *McInnes* classification of cases the matter falls into.[3]

1 [2010] EWHC 508 (QB) at para 24 of his main judgment.
2 Although his point 4, [at para 37, cited above at footnote 1 arguably suggests there may be review, albeit on a less intense basis, even where the right to work is not affected.
3 Although it is arguable that his analysis carries with it a flavour of the standard being flexible and dependent on all the circumstances.

7.36 In *Pontypool v WRU*,[1] the club alleged that the WRU had breached its own league rules on the selection of the clubs to play in the Welsh Premier Division in the season 2012/2013. Those rules, set in order to reduce the size of that division, provided that the division would be made up of ten clubs, that to be eligible a club had to have been granted an 'A licence', and that if more than ten had been granted such a licence, a 'meritocracy ranking' would be applied to identify the top ten. Pontypool, which had an A licence, contended that other clubs higher than it in the meritocracy ranking ought not to have A licences and so should not be in the division in its place. Pontypool contended that the WRU owed it a contractual obligation to assess those other clubs' entitlement to an A licence in accordance with the facilities criteria, and that if the WRU had done so it would not have granted them A licences and so would have excluded them and admitted Pontypool instead. Alternatively, Pontypool contended that the WRU was in breach of its *Bradley* duty to act fairly, rationally and in accordance with the rules. The court concluded that there was a contract between the WRU and each individual club that its entitlement to an A licence would be assessed in accordance with the facilities criteria,[2] and that if the club satisfied them, it would be entitled to an A licence and a place in the premier division, subject to the meritocracy ranking applying if more than the necessary number of clubs satisfied those criteria. However, there was no contractual obligation owed by the WRU to a club in Pontypool's position, to apply the facilities criteria strictly vis-à-vis other clubs, and not for example to afford an extension of time or a waiver to another club.[3] The WRU's only obligation to a club in Pontypool's position was the *Bradley* duty (if necessary, implied as a contractual term) not to act unfairly or irrationally between clubs in deciding whether to grant a waiver or an extension of time. Under the principles in *Bradley* and *Stevenage*, the courts should not second-guess the WRU's decision in that context. Further, there was no obligation at all under the league rules to appoint an independent assessor of certain facilities as alleged,[4] and the WRU was entitled to rely on clubs' statements of truth as to their satisfaction of local authority-administered safety requirements at grounds.[5] The WRU was therefore not in breach of any obligation in relation to how it had assessed the other clubs' entitlement to an A licence. The fact that later the WRU agreed with the Welsh regions to add two other clubs subject to their satisfying the conditions did not avail Pontypool.[6]

1 *Park Promotion Ltd (t/a Pontypool Rugby Football Club) v Welsh Rugby Union Ltd* [2012] EWHC 1919 (QB), 11 July 2012.
2 At para 44.
3 At para 45.
4 At paras 47 to 49, 51.
5 At paras 50 to 52.
6 At paras 53, 54.

7.37 In *Cronin v Greyhound Board of Great Britain Ltd*,[1] the claimant was a licensed greyhound trainer. The Greyhound Board's disciplinary committee found the claimant guilty of a breach of the rules, gave him a severe reprimand, fined him £750, and ordered him to pay £10,000 towards the Board's costs. The rules did not include a requirement for reasons to be given for a decision, but did provide for an appeal to an internal appeal board. The claimant did not pursue such an appeal and did not pay the fine or costs. The Board served a statutory demand upon the claimant, at which point he commenced proceedings in the county court challenging the disciplinary committee's decision on various grounds, including a failure to provide reasons. The challenge ended up in the Court of Appeal. Maurice Kay LJ held that the Greyhound Board was '...*a private sector regulator constructed on contractual foundations but* *which, when exercising its disciplinary powers, is subject to requirements of fairness, whether or not they are expressed in the rules it has adopted'.*[2] He held that the Board's *'absolutist'* argument that it owed no duty to give any reasons at all was arguably wrong,[3] but that it was *'...axiomatic that in a case such as this the ultimate concern is with the overall fairness of the available procedure'*[4] and that the claimant was in no position to make a complaint of overall unfairness having failed to exercise his right to appeal to the internal appeal board, with the result that *'...looking at the internal procedures as a whole'*, it was not arguable that *'the initial absence of reasoning from the DC points to overall unfairness'.*[5] The claimant's case accordingly failed, in view of the overall fairness of the procedure and notwithstanding an arguable case based on lack of reasons.

1 *Cronin v Greyhound Board of Great Britain Ltd* [2013] EWCA Civ 668, 18 June 2013.
2 At para 1.
3 At paras 14 to 16.
4 At para 17.
5 At paras 19 to 21.

(i) The current position on the authorities

7.38   The current position on the authorities can be stated as follows. Sports governing bodies, and their separate disciplinary bodies, are not public bodies for the purposes of CPR Pt 54 judicial review. At least some of them nevertheless exercise control over and regulate a sport or aspects of it, in a way that affects to varying degrees the participants in it, often but not always such as to limit a participant in its trade.

7.39   Where that control exists, it warrants courts or arbitral tribunals exercising a non-contractual supervisory jurisdiction over the regulatory actions of the sports governing body and its separate disciplinary bodies irrespective of whether any contract arises between governing body and the participant. In the context of disciplinary actions, the supervisory jurisdiction falls to be exercised over decisions on both liability and penalty. The supervisory jurisdiction extends beyond disciplinary actions to other regulatory actions.

7.40   While the precise degrees of control and of effect that are sufficient to trigger this non-contractual jurisdiction are undefined (and of their nature are likely to remain so), in the authors' view it is not or ought not to be necessary that the sports governing body controls the entire sport. Instead, it is or ought to be sufficient that the sports governing body exercises control through a set of rules over a significant aspect of the participant's life. It is, furthermore, arguably anomalous to limit the non-contractual supervisory jurisdiction, as indicated by *Bradley* and *Chambers*, to decisions limiting the participant in his, her or its trade. Where the existing relationship can be characterised as contractual, the supervisory jurisdiction appears to arise whatever the level at which the sport is played by the claimant, whatever the sport and whatever the degree of power and influence the sports governing body has. Given that the courts have an equivalent contractual supervisory jurisdiction over bodies in that position where a contract can be identified, often artificially,[1] then it would seem odd for there to be no jurisdiction in circumstances that are identical save for the fact that the artificial contract cannot be identified. The decision is the same in both instances and its effects are the same in both instances.

1 See for example the debate in *Modahl*: para **7.13**.

7.41   The supervisory standard and grounds for review that apply on this non-contractual basis are the equivalent to those to which a public body is subject through judicial review proceedings before the Administrative Court under CPR Pt 54. As public law develops, so too will the standard and grounds for review that apply to a sports governing body. Broadly, the governing body (and its separate disciplinary bodies) cannot exercise its regulatory functions in a way:[1]

(a)   that is contrary to or outside its powers in its rules and regulations,[2] or contrary to the general law; or

(b)   in a manner that is procedurally unfair or contrary to natural justice;[3] or

(c)   that takes into account irrelevant considerations or fails to take into account relevant considerations; or

(d)   that has no factual basis; or

(e)   that is contrary to a legitimate expectation; or

(f)   that is irrational, perverse, arbitrary or capricious.

These grounds for review will be applied in the same way as the Administrative Court would apply them to a public law body. This means that in relation to some of them, such as irrationality, the court will give considerable deference to the expert decision maker, will examine only how the decision was made, as opposed to its substantive merits, and will not substitute its view for that of the decision-maker. In relation to others (sometimes described as 'hard-edged'), such as a claim that the governing body had breached its own written rules and regulations or a separate legal provision of general application, the court or tribunal will look at the substantive merits.

1 Each of these is addressed further below at paras **7.47–7.80** in the context of sport, but resort should also be had to administrative law texts.

2 The requirement that a public law body properly instruct itself as to, and act in accordance with, the law translates into a requirement that a sports governing body properly instruct itself as to and act in accordance with its rules as well as the law.

3 It will of course always be the case that the precise content of the obligation to act consistently with natural justice and in a procedurally fair manner varies from case to case: that is the public law position. Much of what is said in *Onslow-Fane* would therefore still apply. Where however the standard of natural justice and fairness set out in *Onslow-Fane* would offer less protection than would be the case in a public law context involving the same type of application or disciplinary proceedings, the court would now insist on the greater degree of protection.

7.42   Although the authorities discussed in this chapter identify their own criteria as to when the non-contractual supervisory jurisdiction exists, such as the existence of an impact on the right to work, public law standards may be relevant to whether a claimant has sufficient standing. On a public law standing-based approach, the principal factor would be the degree of the effect of the action on the claimant.

7.43   Where a contract exists between the governing body and the claimant, it will be implicit in it that the decisions of the governing body are subject to the same grounds for review as apply on the non-contractual basis, which will continue to be available. Prudence would dictate that both causes of action should be pleaded. Where a contract exists, it would not appear that any particular degree of control over the sport need be established in order to establish jurisdiction. The same supervisory standard will apply. This means that even in a contractual context, the court or arbitral tribunal will carry out the same exercise as would the Administrative Court on an application for judicial review. However, whether a cause of action sounding in damages arises against the governing body depends on first, the nature of what has been done wrong, and secondly on whether the decision-maker was the sports governing body or a separate disciplinary body.

7.44   Where a contract exists on the terms of the sports governing body's rules and regulations, a breach of the express terms of those rules and regulations by the sports governing body itself gives rise to a contractual cause of action in damages. Where a sports governing body has been found to have acted in a way that is impermissible under one of the other grounds for review, by reference to the same supervisory standard that would apply irrespective of contract, it would appear (subject to the proper construction of the contract in all its circumstances) that the sports governing body is in breach of an implied requirement in the contract that it should not do so, and a cause of action in damages may arise. This would be notwithstanding that damages would not be available in public law, and there remains an untested argument that the proposition that there should be the same standard of review irrespective of implied contractual obligation means that the remedies available should also be the same, consequently excluding damages.

7.45   Where on the other hand a disciplinary body created by, but separate from, the sports governing body takes a decision that has been found to be impermissible under any of the grounds for review, by reference to the same supervisory standard that would apply irrespective of contract, it is less likely that a cause of action in damages arises against the sports governing body with whom the participant has a contract. In these circumstances, it has been said that the extent of the obligation on the sports governing body is to establish a fair process. It would however appear that the sports governing body may also owe implied contractual obligations to *enforce* the decision made by the separate disciplinary body (and nothing else), but *only* if the decision was reached in accordance with the public law standards applicable in a supervisory review. It would appear that breach of those obligations would sound in damages against the sports governing body. The basis for this lies in Richards J's judgment in *Bradley*, but it is to be remembered that he did not expressly state that breach of his implied terms sounded in damages; there was no claim for damages before him; his statement of the existence of the second implied term was arguably equivocal; and such a result would arguably go further than what had been contemplated in the cases on which he relied. Furthermore, there would again be the untested argument that if the same standard of review is to apply, then so too should the same remedies, excluding damages.

7.46   It remains unclear whether the law has developed sufficiently to cast doubt on the principle that a sports governing body cannot be forced to take a person or body as a member. In the authors' view, given that (irrespective of contract) sports governing bodies are subject to a standard of review equivalent to that applied to public law bodies, then there is little justification for an argument that they cannot be forced to accept a member on the grounds that this would amount to forcing them to enter into a contract. As stated in *Nagle v Feilden*,[1] the contract that the sports governing body would be forced into is an artificial construct in a context where the reality is that the sports governing body controls access to the sport and being excluded from membership prevents the claimant from participating in the sport. Membership in this context is something very different from membership of a private club.[2] One way to test this is to ask what Carnwath J would have gone on to do had he not dismissed Stevenage's case on grounds of delay.[3] If he had decided that Stevenage had been unlawfully excluded from promotion by reason of the imposition of unjustifiably restrictive criteria, would he have gone on to say that the court was powerless to order The Football League to promote the club? That seems to the authors to be unlikely. Instead he would in the authors' view have forced the league to take Stevenage as a member. That said, it is clear that the courts are still reluctant to force membership even in the presence of a contractual entitlement.[4]

1 [1966] 2 QB 633, and see para **7.6**.
2 As in *Collins v Lane*, 22 June 1999 CA. Insofar as the reluctance stems from an analogy with the principle that the courts will not compel by injunction the continuance of a personal relationship (*Warren v Mendy* [1989] 1 WLR 853), there will be many applications for membership of sports governing bodies (eg by clubs rather than individuals) that are more analogous to the sort of ordinary commercial relationship where that principle does not apply (*Lauritzencool AB v Lady Navigation Inc* [2005] 1 WLR 3686).
3 Or Sir Raymond Jack in the *Pontypool* case, see para **7.36**.
4 See *Alwyn Treherne (for the Welsh Amateur Boxing Federation) v Amateur Boxing Association of England*, Garland J 27 February 2001 [2001] 3 ISLR 231, [2002] EWCA Civ 381, [2002] All ER (D) 144 (Mar) (Both Garland J and Buxton LJ felt that, even if there had been such a contract, it would not have been appropriate to grant an injunction to force the ABAE to admit the clubs).

B   THE REQUIREMENT TO ACT LAWFULLY AND IN ACCORDANCE WITH THE SPORTS GOVERNING BODY'S RULES

(a)   Acting in accordance with the rules

7.47   The first ground of review is failure to comply with the requirement that a sports governing body and its separate disciplinary bodies follow its rules and not step outside them, and act in accordance with the general law. This ground for review is equivalent to the requirement that a public body not make an error of law, and reliance may be placed on the principles developed by the courts in that context.[1] The sports governing body is required properly to instruct itself as to its rules and to act lawfully in accordance with them.[2] This is not only a negative prohibition of breach of the rules, but also a positive requirement to do what the rules provide.[3] In disciplinary proceedings, for example, the charge brought must be one that can be made under the rules and it must be formulated in accordance with the rules. Any sanction must be permissible under the rules. If the rules provide for a discretion, then the discretion must be exercised and not ignored by applying an inflexible criterion or vitiated by acting for an improper purpose.[4] The advantage of a challenge on grounds of illegality (whether based on non-compliance with the rules or the general law) is that it is broadly either right or wrong, and the court ought not to decline to intervene on the basis that it is a matter for the sports governing body.[5]

1 For a detailed description of those principles, see Fordham, *Judicial Review* (6th edn, Hart, 2012) Chapters P7, P16 and P46 to P48.
2 *Modahl* [2002] 1 WLR 1192 at 1209, per Latham LJ at paras 52 to 54. A sports governing body may not misdirect itself as to its rules: *Badrick v British Judo Association*, [2004] EWHC 1891 (mis-listed in some databases as 1605) Ch 1 July 2004 Lightman J, at paras 17–18.
3 The club or player has the right to have a rule properly applied: see *Stevenage Borough Football Club v Football League Ltd*, Carnwath J, (1996) Times, 1 August; CA [1996] 9 Admin LR 109.
4 *Auckland Boxing Association v New Zealand Boxing Association* [2001] NZLR 847 (improper use of suspension as punitive measure).
5 The construction of rules is a matter for the court: *Modahl v BAF* 28 June 1996, Popplewell J at pp 13.3–14.8 of the shorthand writers' transcript; *Tyrrell Racing Organisation v RAC Motor Sports Association and the Fédération Internationale du Sport Automobile*, 20 July 1984 Hirst J at p 11 of Lexis transcript; *Enderby Town Football Club v Football Association* [1971] Ch 591 at 605; *Reel v Holder* [1981] 1 WLR

1226 per Lord Denning MR at 1230 to 1231 (on the proper construction of the IAAF Rules, which was for the court, the Taiwanese athletic association could not be expelled); *Lee v Showmen's Guild* [1952] 2 QB 329 at 354.

7.48   That said, the courts will not interpret the rules of a sports governing body as if they were a statute, or even a technical legal document such as a conveyance. The courts accept that often they have not been drafted by lawyers and should not be given an unduly legalistic interpretation.[1] They will be interpreted so as to give effect to their purpose, and so as not to conflict with the requirements of procedural fairness and natural justice.[2]

1 *Cowley v Heatley* (1986) Times 24 July, Browne-Wilkinson V-C, p 4 of the Lexis transcript.
2 *Modahl v BAF*, 28 July 1997 CA per Lord Woolf MR at pp 16F–17B, where Lord Woolf MR also pointed out that national governing body rules should be interpreted in the light of international governing body rules, with which they must be consistent; *R v BBA, ex p Mickan*, 17 March 1981 CA at p 5 of the Lexis transcript (rules to be construed so as to give effect to their purpose, and in the light of their context).

7.49   There ought to be no difference in approach depending upon whether or not the rules constitute a contract between the sports governing body and the claimant. Whether they do constitute a contract depends upon their proper construction in all the circumstances.[1] Where they do constitute such a contract, the requirement that the governing body act in accordance with its rules is a requirement to comply with its contractual obligations, enforceable in the normal way (at least so far as express obligations are concerned) through injunction, declaration or damages. Where there is no contract, and no other cause of action, a player or other participant can nevertheless seek a declaration that the governing body has not acted in compliance with its rules,[2] and possibly an injunction to require it to do so.

1 Some rules, such as those of the FA Premier League, specifically state that they constitute a contract between each member and the Premier League, and indeed between each member and each other member: see the *Sheffield v West Ham* litigation. Under the companies legislation the articles of association of a company constitute a contract between members.
2 See *Gasser v Stinson* 15 June 1988, unreported, Scott J at p 24H of the shorthand writers' transcript; *Korda v ITF* (1999) Times, 4 February, [1999] All ER (D) 84; revsd [1999] All ER (D) 337, CA 25 March 1999; *Davis v Carew-Pole* [1956] 2 All ER 524 (where the court found that a contract arose but held that even if there was no contract a declaration would still lie where a sports governing body went outside its rules).

7.50   The most common circumstances where a challenge is made to a wrongful interpretation of rules that do not constitute a contract between the claimant and the sports governing body[1] are where the claimant is seeking access to the sport or to a particular level of competition[2] and where a governing body has found there to be a doping offence.[3]

1 Although there may be a contract in these contexts also.
2 See for example *Cowley v Heatley* (1986) Times, 24 July (Browne-Wilkinson V-C), in which the applicant raised a 'pure question of law' (p 3 of the Lexis transcript) as to whether she enjoyed the requisite 'domicile' under the applicable rules, on which issue the court favoured the non-technical meaning attributed to it by the sports governing body.
3 See for example *Modahl v British Athletics Federation*, Popplewell J 28 June 1996, CA 28 July 1997, HL 22 July 1998, Douglas Brown J 14 December 2000 and [2002] 1 WLR 1192, CA 8 October 2001.

7.51   The range of circumstances in which a lawfulness argument can arise on the proper construction of the rules is however as wide as the variety of rules that exist. Cases that have arisen include disputes over the proper application of the actual rules of competition,[1] end-of-season promotion rights under the rules,[2] the extent of a contractual right to stay in an association or league,[3] the contractual right to play pending the outcome of proceedings based on a breach of the rules,[4] the allocation of functions between internal organs of the sports governing body,[5] the constituents of an offence and availability of opportunity to impose a further sanction,[6] criteria for selection,[7] the existence of a right to appeal for the sports governing body against a decision of its own disciplinary body,[8] the existence of a power to award costs,[9] whether or not the rights of a competitor can be assigned to another competitor,[10] whether the rules require clubs to release players for an international match that clashed with club matches,[11] and whether one sports governing body's rules on their proper construction preclude another body adopting an inconsistent rule.[12]

1 Sailing's Americas Cup is an example of an event where detailed rules give rise to many challenges based on breach of them, both in the courts and before the America's Cup Jury. For examples of court challenges see the various *Golden Gate Yacht Club v Société Nautique De Genève* cases before the New York courts between April and November 2009 described in 'America's Cup – whether challenging yacht club required to have held annual regatta on the sea prior to issuing challenge' (2009) Lloyd's Maritime Law Newsletter 768, 3–4.

2 Whether a champion of a second division had the right under the rules and agreements to form part of an expanded first division operated by the same sports governing body: *Rotherham and English Second Division Rugby Ltd v English First Division Rugby Ltd and the RFU*, 16 August 1999 Ferris J, [2000] 1 ISLR 33; *Aberavon & Port Talbot v WRU* [2003] EWCA Civ 584, 9 April 2003 May LJ, Laws LJ, [2003] SLJ Iss 2 p 185 (the judge had reached the correct conclusion in ordering summary judgment against the claimant rugby football club, which claimed that it was contractually entitled to a promotion that the Welsh Rugby Union did not grant).

3 For example *Park Promotion Ltd (t/a Pontypool Rugby Football Club) v Welsh Rugby Union Ltd* [2012] EWHC 1919 QB, 11 July 2012 (no contractual obligation owed by the WRU to a club excluded from reduced size league, that the WRU would strictly apply A licence criteria to other clubs, without waiver or extension of time, when an A licence was a prerequisite of membership of reduced size league); *Widnes v Rugby Football League*, 26 May 1995 Parker J.

4 For example, whether on the proper construction of the rules a sanction has to be suspended pending the hearing of an appeal: *Tyrrell Racing Organisation v RAC Motor Sports Association and the Fédération Internationale du Sport Automobile*, 20 July 1984 Hirst J at p 10 of the Lexis transcript.

5 For example, how under the rules jurisdiction is to be allocated between the governing body's committees and tribunals and the effect on earlier rulings of subsequent decisions: *Robert C Allan v Scottish Auto Cycle Union* (1985) Outer House Cases 32 and see also *Anderlecht v UEFA*, CAS 98/185, *Digest of CAS Awards II 1998–2000*, p 469 (decision taken by the wrong UEFA body).

6 For example, whether a further sanction can be imposed: *Re Duncan Ferguson (Ferguson v Scottish Football Association)* (1996) Outer House Cases Lord Macfadyen 1 February 1996; *Rangers Football Club Plc, Petitioner* [2012] CSOH 95; 2012 GWD 20-402; Court of Session (Outer House) 6 June 2012.

7 For example, what criteria for selection are provided by the rules: *Cowley v Heatley* (1986) Times, 24 July, Browne-Wilkinson VC.

8 In *Korda v ITF* (1999) Times, 4 February, [1999] All ER (D) 84; revsd [1999] All ER (D) 337, CA 25 March 1999, an independent Appeals Committee convened under the terms of the ITF Anti-Doping Programme upheld the finding of an offence, but found that 'exceptional circumstances' existed – namely the player's lack of knowledge of how the substance got into his body – that warranted a waiver of any suspension. The ITF filed an appeal to the CAS against that decision. Lightman J granted the player a declaration that the ITF could not appeal its own decision to the CAS, but his decision was overturned by the Court of Appeal and the ITF was allowed to pursue its appeal to the CAS).

9 *TWR v RAC* (1985) Times, 12 October (where there was power to award costs).

10 *Phoenix v Fédération International de l'Automobile, Formula One Management and Formula One Administration* [2002] EWHC 1028 Ch, Morritt VC.

11 See *Premier Rugby v RFU* [2006] EWHC 2068 (Comm) 27 Jul 06 (extra international match clashing with club matches: interpretation of the contract to resolve such matters). Cf *Welsh Rugby Union Ltd v Cardiff Blues* [2008] EWHC 3399 (QB), 24 October 2008, where an injunction was granted to the WRU to enforce a player release rule.

12 *British Olympic Association v World Anti-Doping Agency*, CAS 2011/A/2658, award dated 30 April 2012.

(b)   Acting in accordance with the general law and the validity of the rules

7.52   A lawfulness argument may also arise on the basis that the sports governing body has failed to act in accordance with the general law.[1] A particular aspect of this is an argument that a specific rule that the sports governing body is seeking to apply is unlawful. It could be unlawful as being in unreasonable restraint of trade,[2] or as being contrary to the competition rules,[3] or the free movement rules,[4] or the equality legislation,[5] or on public policy grounds if the rule runs directly contrary to the requirement to act fairly and in accordance with natural justice.[6] A particular rule could also be unlawful because it was 'unconstitutional' or ultra vires, in the sense that the sports governing body did not have the power to adopt it,[7] or because it was adopted in the wrong way.

1   The leading authority (although it was not itself an error of law case) is now *Bradley* per Richards J at para 37.
2   A leading recent example is *Chambers* (cited above at paras **7.31–7.32**).
3   A leading recent example is *London Welsh v Rugby Football Union, Newcastle Falcons intervening*, RFU Arbitration 29 June 2012, James Dingemans QC, Ian Mill QC and Tim Ward QC (promotion rules successfully challenged on competition law grounds).
4   See paras **12.1–12.5**.
5   The Equality Act 2010, the European Convention on Human Rights and in some instances EU law and the common law.
6   Under the European Convention on Human Rights and the common law. A leading recent example is *Stretford v The FA* (cited above at para **7.26**).
7   For example because it was outside its objects: *Baker v Jones (for British Amateur Weightlifters Association)* [1954] 2 All ER 553.

C   THE REQUIREMENT TO ACT FAIRLY IN A PROCEDURAL SENSE, OR 'NATURAL JUSTICE'

(a)   General points

7.53   Sports governing bodies and their separate disciplinary bodies are generally required to afford minimum standards[1] of procedural protection to the individual, club or other constituent affected by their actions, and to act fairly.[2] That requirement cannot be excluded by contract.[3] The content of the requirement to act fairly in a procedural sense is, at least in most situations, equivalent to that owed by a public body, and so reliance may be placed on the principles developed by the courts in that context.[4] There are a number of general points to note about this ground for review before turning to the various types of procedural protection that the courts are likely to expect sports governing bodies to offer to their constituents.

1   Their rules can expressly provide for a greater degree of protection, but there is a floor that will apply in any event. The obligation is categorically not an obligation to reach the right conclusion, only an obligation to apply a fair process: see *Colgan v Kennel Club*, 26 October 2001 Cooke J; and *Modahl* CA [2001] EWCA Civ 1447, [2002] 1 WLR 1192 per Latham LJ at paras 52 to 54, Jonathan Parker LJ at paras 85 to 88 and Mance LJ at paras 120 to 122.
2   The leading authority (although it was not itself a procedural fairness case) is now Richards J at para 37, approved by the Court of Appeal, in *Bradley v Jockey Club* [2004] EWHC 2164 QB, 1 October 2004 Richards J, [2004] All ER (D) 11; upheld on appeal [2005] EWCA Civ 1056, 12 June 2005, Lord Phillips MR, Buxton LJ, Scott Baker LJ, (2005) Times, 14 July.
3   See para **7.7** note 3.
4   For a detailed description of those principles, see Fordham, *Judicial Review* (6th edn, Hart, 2012) Chapters P7, and P60 to P62.

7.54   First, the extent of the requirement to act fairly in a procedural sense varies from case to case, in the light of all the circumstances, such as in particular into which of the three *McInnes v Onslow-Fane* categories of application, expectation and forfeiture[1] the case falls. The greater the entitlement of the participant and the greater the effect, the greater the degree of procedural protection that is required.[2] Those circumstances also include the fact that sports governing bodies, and the disciplinary bodies or committees that they establish, are not courts of law. They are not bound by the same evidential and procedural constraints. The circumstances may also include the fact that participants have often contractually agreed to particular procedures.[3]

1 See para **7.8** above.
2 Increased commercialisation of sport arguably warrants greater protection than might have been the case in the past: *Jones v WRU*, cited above at para **7.11**.
3 *Sankofa and Charlton v The FA* [2007] 12 January 2007 Comm Ct Simon J, at para 20.

7.55   Secondly, the law on procedural fairness is fluid, and the extent of protection that the courts are prepared to ensure is likely steadily to increase across the board. This process is likely to be encouraged by the increasing number of cases under the Human Rights Act 1998 in relation to the right to a fair trial protected in Art 6 of the European Convention on Human Rights. Even if a claim cannot be made under the Act, the courts will be informed by Art 6 considerations and precedents when determining the level of behaviour to be expected of sports governing bodies. Consequently the categories of protection dealt with below are not exhaustive, and the current position on the authorities is not definitive. Ultimately, if the court thinks that a player's treatment has been unfair, it will say so. The question for the practitioner is therefore first and foremost whether what has happened has really been unfair in the ordinary sense of the word.

7.56   Thirdly, what falls to be assessed is the procedural fairness of the process as a whole, not simply one stage of it.[1] For example, a peremptory first decision might nevertheless be lawful if a full appeal was available. This is of particular importance in cases where the challenge is based on, or seeks to draw on, Art 6 ECHR.[2]

1 *Cronin v Greyhound Board of Great Britain Ltd* [2013] EWCA Civ 668 18 June 2013, per Maurice Kay LJ at para 17.
2 See for example the Jockey Club Appeal Board's decision in *Bradley v Jockey Club* [2003] ISLR-SLR 71, that the full process set out in the Jockey Club's rules complied with Art 6 due to the independence and impartiality of the Appeal Board, failing which due to the supervisory jurisdiction exercised over the process by the High Court.

7.57   Fourthly, the obligation to afford procedural fairness appears to be owed to the defendant to a procedure, and not necessarily to the complainant.[1]

1 See *Elias Karigiannis v Football Federation Australia Ltd* [2010] NSWSC 1454, 17 December 2010 (sports governing body's obligation to observe the rules of natural justice was owed to those who might be the subject of disciplinary sanction, but it was not owed on the facts of the case to a complainant who was not in jeopardy of any sanction; it was not the role of the court to examine the merits of a sports governing body's decision).

7.58   Fifthly, a disadvantage of an argument based on procedural unfairness is that it impugns only the particular decision. That decision will generally be remitted to be taken again. The sports governing body can often legitimately go back and make a decision that is procedurally fair,[1] but that is to the same effect as the original decision.[2] It could even do so before final resolution of the challenge on procedural grounds to the legality of the first decision.[3] Equally, a court might even refuse to remit a procedurally flawed decision for reconsideration, for example because of delay or (more questionably) on the basis that procedurally lawful treatment would have made no difference to the outcome.[4]

1   See Fordham, *Judicial Review* (6th edn, Hart, 2012) Chapter P3, and paras 13.26 to 13.27.
2   There may be cases where this is not the case, for example where the decision-making panel was biased and cannot be reconstituted with people who are unaffected.
3   As in *Jones v WRU*, cited above at para **7.11**.
4   In this context there may be scope for application by analogy of the developing case law under s 31(2A) of the Senior Courts Act 1981.

7.59   Finally, there may be a question as to when a procedural fairness point should be taken, whether at the hearing before the sports governing body or its separate disciplinary body that is to take the decision, or in court before that decision is taken.[1] If the point is not taken in one of these two ways, care must be taken to ensure that it is not waived, precluding it subsequently being raised in court.

1   See *Enderby Football Club v FA* [1971] Ch 591 at 606.

(b)   Proper opportunity to be heard

7.60   Sports governing bodies must afford the player, club or other participant a fair opportunity to put his, her or its case.[1] What this means will vary from case to case, depending amongst other things on the nature of the dispute and the severity of the consequences, and on whether the sports governing body is considering an application by the player, club or other participant to exercise its regulatory powers in some way, or is rather pursuing disciplinary proceedings against the player, club or other participant. The starting point is however that in order to have a proper opportunity to be heard, there must be a proper preparatory process. The player, club or other participant must actually be informed that the matter is to be considered, and when.[2] The case put against the player, club or other participant must be fully disclosed: the respondent to disciplinary proceedings must know the details of the charge, and the applicant for a licence must know the objections, if any, to its being granted.[3] Sufficient time must be given to allow the sports governing body's case to be considered and the player, club or other participant to prepare his, her or its case.[4] The requirement to which the governing body is subject probably does not extend to conducting further investigations at the request of the player, club or other participant.[5]

1   For the generally applicable position, see Fordham, *Judicial Review* (6th edn, Hart, 2012), Chapter P60.
2   *Collins v Lane*, 22 June 1999 CA at p 11 of the shorthand writers' transcript (club member must be informed of intention to consider complaints against him).
3   In *Lovell v Pembroke County Cricket Club* (cited above at para **7.6**), one of the requirements that Neuberger J held (at para 53) to arise notwithstanding that the circumstances warranted relatively limited protection, was a requirement that the club inform the claimant fully and fairly of the nature of the complaint made against him.
4   See *Tyrrell Racing Organisation v RAC Motor Sports Association and the Fédération Internationale de l'Automobile*, n 3 at p 11 of the Lexis transcript. The deadlines set must be reasonable: *G v International Equestrian Federation* CAS 91/53, *Digest of CAS Awards 1986–1998*, p 79 at paras 10–12.
5   See *Wright v Jockey Club* QB Sir Haydn Tudor Evans, (1995) Times, 16 June, at p 11 of the Lexis transcript.

7.61   At the decision-making stage, the player, club or other participant must have an adequate opportunity to convey his, her or its case to the decision-making body.[1] Within reason, the player, club or other participant should not be prevented from making points which he, she or it believes to be pertinent to the issue.[2] While it is possible that in some instances written submissions may be sufficient, in most cases the player, club or other participant should have the option of a full oral hearing at which to present evidence and arguments.[3] Whether representation must be allowed will vary from case to case, as will whether *legal* representation must be allowed.[4] Whether the player, club or other participant must be permitted to call witnesses or to cross-examine the sports governing body's witnesses,[5] and whether submissions must be allowed to take the particular form that the player, club or other participant wishes,[6] will also depend on the circumstances. It is to be borne in mind that under Art 6 ECHR, to which reviewing courts may look for inspiration, some of the elements of procedural protection set out above are mandatory. Further, under Art 6 a person is entitled to have their 'civil rights and obligations' determined in *public*, a requirement that is not an element of common law procedural fairness.

1 In *Lovell v Pembroke County Cricket Club* (cited above at para **7.6**), one of the requirements that Neuberger J held (at para 53) to arise notwithstanding that the circumstances warranted relatively limited protection, was a requirement that the club provide the claimant an adequate opportunity to present his case. See also *Andrade v Cape Verde NOC* CAS OG 1996/005, *Digest of CAS Awards 1986–1998*, p 397 (withdrawal of accreditation by a governing body not possible without an opportunity to answer charge).

2 Whether preventing a defendant raising on appeal a point not taken below is procedurally unfair will depend on the circumstances. In *McKeown v British Horseracing Authority* [2010] EWHC 508 (QB), 12 March 2010, see paras **7.33–7.35**, Stadlen J ordered the matter to be remitted to allow the jockey to argue a point that the appeal board had prevented him from taking.

3 Based on *McInnes v Onslow-Fane* [1978] 1 WLR 1520, it appears that an oral hearing would be required in forfeiture and legitimate expectation cases, but not application cases. In *Currie v Barton* 26 March 1987, unreported, Scott J; 11 February 1988, unreported, CA, (1988) Times, 12 February, the absence of an oral hearing was held on the facts not to amount to a breach of natural justice.

4 If the rules provide for representation, they must of course be followed. If they do not, the circumstances may dictate that representation, and even legal representation, should be allowed. Sports governing bodies are not required always to allow such representation, but they must not rule out the possibility of doing so altogether: *Enderby Town Football Club v Football Association* [1971] Ch 591 at 605 per Lord Denning.

5 See *Jones v WRU*, cited above at para **7.11** (on an interlocutory hearing, Ebsworth J held, at p 9 of the Lexis transcript, that it was arguable that preventing the player calling evidence or questioning witnesses in the context of disciplinary proceedings in a professional sport was contrary to natural justice. The Court of Appeal upheld this interlocutory conclusion: see Potter LJ at p 17 of the transcript).

6 See *Jones v WRU*, cited above at para **7.11** (Ebsworth J held, at pp 7 and 9 of the Lexis transcript, that it was arguable that refusing Jones permission to make submissions on the content of a video of the incident while the video was being played was contrary to natural justice).

(c) Burden and standard of proof and presumptions

7.62   An unfair burden and standard of proof must not be placed on the player, club or other participant, for example that they must prove innocence beyond all reasonable doubt. This does not mean that the onus must be on the sporting body to establish guilt beyond all reasonable doubt, although this is often the burden and standard set by the rules.[1] In the normal course, in the absence of specific provision, the burden will be on the sports governing body and the standard of proof will be the 'civil' standard of balance of probabilities, although within that measure the graver the offence, the better the quality of evidence necessary to satisfy the court or tribunal on that standard.[2] It remains open however to sports governing bodies to provide for presumptions in their rules if the circumstances dictate.

1 For example, in the ICC Anti-Corruption Code, which means that was the standard to which the spot-fixing charges against the three Pakistani cricketers had to be proved in *ICC v Butt, Asif and Amir*, Anti-Corruption Tribunal decision dated 5 February 2011; appeals denied, *Asif v ICC*, CAS 2011/A/2362, award dated 17 April 2013; *Butt v ICC*, CAS 2011/A/2364, award dated 17 April 2013.

2 *Korneev*, CAS OG 1996/003–4, award dated 4 August 1996 (standard of satisfaction must reflect the nature of the offence and evidence must be sufficient; the governing body must prove its case to the 'comfortable satisfaction' of the tribunal). For English law on the standard and burden of proof, see *Re B* [2008] UKHL 35. For CAS's approach (or one of them), see *WADA and UCI v Contador* CAS 2011/A/2384 and 2386, 6 February 2012.

(d)   Reliance on criminal charges, convictions, or acquittals

7.63   Where a participant is the subject of serious criminal charges[1] or conviction,[2] the degree of procedural protection to be afforded may be reduced, and reliance placed on the position before the criminal courts. Conversely, a tribunal applying a sports governing body's rules as opposed to the criminal law, and a different standard of proof, may not be constrained by an acquittal on criminal charges.[3]

1 At least in the context of a sports governing body's imposition of an interim suspension pending determination of the criminal charges. See *Fallon v Horseracing Regulatory Auth* [2006] EWHC 1898 QB, 28 July 2006, Davis J, [2006] All ER (D) 427, at paras 20 to 52. In *R v Terry* and *FA v Terry* (note 3 below), disciplinary proceedings against the player were stayed pending criminal trial, but he was not suspended (although he was not selected as England captain) and so was able to play at the European Championships. In 2011 and 2012, following ICC disciplinary action suspending them for many years (*ICC v Butt, Asif and Amir*, Anti-Corruption Tribunal decision dated 5 February 2011; appeals denied, *Asif v ICC*, CAS 2011/A/2362, award dated 17 April 2013; *Butt v ICC*, CAS 2011/A/2364, award dated 17 April 2013), three cricketers were criminally convicted in respect of spot fixing, and received significant sentences: *R v Amir (Mohammad), R v Butt (Salman)* [2011] EWCA Crim 2914; [2012] 2 Cr App R (S) 17 (CA (Crim Div)).
2 Where a criminal court has been satisfied on the higher standard of proof of the commission of an offence, there is little point (absent differently worded rules) in the sports governing body having to conduct a hearing with the same level of procedural protection. In *Colgan v Kennel Club*, unreported, Cooke J, 26 October 2001, it was held that the lack of an oral hearing was not unfair in circumstances where there had already been a criminal conviction.
3 In 2012 in *R v Terry*, Westminster Magistrates' Court, 13 July 2012, former England captain John Terry was acquitted on the facts of racially insulting Anton Ferdinand on the pitch. In *FA v Terry*, FA Regulatory Commission decision dated 27 September 2012, FA disciplinary proceedings that had been suspended pending the criminal case continued after the acquittal and in September 2012 Terry was found to have committed a breach of the FA rules (differently worded to the criminal legislation and subject to a lower standard of proof) and fined and banned for four matches.

(e)   Unfairness of decision to initiate disciplinary proceedings

7.64   In some limited circumstances, it may be unfair to initiate disciplinary proceedings notwithstanding that there is an arguable case of breach, for example where the breach has been caused by the sports governing body itself,[1] or where the rules fall to be construed as limiting the circumstances where such a case can be brought,[2] or if there has been some culpable delay in bringing the proceedings that has materially prejudiced the defendant's ability to defend him or herself.[3]

1 As in the ATP nandrolene cases where the suggestion was that electrolyte tablets handed out by ATP trainers may have been the source: see *ATP v Ulirach*, Anti-Doping Tribunal decision dated 7 July 2003.
2 For example, in *Re Duncan Ferguson (Ferguson v Scottish Football Association)* (1996) Outer House Cases, Lord Macfadyen 1 February 1996, it was held that the SFA on its rules was unable to discipline a player not cautioned at the time by the referee. See further *European Rugby Cup v Richards, Brennan, Chapman and Harlequins* (2010) International Sports Law Review 1, SLR9-43, ERC Appeal Committee (no jurisdiction over Dr Chapman in context of 'Bloodgate').
3 See, eg, *UCI v Ullrich*, CAS 2010/A/2083, award dated 9 February 2012, para 32b (failure to issue summons to athlete by deadline specified in UCI rules did not entitle athlete to relief, because it did not result in 'any prejudice to Ullrich that will affect these proceedings. This Panel concludes that Ullrich

did not suffer prejudice in this regard, not least because he was fully aware of the UCI's investigation at the time, in particular by reason of his dismissal from his team for suspicion of involvement in Operation Puerto. There is no evidence that Ullrich's ability to mount a defence has not [*sic*] been compromised, and Ullrich's procedural objections to the UCI Rules have not featured any factual allegation that his ability to put forward any facts or arguments or otherwise mount his defence has been compromised'); *ITF v Burdekin*, Anti-Doping Tribunal decision dated 4 April 2005, paras 59, 61–62 ('The Tribunal is prepared to accept that [the athlete] should have been notified of the adverse test result by about the last week of August 2004. It does not follow that the entire charge should be dismissed. The Tribunal, having heard and weighed all the evidence, does not accept that the player suffered any real rather than theoretical prejudice through lapse of time').

(f) Good faith and prejudging the issue

7.65 The committee or panel of the sports governing body or separate disciplinary body that is to take the decision must approach the matter with an open mind.[1] It must make the decision for the right reasons, not for some ulterior and improper motive, and must act in good faith.[2] It must exercise its discretion in light of the circumstances of the case before it, and cannot simply apply an over-rigid policy.[3]

1 For the generally applicable position, see Fordham, *Judicial Review* (6th edn, Hart, 2012), Chapters P50 and P51.
2 For the generally applicable position, see Fordham, *Judicial Review* (6th edn, Hart, 2012), Chapter P52; *Wright v Jockey Club* QB Sir Haydn Tudor Evans, (1995) Times 16 June, at p 9 of the Lexis transcript. A sports governing body cannot go back on a policy it has adopted for entry deadlines for a competition: *US Swimming v FINA* CAS OG 1996/001, *Digest of CAS Awards 1986–1998*, p 377. Nor can it go back on the selection of an athlete: *Watts v Australian Cycling Federation* CAS 96/153, *Digest of CAS Awards 1986–1998*, p 335.
3 In *Wimbledon Football Club v Football League*, FA Arbitration Panel decision dated 29 January 2002, the panel remitted the club's application to move ground to The Football League on the basis that The League's decision had been procedurally flawed because it applied an over-rigid policy without considering in detail the particular facts of the matter or the restraint of trade argument advanced. The League referred the matter to an FA Commission to make the decision, and it was decided that the club should be allowed to move.

(g) Bias and independence and impartiality

7.66 The committee or panel of the sports governing body or separate disciplinary body that is to take the decision must not be actually biased, and must not have the appearance of being biased, against the player, club or other participant.[1]

1 For the generally applicable position, see Fordham, *Judicial Review* (6th edn, Hart, 2012), Chapter P61. In contrast to what the position would be in England, a CAS arbitrator will have an appearance of bias if he is a member of the same chambers as a barrister instructed by one of the parties: see *Brescia Calcio SpA v West Ham United FC*, 26 June 2012, ICAS, (2012) International Sports Law Review 3, SLR40-53.

7.67 The test for actual bias is whether the facts demonstrate an actual predisposition against one party's case for reasons unconnected with the merits of the issues.[1] The decision-making body must be free from any interest, such as a financial interest,[2] in the outcome.

1 In *Re Medicaments* and *Related Classes Goods (No 2)* [2001] 1 WLR 700, Lord Phillips MR stated at 726 para 38 that 'the phrase 'actual bias' has not been used with great precision and has been applied to the situation (1) where a judge has been influenced by partiality or prejudice in reaching his decision and (2) where it has been demonstrated that a judge is actually prejudiced in favour of or against a party' (see also para 37).
2 *Barnard v Jockey Club of South Africa* (1984) 2 SALR 35 (member of panel was a partner in the firm of lawyers representing the Jockey Club).

7.68   The test for an appearance of bias is 'whether the fair-minded and informed observer, having considered the facts, would conclude that there was a real possibility that the tribunal was biased'.[1] An appearance of bias can arise if the decision-making body includes individuals who have previously been connected with the dispute to be decided upon, for example if they have participated in an anterior decision to make the charges or to refuse an application,[2] or who have made a statement as to what the outcome should be.[3] Any statements to the press should come from people who will not take part in the decision-making process. There should be a separation between the roles of prosecutor and judge,[4] and care should be taken (for example) that a representative of the executive does not retire with the decision-making body.[5] It may be that members of the council of the sports governing body should not sit on that body.[6] The question of whether there has been a lack of procedural fairness due to bias falls to be measured over the procedure as a whole.[7] An untainted appeal body may therefore cure any deficiency in a first instance body, most likely where the appeal body undertakes a full merits review.[8]

1 See *Modahl*, para **7.13**, in the second CA case, per Mance LJ at para 128 and *Flaherty v NGRC*, para **7.22**, per Scott Baker LJ in the CA at paras 26–31. See further generally *Porter v Magill* [2001] UKHL 67, [2002] 2 AC 357.

2 In *Collins v Lane*, 22 June 1999 CA, at p 11 of the shorthand writers' transcript, the principle was regarded as infringed where the official who made the complaint against the shooter also participated in the disciplinary decision.

3 *Modahl v BAF*, para **7.13**, [2002] 1 WLR 1192, CA at para 68 (panel member alleged to have said that all athletes are guilty of doping until they have proved their innocence); *Revie v Football Association*, Cantley J, (1979) Times, 14 December (FA tribunal members had expressed a view on the merits of an action against Don Revie before hearing the charges).

4 *Freedman v Petty and Greyhound Racing Control Board* [1981] VR 1001 (contrary to natural justice for the Board to act as both prosecutor and judge).

5 In *Flaherty v NGRC*, para **7.22**, Evans-Lombe J held at first instance that the decision was also undermined by the fact that the chief executive of the NGRC retired with the disciplinary body and therefore there was an appearance of interference in the deliberations of the tribunal. The Court of Appeal held that while it was certainly not best practice to allow this to happen (para 68), there was no appearance of bias in the light of the evidence as to the chief executive's actions when he was together with the disciplinary body (para 76).

6 See *R (Kaur) v (1) Institute of Legal Executives Appeal Tribunal and (2) The Institute of Legal Executives* [2011] EWCA Civ 1168, [2012] 1 All ER 1435 (Vice-President of the Institute of Legal Executives held to be disqualified from sitting on an ILEX disciplinary or appeal tribunal by reason of her inevitable interest in ILEX's policy of disciplinary regulation, as a result of which she was not free of an influence which could prevent the bringing of an objective judgment to bear).

7 *Modahl v BAF*, cited above at para **7.13**.

8 The issue is whether in the end there had been a fair result matched by fair methods: *Calvin v Carr* [1980] AC 574 at para 59. For the position under Art 6 ECHR, see *Tsfayo v United Kingdom* (2009) 48 EHRR 18; *R (King) v Secretary of State for Justice* [2015] 3 WLR 457 at paras 123–126 per Lord Reed.

7.69   Again the influence of Art 6 ECHR may lead to the imposition of more rigorous standards: that article requires any determination of the 'civil rights and obligations' of a person to be carried out by an 'independent and impartial' tribunal. While the test for impartiality is the same as for bias,[1] the requirement of independence goes beyond the common law requirements.[2]

1 See *Flaherty*, CA at para 26 (cited above at para **7.22**).

2 The concept of independence requires those on a decision-making body subject to Art 6 to be free of any hierarchical or other links with another actor in the proceedings: *Kyprianou v Cyprus* (2007) 44 EHRR 27 at para 121 (Grand Chamber). This is a rigorous standard, which may not be satisfied for example where a decision-maker is subject to reappointment by the disciplining authority, even if there is no credible basis for suggesting that he would tailor his or her decisions in order to ensure renewed appointment.

(h) Delay and interim suspension

7.70 Justice delayed is justice denied. The case must come on within a reasonable time.[1] This is a specific requirement of Art 6 ECHR. The extent of any delay is an important factor in deciding whether there can lawfully be an interim suspension pending disciplinary proceedings, particularly if they are stayed pending some extraneous event, such as a criminal trial.

1 For the generally applicable position, see Fordham, *Judicial Review* (6th edn, Hart, 2012), para 32.2.3. For a case in the sports context, see *Barrieau v US Trotting Association* (1986) 78 NBR (2d) 128, 198 APR 128.

(i) Reasons and public decision

7.71 Perhaps surprisingly, it is not yet established that there is a requirement that sports governing bodies and their separate disciplinary bodies must give reasons for their decisions: it will depend upon the circumstances.[1] That said, it is better (and more usually adopted) practice, and generally likely to be wiser, for a sports governing body or separate disciplinary body to provide the reasons for its decisions, particularly if there is an appeal process that involves something other than a complete rehearing.[2] Again the influence of Art 6 ECHR may lead to the imposition of more rigorous standards: Art 6 requires a decision determining a person's 'civil rights and obligations' to be a public one, which is not a requirement of common law procedural fairness.

1 For the generally applicable position, see Fordham, *Judicial Review* (6th edn, Hart, 2012), Chapter P62. See also *McInnes v Onslow-Fane* [1978] 1 WLR 1520 (no requirement to give reasons in an application case); *Fisher v National Greyhound Racing Club*, 31 July 1985 CA per Oliver LJ at pp 8–9 of the Lexis transcript (arguable that a right to reasons arises on an *Onslow-Fane* expectation case); *Sankofa and Charlton v The FA* [2007] 12 January 2007, Comm Ct, Simon J at para 20 (where there is urgency and the extent of the sanction is limited, as for example in the context of one or two match bans imposed on footballers pursuant to the FA's written fast track procedure, reasons may not be required, but might be desirable).
2 In *Dundee United Football Club v Scottish Football Association*, 3 February 1988 (1988) Outer House Cases, 1998 SLT 1244, it was held that on the facts the failure to give reasons did not amount to a denial of natural justice, but that in general where there is a right of appeal reasons should be given.

(j) Possibility of appeal

7.72 The authors are not aware of any case holding that procedural fairness requires that there be a right to appeal against the decision of a sports governing body.[1] On the other hand the great benefit for a sports governing body of providing for a right of appeal is that a properly carried out appeal can cure defects in earlier stages of the process (because it is the fairness of the process as a whole that will be assessed[2]). If there is to be no right of appeal, then the single stage determination must be unimpeachable.

1 For the generally applicable position, see Wade, *Administrative Law* (8th edn, Oxford University Press, 2000) at pp 520–523; *Jones v WRU*, 27 February 1997, unreported, Ebsworth J, (1997) Times, 6 March (absence of an appeal not a ground of unfairness).
2 In *Stewart v Judicial Committee of the Auckland Racing Club* [1992] 3 NZLR 693 the appeal provided for was construed as involving a full rehearing in order to provide a fair procedure overall in the light of the fact that the first hearing was peremptory.

(k)   Costs

7.73   The authors are not aware of any common law authority that fairness requires costs to be awarded to a player, club or other participant if he she or it succeeds in an action. It may be required under Art 6 however, which the English courts may take into account in developing the law in this context.

D   THE REQUIREMENT TO TAKE INTO ACCOUNT ONLY RELEVANT CONSIDERATIONS

7.74   Sports governing bodies and their separate disciplinary bodies must make their regulatory decisions on the basis of only relevant considerations. This is a twofold requirement: they must take into account all considerations that are relevant, and they must not take into account any considerations that are irrelevant.[1] In some circumstances, this requirement may be a 'hard-edged' one, if the rules of the governing body expressly or by implication require that particular matters are taken into account and other matters are not. If the decision-maker has failed in a material way to do this, it is a ground for review. If however the rules cannot be said to contain this requirement, then what considerations are relevant (and how much weight is to be attached to them[2]) is a matter for the decision-maker and the requirement is reduced to an aspect of irrationality.[3]

1 For a detailed description of this requirement, see Fordham, *Judicial Review* (6th edn, Hart, 2012), Chapter P56. In the context of sport, see *Wilander and Novacek v Tobin and Jude* [1997] 2 Lloyd's Rep 296, per Lord Woolf MR at 300 col 1; *Fallon v Horseracing Regulatory Auth* [2006] EWHC 1898 (QB), 28 July 2006, Davis J, [2006] All ER (D) 427 at paras 9 and 32 et seq, where the argument was run and rejected.
2 *Le Roux v NZRFU* unreported, Eichelbaum CJ, New Zealand High Court, 14 March 1995, at p 3 to 10 of the transcript. The argument was rejected because the claimant was in reality complaining about the weight attached to the factors rather than whether they should or not have been taken into account.
3 *R (Khatun) v London Borough of Newham* [2005] QB 37 per Laws LJ at para 35.

7.75   In *Sheffield United v FAPL*,[1] Sheffield United challenged the FAPL disciplinary body's decision on the basis that it had ignored relevant considerations and taken into account irrelevant considerations. The arbitral panel stated that had it sat in place of the disciplinary body it would have deducted points,[2] but that the decision only to fine did not fall outside the range of decisions reasonably open to the disciplinary body, which was free to attach whatever weight it saw fit to each consideration.[3]

1 *Sheffield United v FAPL*, award dated 3 July 2007, [2007] ISLR-SLR 77, and paras **7.27–7.30**.
2 At para 36.
3 At paras 37–39.

E   THE REQUIREMENT THAT THE BODY INSTRUCT ITSELF PROPERLY AS TO THE FACTS

7.76   A sports governing body and its separate disciplinary bodies cannot make a decision for which there is no evidential basis, and must instruct themselves properly as to the facts before reaching a decision.[1] There is a distinction in this context between facts *stricto sensu*, and evaluative conclusions, as to which the decision maker enjoys a margin of appreciation.[2]

1 For the generally applicable position, see Fordham, *Judicial Review* (6th edn, Hart, 2012), Chapters P49 and P51. In the context of sport, see *Wilander and Novacek v Tobin and Jude* [1997] 2 Lloyd's Rep 296, per Lord Woolf MR at 300 col 1; *Wright v Jockey Club* Sir Haydn Tudor Evans, (1995) Times, 16 June (QBD), at p 11 of the Lexis transcript.
2 *McKeown v British Horseracing Authority* [2010] EWHC 508 (QB), 12 March 2010 paras 32 and following.

F   THE REQUIREMENT NOT TO ACT CONTRARY TO A LEGITIMATE EXPECTATION

7.77   In the past, the only legitimate expectation protected by the courts has been the right to be consulted before a policy is changed for the future,[1] or to be given a fair opportunity to explain why a particular state of affairs, such as the licensed status of a participant, should not be altered.[2] In other words, the requirement has been essentially procedural. There has however been movement in the law generally, raising the possibility that in certain circumstances the courts will protect a substantive legitimate expectation of a particular outcome, as opposed to simply of a fair opportunity to make a case before something happens. It is now possible that a court may hold that a sports governing body and its separate disciplinary bodies are precluded from departing from a previously stated policy giving rise to a substantive legitimate expectation.[3]

1 For the generally applicable position, see Fordham, *Judicial Review* (6th edn, Hart, 2012), Chapter P54; *R v Jockey Club, ex p RAM Racecourses* [1993] 2 All ER 225, DC.
2 As in *McInnes v Onslow-Fane* [1978] 1 WLR 1520.
3 *R v North and East Devon Health Authority, ex p Coughlan* [2001] QB 213. For a convenient summary of the case law and the relevant principles, see *UKAFPO v Secretary of State for Environment, Food and Rural Affairs* [2013] EWHC 1959 (Admin) per Cranston J at paras 80–98.

G   THE REQUIREMENT NOT TO ACT UNREASONABLY, IRRATIONALLY, ARBITRARILY OR CAPRICIOUSLY

(a)   Reasonableness of the substantive decision

7.78   Sports governing bodies and their separate disciplinary bodies must not act irrationally, arbitrarily or capriciously.[1] The test of rationality in this context has traditionally been regarded as a high one for a challenger to overcome, although there have been a number of decisions at the highest appellate level in recent years that suggest a lowering of the threshold wherever fundamental rights are in issue.[2] The court will not substitute its view of the merits for that of the expert decision-maker; instead, it will only overturn a decision on this ground if it was one which no sports governing body or separate disciplinary body properly instructing itself as to the facts and the law could have made, and the decision consequently falls outside the range reasonably open to the decision-maker, on the basis of the material available to it at the time.[3] That said, there are a number of circumstances that are indicative of an irrational decision that may not be quite so difficult to establish. For example, sports governing bodies must not treat like situations differently or unlike situations the same.[4] Even where it cannot be said that the sports governing body's rules expressly or by implication contemplate what must and must not be taken into account such that non-compliance amounts to a 'hard-edged' ground for review,[5] the factors that the decision-makers have relied upon or ignored may take their decision outside the range of decisions reasonably open to them, and so create a ground for challenge for irrationality.[6]

1 For the generally applicable position, see Fordham *Judicial Review* (6th edn, Hart, 2012), Chapters P7 and P55 to P58.
2 *Kennedy v Charity Commission* [2015] AC 455 per Lord Mance at paras 51–55; *Pham v Secretary of State for the Home Department* [2015] 1 WLR 1591 per Lord Carnwath at para 60; *Keyu v Secretary of State for Foreign and Commonwealth Affairs* [2015] 3 WLR 1665 per Lord Neuberger at paras 132–133; *Youssef v Secretary of State for Foreign and Commonwealth Affairs* [2016] UKSC 3 per Lord Carnwath at paras 52–58.
3 *Bradley*, per Richards J at paras 37 ('whether any exercise of judgment or discretion fell within the limits open to the decision-maker') and paras 43–44 ('the court's role, in the exercise of its supervisory jurisdiction, is to determine whether the decision reached falls within the limits of the decision-maker's discretionary area of judgment').
4 *Nagle v Feilden* [1966] 2 QB 633. A decision may be irrational if it is discriminatory in some respect which is incapable of objective justification: *Matadeen v MGC Pointou (Mauritius)* [1999] 1 AC 98 per Lord Hoffmann at 109C; *Bank Mellat v HM Treasury* [2014] AC 700 per Lord Sumption at para 25. Note that in some circumstances discriminatory behaviour may breach domestic equality legislation or EU law or ECHR law, raising an unlawfulness argument: see para **7.52**.
5 See para **7.74**.
6 The weight they attach to relevant factors is however a matter for them: *Sheffield Utd*, at para 39; *Fallon*, at para 63.

(b)   Proportionality as an element of reasonableness

7.79   In the past, a distinction has been drawn for public law purposes between reasonableness and proportionality.[1] Whereas reasonableness has been seen as a test to be applied in the fulfilment of a purely supervisory jurisdiction, proportionality has been characterised as a test that (while still supervisory) trespasses to a greater degree on the merits. Proportionality involves balancing the legitimate aim pursued against the impact of the action chosen. To be proportionate, the action must go no further than is reasonably necessary in the pursuit of the legitimate aim. If the adverse consequences are out of proportion to the benefit gained, or if a less onerous course could have been adopted with the same results, the action will be disproportionate. In fact, the proportionality test allows a margin of appreciation, or latitude, to the decision-maker, just as does the reasonableness test.[2] It too is a flexible concept, and the extent of the margin of appreciation will vary from context to context. Developments in the public law test for review may make it arguable that proportionality is a part of the public law test in this context.[3] The logic of the *Modahl*,[4] *Wilander*[5] and *Bradley* decisions is that as the public law test develops, so too does the test to be applied to sports governing bodies.

1 Proportionality in various forms is the standard in EU competition and free movement and in ECHR law. It also has a role to play in the common law restraint of trade.
2 *Bradley* per Richards J at paras 43–44. See further the quartet of Supreme Court decisions during 2014, 2015 and 2016 cited at n2 in para **7.78**.
3 But this would require a development of the law: *Keyu v Secretary of State for Foreign and Commonwealth Affairs* [2015] 3 WLR 1665 per Lord Neuberger at paras 132–133.
4 *Modahl v British Athletics Federation*, 28 June 1996 Popplewell J; CA 28 July 1997; HL 22 July 1998; Douglas Brown J 14 December 2000 and [2002] 1 WLR 1192, CA 8 October 2001.
5 *Wilander and Novacek v Tobin and Jude*, 19 March 1996 Lightman J; CA (1996) Times, 8 April; [1997] 1 Lloyd's Rep 195, Lightman J; revsd [1997] 2 Lloyd's Rep 296, CA.

(c) Availability and proportionality of sanctions

7.80   A sports governing body or its separate disciplinary bodies may not impose sanctions that are out of proportion to the gravity of the offence involved.[1] In this sense a lack of proportionality is already an established ground for review, but the question remains whether the sanction fell outside the range of sanctions reasonably open to the decision-maker. The same proportionality principle is applied by the CAS.[2] A disproportionate sanction can also be challenged as a matter of competition law.[3]

1 Richards J at paras 43–44 in *Bradley*; Davis J at paras 53 et seq in *Fallon*.
2 *Squizzato v FINA*, CAS 2005/A/830 at paras 10.19–10.26; *Puerta v ITF*, CAS 2006/A/1025 at paras 11.7.1–11.7.34; *FINA v Mellouli*, CAS 2007/A/1252 at paras 36–40; *I. v FIA*, CAS 2010/A/2268.
3 *Meca-Medina v Commission* (T-313/02) Court of First Instance 30 September 2004, [2004] ECR II-3291, [2004] 3 CMLR 1314, [2004] All ER (D) 184; C-519/04P European Court of Justice, 18 July 2006 [2006] ECR I-6991; [2006] ISLR SLR-175; [2006] All ER (EC) 1057.

CHAPTER 8

Contract

8.1   For the reasons developed above, the standard of review will be the same, at least in the absence of an express term rendering such review more intrusive, whether or not a contract is found to exist between a sports governing body and the claimant. However, it remains the case that a challenge to the actions of a sports governing body in pursuit of its regulatory powers is assisted if it can be established that there is a contract to which it and the claimant are parties, and of which it is in breach. The source for such a contract, and its contents, vary as much in the sports sector as in any other. And, as in any other sector, whether there is such a contract and what its terms are depend upon all the circumstances. Contract of course also forms the basis for other legal actions involving the non-regulatory, purely commercial actions of sports governing bodies, and indeed for most other legal actions in the sports sector not involving sports governing bodies, for example as between players,[1] clubs,[2] other participants,[3] and commercial partners.

1 Players are generally in a contractual relationship with their club (or its members), whether it be a contract based on membership of the club or a contract of employment.
2 There may be an implied contract between the competitors in the same event to comply with the rules: *Clarke v Earl of Dunraven, The Satanita* [1897] AC 59, HL, but see *Chitty on Contracts* (32nd edn, Sweet and Maxwell, 2015) at para 18-013 for criticism of this analysis. The rules of a sports governing body may expressly provide that they constitute a contract not only between it and its members, and between it and anyone else who agrees to be bound by the rules, but also between each member and each other member. It was on this basis that Sheffield United recovered damages against West Ham, following the rejection of its claim against the FA Premier League: *Sheffield United v West Ham* FA Rule K arbitration, Lord Griffiths, Sir Anthony Colman, Robert Englehart QC.
3 For example, contracts involving the right to mount the next challenge to a boxing champion, as in *Lewis v WBC and Bruno*, 3 November 1995 Rattee J (failed attempt to prevent WBC bout between Bruno and Tyson on basis of an alleged contractual entitlement of Lewis to fight Bruno first).

A THE SOURCES OF CONTRACTS TO WHICH SPORTS GOVERNING BODIES ARE PARTY

(a) Written contracts between sports governing bodies and commercial partners

8.2   The most obvious contracts to which a sports governing body is party are the straightforward contracts (generally written or at least evidenced in writing) that it enters into[1] with commercial partners.[2] Breaches of these arrangements can obviously be the subject of legal action in the normal way, and subject to the normal defences. Ostensibly the contractual obligations owed by sports governing bodies in the context of a purely commercial contract (as opposed to the exercise of some regulatory function) do not include the requirements of procedural fairness and rationality and the other requirements equivalent to those in public law, dealt with in Chapter 7.[3]

1 Assuming that it has legal personality. Otherwise representatives will have to contract on behalf of the membership.
2 Or customers, for that matter, for example when a sports governing body sells a ticket to a spectator.
3 Although even in the purely commercial context analogous obligations may arise as a matter of contract: see eg *Blackpool and Fylde Aero Club v Blackpool Borough Council* [1990] 1 WLR 1195.

(b) The sports governing body's rules as a contract between the sports governing body and its members

8.3   In many circumstances, the rules of a sports governing body will constitute a contract between the members of the sports governing body, and between each member and the sports governing body itself. The principal way in which such a contract arises is that the rules themselves expressly so provide.[1] Where the association is unincorporated, the rules of the association may provide that each of the members enters into a contract with the other members when it joins, on the terms of the rules of the association.[2] Where the association is incorporated, for example as a limited company, then under the companies legislation there is a contract on the terms of the memorandum and articles of association between all the members and between each member and the association itself.[3] But that does not necessarily mean that the rules, or all the rules, produced pursuant to the memorandum and articles of association constitute a contract. If it is not expressly so provided (whether in the context of an unincorporated or an incorporated association), it will be necessary to examine all the circumstances to evaluate whether there is such a contract on the basis of the rules, and what its terms are.[4] Even if it is implicit that there is a contract on the basis of the rules, that does not necessarily mean that all the levels of the sports governing body's rules form part of that contract, or that the contract confers an entitlement to sue the governing body, for example in relation to its treatment of a third party.[5]

1 Some rules, such as those of the FA Premier League, specifically state that they constitute a contract between each member and the Premier League, and indeed between each member and each other member: see the *Sheffield United v West Ham* litigation, para **7.49** note 1. Perceived breaches of those rules can therefore be the subject of legal action in the normal way. Actions have been brought on the basis of breach of a sports governing body's rules as a contract in a wide range of circumstances.
2 For example World Rugby is an unincorporated association made up of the rugby unions of each rugby-playing nation. In turn the individual unions are made up of the individual rugby clubs in each nation, each of which is bound by its union's rules. Some individual unions may have become incorporated, but there remains a contract between the members, which may now have become shareholders, on the basis of the rules. See World Rugby Bye-Law 7.
3 Under s 33(1) of the Companies Act 2006, which provides: 'The provisions of a company's constitution bind the company and its members to the same extent as if there were covenants on the part of the company and of each member to observe those provisions'. Shareholder members can enter into their own shareholder agreements and have available to them shareholders' remedies against the company as a matter of company law.
4 *Park Promotion Ltd (t/a Pontypool Rugby Football Club) v Welsh Rugby Union Ltd* [2012] EWHC 1919 (QB), 11 July 2012, per Sir Raymond Jack at para 35.

5 *Pontypool*, n 4 above, paras 44-45. See also *Miller v Australian Cycling Federation Inc* [2012] WASC
74 (Supreme Court of Western Australia, 6 March 2012) at paras 22, 28, 42 and 48.

8.4   Where there is a contract on the basis of the rules, it would appear to
be on the basis of the rules from time to time in force: in other words the parties
agree to that in advance. It would appear on this basis that the rules can be changed
periodically in accordance with defined procedures and that the parties continue in
a contractual relationship on the basis of the changed rules.[1] It may be, however,
that new rules, even where adopted in accordance with those procedures, must at
least have been published or available for inspection by a party before they are
incorporated. Departure from the procedures may however preclude the incorporation
of the change into the rules.

1 *Doyle v White City Stadium Ltd* (1935) 1 KB 110 (CA), per Lord Harnworth MR at 120–121.

(c) Side contracts between sports governing body and some members

8.5   There may also be side contracts between specific member clubs and the
sports governing body. The so-called 'European Model of Sport' is pyramidical in
structure, with each level from the top to the bottom linked by the possibility of
promotion and relegation. As a result, sports governing bodies regulate a diverse
group, ranging from amateur sides playing in the park to professional clubs turning
over many millions of pounds. The interests, expectations and entitlements of these
completely different constituents are wholly different, for example in terms of the
funds to be received from the central selling of broadcasting and other rights that
are derived solely from the activities of the elite clubs. Side contracts have been
used by sports governing bodies to define specific obligations and rights that apply
between the sports governing body and only some of the clubs that are members of
it. That may well often be entirely legitimate, but on occasions clubs have sought to
challenge the imposition of side contracts, or of terms in them, on the basis that they
constitute attempts by the sports governing body to prevent them breaking away and
keeping the broadcasting revenue for themselves.[1]

1 See *Premier Rugby v RFU* [2006] EWHC 2068 (Comm) 27 July 2006; *Williams and Cardiff RFC v
Pugh*, later known as *Williams and Cardiff RFC v WRU (IRB intervening)*, interim injunction hearings,
Popplewell J, 23 July 1997 and CA, 1 August 1997; application for a stay hearings, Buckley J, 17 March
1998; Eady J, 29 July 1998 [1999] Eu LR 195; the 'Superleague case', *News Ltd v Australian Rugby
League* (1996) 135 ALR 33; and *News Ltd v Australian Rugby League (No 2)* (1996) 139 ALR 193.
Cf *Scottish Football League v Smith* 1998 SLT 608.

(d) The contractual relationship between the rules of international sports governing bodies and national sports governing bodies

8.6   In the same way that the clubs that are the members of a national sports
governing body are bound by its rules and may well be in a contractual relationship
with it and with each other, the national sports governing bodies are likely to be
members of an international sports governing body, bound by its rules, and may
well also be in a contractual relationship with it and with each other.[1] If there is
such a contract, it too can be enforced by action in the courts[2] or before an arbitral
tribunal.[3] It is through this obligation to comply with the international rules that the

national sports governing bodies maintain the structure of the sport along national lines: a national sports governing body in one country can (if necessary through the intervention of the international sports governing body) cause a national sports governing body in another country to act in a particular way towards a member of the former.[4]

1 For example, as set out above, World Rugby is made up of the national rugby unions which are in turn made up of the clubs in each country: see n 2 to para **8.3** above. In football broadly the same arrangements apply, although each national association is a member not only of the international governing body or 'federation', FIFA, but also of a regional association or 'confederation', such as (in Europe) UEFA. Contracts between national governing bodies may also arise outside the international governing body's rules: see *Alwyn Treherne v ABAE* 27 February 2001 Garland J, [2001] 3 ISLR 231; 11 March 2002 CA [2002] EWCA Civ 381, [2002] All ER (D) 144 (Mar).
2 See in relation to membership, *Reel v Holder (for IAAF)* [1979] 1 WLR 1252; affd [1981] 1 WLR 1226, CA (the Taiwanese athletics governing body obtained a declaration that the IAAF was not entitled to expel it from membership). In *Walker v UKA and IAAF*, 3 July 2000 Toulson J; 25 July 2000 no judgment Hallett J, the athlete challenged the ability of the IAAF to take UKA to arbitration under UKA's contract of membership of the IAAF, over UKA's acquittal of the athlete on a doping charge.
3 For the hearing of the IAAF's challenge to UKA's acquittal of Walker, see *IAAF v UKA and Walker*, IAAF Arbitration Panel Award 20 August 2000 reported at [2001] 4 ISLR 264, see also [2000] 2 ISLR 41.
4 See *Newport v Football Association of Wales* interlocutory hearing Jacob J [1995] 2 All ER 87, trial 12 April 1995, Blackburne J (Football Association of Wales persuaded The FA not to allow the Welsh clubs to play their home games in the English league at their grounds in Wales).

8.7 The issue may arise as to the nature of the relationship between a club and the international governing body, given that the club is a member of the relevant national body but not of the international body. Often the international body's rules are expressly incorporated by reference into the rules of the national body; indeed, the international body's rules may require the national body to do this.[1] This allows such rules of the international body to be enforced by the national body against the clubs that are its members (and vice versa), but ostensibly it does not give rise to a contract between the members of the national body and the international body capable of enforcement by either of them against the other.[2] Such a contract would have to be found elsewhere, in the same way as a contract between a national sports governing body and a non-member player or participant.

1 Such as World Rugby's rules. See *Williams and Cardiff RFC v Pugh*, later known as *Williams and Cardiff RFC v WRU (IRB intervening)*, interim injunction hearings, 23 July 1997 Popplewell J; 1 August 1997, CA; application for a stay hearings 17 March 1998 Buckley J, [1999] Eu LR 195.
2 In *Walker v UKA and IAAF* 3 July 2000 Toulson J; 25 July 2000 no judgment Hallett J; IAAF Arbitral Award 20 August 2000 reported at [2001] 4 ISLR 264, see also [2000] 2 ISLR 41 and para **8.12** below, one issue was whether the IAAF had a contractual entitlement to sanction the athlete for a doping offence after he had been cleared by UKA.

8.8 In addition to international associations of national associations, there may be other types of international sports governing body, for example those with responsibility for particular areas such as the World Anti-Doping Agency, with which both national and international sports governing bodies may have a relationship, which may be contractual. In 2012, CAS had to examine the validity of a British Olympic Association rule controlling eligibility for selection for Team GB[1] and an International Olympic Committee rule controlling eligibility for the Olympic Games.[2] CAS held that the IOC and BOA rules were unlawful because they were not compliant with the World Anti-Doping Code requirement that the only sanction for a first doping offence was a period of two years' ineligibility. CAS regarded compliance with that requirement as a contractual obligation on the sports governing bodies as signatories to the Code.

1 *British Olympic Association v World Anti-Doping Agency*, CAS 2011/A2658, award dated 30 April 2012.
2 *United States Olympic Committee v International Olympic Committee*, CAS award dated 4 October 2011.

(e)   Express contracts between individual participants and sports governing bodies

8.9   It is often an important question whether there is a contract between individual participants and the sports governing body.[1] In many instances, the answer is relatively straightforward because an express contract can be identified. First, in some sports the participant is actually a member of the sports governing body and in an express, or possibly implied, contractual relationship on the basis of the rules and able to sue and be sued on the basis of them. In other instances the participant is not a member but enters into a direct written contract with the sports governing body.[2] A written contract including an obligation to abide by the governing body's rules sometimes arises when participants obtain licences,[3] or complete event entry forms.[4] A written contract may also arise in relation to compliance with a drugs testing regime.[5] In some cases a contract may arise out of previous participation.[6] In other cases, the participant may be bound by the rules of the sports governing body because his or her contract with the *club* includes a requirement to comply with the rules.[7] Again however that does not necessarily give rise to a contract between the participant and the sports governing body.[8]

1 An example is the *Modahl* litigation: see paras **8.11-8.13** below.
2 In Formula One, for example, the teams are contractually bound by the FIA rules. The purely contractual nature of a fine imposed by a sports governing body was demonstrated in *McLaren Racing Limited TC02278* [2012] UKFTT 601 (TC), 7 September 2012. The record multi-million dollar fine imposed on McLaren by the FIA in the 2007 case known as 'Spygate' was held to be deductible in the calculation of McLaren's trading profits for the purposes of corporation tax, because it was a penalty that McLaren was contractually obliged to pay and did not result from the action of an 'external regulator'. This was reversed by the Upper Tribunal in [2014] UKUT 269 (TCC).
3 As in *Stretford v The FA* [2006] EWHC 479 (Ch) 17 March 2006 Morritt C, [2006] All ER (D) 275; [2007] EWCA Civ 238, 21 March 2007, Clarke MR, Waller and Sedley LJJ (agent contractually bound to comply with the rules on the basis that he had taken a licence that specified that it was taken on the basis that he would do so).
4 *Earl of Ellesmere v Wallace* [1929] 2 Ch 1, CA (each entrant to a race regarded as having a contract with the Jockey Club and not each other). Cf *Clarke v Dunraven, The Satanita* [1897] AC 59, HL (each entrant regarded as having a contract with all of the other entrants).
5 By the player similarly signing a form. See for example *Korda v ITF* (1999) Times, 4 February, [1999] All ER (D) 84; revsd [1999] All ER (D) 337, CA 25 March 1999.
6 See *Lewis v WBC and Bruno*, 3 November 1995 Rattee J.
7 For example, the standard FA Premier League/Football League player contracts require football players to abide by The FA's rules.
8 Equally, the fact that a football players' agent has an obligation to comply with The FA's rules has been held not to be an obligation contained in his contract with a player: *Barry Silkman Soccer Consultancy Ltd v Colchester* Morland J, 15 June 2001, (2001) WL 825218 (p 1 and p 9 col 2).

(f) Implied contracts between individual participants and sports governing bodies

8.10   A more difficult situation arises where there is no express contract and the parties have instead sought to argue that an implied contract arises out of the circumstances and the conduct of the parties. In that context the traditional approach was that it is not for the courts to invent fictitious contracts where the standard essentials of a bargain (intent to create legal relations, offer and acceptance of terms, and consideration) are not proven. Recently, however, as explained below, the courts have shown a greater willingness to find a contractual relationship in order to confer effective rights on participants who have been supposedly badly treated at the hands of a sports governing body.[1]

1 The modern test for the implication of a contract is one of necessity: *Baird Textile Holdings Ltd v Marks & Spencer plc* [2002] 1 All ER (Comm) 737 per Sir Andrew Morritt V-C at paras 17 to 21, Judge LJ at para 48 and Mance LJ at paras 60 to 61.

8.11   At the trial of *Modahl v BAF*,[1] Douglas Brown J conducted a review of the earlier cases.[2] He pointed to exhortations from Lord Denning MR in *Nagle v Feilden*[3] and Scott J in *Gasser v Stinson*[4] not to create fictitious contracts, and concluded that it was quite artificial to identify a contract as arising between the athlete and the BAF out of either her membership of Sale Harriers, her participation in other meetings organised by the governing bodies or her submission to doping control at an international event abroad run by a different organisation.[5] He identified that she was not without any remedy at all, because the free-standing grounds for review applied, but that only by establishing a contract could she set up a right to damages. He then went on to hold that in any event, even if there had been a contract, the term would only extend to an obligation to provide a disciplinary process that was fair overall,[6] and there was no breach of that obligation, because the first instance body was not and did not appear to be biased,[7] and Diane Modahl had had a fair disciplinary process overall.

1 14 December 2000 Douglas Brown J. His finding that there was no contract was subsequently overturned by a margin of two to one in the Court of Appeal: see para **8.13** below.
2 At pp 4 to 11 of the shorthand-writers' transcript of 14 December 2000.
3 *Nagle v Feilden* [1966] 2 QB 633 at 644 to 646 (646 in particular). See also per Lord Salmon at 652. He could also have pointed to Lord Denning's reiteration of the point in *Enderby Town Football Club v Football Association* [1971] Ch 591 at 606, [1970] 3 WLR 1021 at 1026.
4 *Gasser v Stinson*, 15 June 1988 Scott J at p 24 of the shorthand writers' transcript.
5 At pp 8 and 11 of the shorthand writers' transcript of 14 December 2000.
6 At p 13 of the shorthand writers' transcript of 14 December 2000.
7 At pp 17, 19, 21 and 23 of the shorthand writers' transcript of 14 December 2000.

8.12   The problem of whether a contract could be inferred between an athlete and a sports governing body arose in a slightly different way in *Walker v UKA and IAAF*.[1] In that case Walker had been acquitted of a doping offence by the UKA disciplinary body. The IAAF disagreed with the verdict and sought to bring disciplinary proceedings before an IAAF arbitral panel against UKA, with the aim of having a ban imposed on the athlete. The athlete sought a declaration in High Court proceedings that he was subject only to the jurisdiction of UKA and not the IAAF and seeking to enjoin UKA from submitting to arbitration or enforcing any decision against him. UKA argued that it had been right to acquit, but equally that the IAAF was entitled to bring arbitration proceedings against that acquittal before the IAAF Arbitration Panel, the decision of which UKA had a right and a duty to enforce. The

IAAF first unsuccessfully challenged the jurisdiction of the court.[2] The IAAF then introduced a new rule to the effect that even if an athlete had been acquitted by his or her national association, the IAAF could require an interim ban to be imposed pending the hearing of the IAAF's action against the national association. The IAAF sought to apply this rule retrospectively to Walker. UKA argued that the IAAF could not impose such a ban. During the hearing of the application,[3] Hallett J indicated her dissatisfaction with such a retrospective change. It was agreed that the athlete would not be banned pending the hearing of the IAAF arbitration, but that he would abide by the result of it. In the event he was found guilty, but because he had chosen not to compete until the issue was resolved completely, he had very little time still to serve. This was the right result. UKA and the IAAF based the contention that the athlete was subject to the IAAF arbitration on two grounds. First, irrespective of whether there was any contract between the IAAF and Walker, the IAAF could require UKA as a result of its contractual relationship with the IAAF to act so as to prevent his being eligible to compete. The IAAF was in control of its own eligibility criteria, one of which was that a player should not have been guilty of a doping offence. If the IAAF held Walker to have been guilty of a doping offence, then he was simply ineligible, and that ineligibility would have to be respected by all members of the IAAF, and indeed as a result of the IAAF's 'contamination rule' (which banned any player who competes in the same event as a player who has already been banned) by fellow athletes as well. Putting it in more general terms, a sports governing body (or an international governing body) can by its contractual authority over a club (or a national governing body) insist on the latter's enforcing the former's own contractual rights further down the chain. In the contract between player and club there may be an obligation on the player to submit to the jurisdiction of the sports governing body. Alternatively, a sports governing body can simply refuse to accept the entry into any event of a player which it has disciplined, on the basis that eligibility to entry is determined by reference to the rules, whether or not they contractually bind the player, and force clubs and other governing bodies to do the same. Secondly, it was argued that there was a contract between the athlete and the IAAF on the basis of the consent given by the athlete to doping control. The athlete, in contrast to Modahl, argued that no contract arose. Neither ground was in the event determined.

1 *Walker v UKA and IAAF*, 3 July 2000, unreported, Toulson J; 25 July 2000, unreported and no judgment, Hallett J; IAAF Arbitral Award 20 August 2000 reported at [2001] 4 ISLR 264, see also [2000] 2 ISLR 41.
2 Before Toulson J, 3 July 2000.
3 Hallett J, 25 July 2000.

8.13   The second Court of Appeal decision in *Modahl*[1] represented a move away from the traditional approach in the cases relied upon by Douglas Brown J at the trial. Latham LJ identified three different bases on which Diane Modahl might have been said to have entered into a contract with the BAF.[2] First, the club acts as agent for its members from time to time in contracting with the governing body (the 'club' basis). Secondly, a contract arises out of repeated participation in events organised by the governing body (the 'participation' basis). Thirdly, a contract arises when a player provides a sample and relies on the appeal process (the 'submission basis'). Latham LJ concluded that the court should consider all the surrounding circumstances to see whether a contract could be implied.[3] He held that the basic structure for a contract was readily identifiable in the fact that the athlete had participated in events under the auspices of the BAF or the IAAF and subject to their rules, and that the governing bodies had accepted responsibility to administer those rules. Contractual intention could be found in the athlete entering those events, even if no entry form was actually completed. Mance LJ agreed, albeit tentatively in the light of the paucity of the evidence, that a contract arose on a combination of the three bases identified by Latham LJ.[4] Jonathan Parker LJ on the other hand was not convinced that a contract arose.[5] The Court of Appeal however held that the terms of the implied contract fell short of those contended for by Diane Modahl. Any implied term was held to be confined to the fairness of the procedure as a whole, and where the decision was actually taken by a separate disciplinary body, such term was confined to an obligation on the sports governing body to establish a fair procedure and did not extend to how the separate disciplinary body carried it out.

1 [2002] 1 WLR 1192, CA.
2 [2002] 1 WLR 1192, para 25.
3 At paras 49 to 52.
4 At para 91 and 103 to 111.
5 At paras 72 to 83.

8.14   In *Bradley*,[1] Richards J held that in the normal course a jockey under licence would be in a contractual relationship with the Jockey Club,[2] but in the case before him Graham Bradley was no longer under licence. Nevertheless, a contract arose because the former jockey had been offered a choice between being dealt with as if he were licensed, or under the warning off provisions, and chose the former.[3] As already discussed,[4] Richards J also held that because the Appeal Board was a separate body from the Jockey Club, there was no implied term making the Appeal Board responsible for its actions.[5] However he went on to hold (arguably equivocally) that what *could* be implied into the contract in the circumstances of the case were (a) an obligation on the Jockey Club to give effect to the decision of the Appeal Board and no more than that decision and (b) an obligation on the Jockey Club that it would only apply a decision of the Appeal Board in so far as it was lawful.[6]

1 *Bradley v Jockey Club* [2004] EWHC 2164 (QB); [2007] L.L.R. 543. See paras **7.15–7.21**.
2 *Bradley*, paras 51–53 per Richards J.
3 *Bradley*, paras 55–56.
4 See para **7.17**.
5 *Bradley*, paras 59–62.
6 Bradley, para 62.

B EXPRESS CONTRACTUAL OBLIGATIONS

8.15   The enforcement of express obligations contained in the rules or in commercial contracts is relatively straightforward. The express obligation is there and must be construed and enforced.[1] The limits of a sports governing body's jurisdiction can be interpreted and set by the courts. The court will ask whether the rules confer the power on the sports governing body that it is purporting to exercise. It may of course also be possible to challenge the existence or validity of the relevant contractual obligation, for example if it has not been correctly adopted or if it is contrary to other pre-existing rules, or on grounds of restraint of trade, competition law, or the free movement rules.

1 See *Martinez v Ellesse SPA*, 30 March 1999 CA, for an exposition in the sporting context of the principles of construction of a commercial contract. For those principles generally, see *Arnold v Britton* [2015] AC 1619 per Lord Neuberger at paras 14–22.

C IMPLIED CONTRACTUAL OBLIGATIONS

(a) The implication of the equivalent of the public law standard of review

8.16 As described above,[1] it is tolerably clear that where a contract does arise between the player, club or other participant and the sports governing body, it will be implicit in such a contract that the decisions of the governing body are subject to the same grounds for review as apply on the non-contractual basis, which mirror the public law standard of review. However, as explained above, whether a cause of action sounding in damages arises against the governing body depends first on the terms of the contract, secondly on the nature of what has been done wrong, and thirdly on whether the decision-maker was the sports governing body or a separate disciplinary body. Where a contract exists on the terms of the rules, a breach of the express terms in the rules by the sports governing body itself can be sued upon as a matter of contract and in such circumstances a cause of action in damages likely arises. Where a sports governing body has been found to have acted in a way that is impermissible under one of the other grounds for review, by reference to the same supervisory standard that would apply irrespective of contract, and proceeds to enforce that action, it would appear that the sports governing body is in breach of an implied requirement in the contract that it should not do so, and a cause of action in damages will arise. Where on the other hand a disciplinary body created by, but separate from, the sports governing body takes a decision that has been found to be impermissible under any of the grounds for review, by reference to the same supervisory standard that would apply irrespective of contract, it is less clear that a cause of action in damages arises against the sports governing body with which the participant has a contract. In these circumstances, it has been said that the extent of the obligation on the sports governing body is to establish a fair process. It would however appear that the sports governing body may also owe implied contractual obligations first to enforce the decision made by the separate disciplinary body (and nothing else), but secondly not to enforce such a decision if it was reached in breach of the supervisory standard of review.

1 See para **7.41** onwards.

(b) The implication of other terms

8.17 As in any other context, other terms may be implicit in the arrangements if the circumstances of the contract so dictate.[1] The normal rules on the implication of terms apply. It is *not* an implied term of a sports governing body's rules that it will not act in unreasonable restraint of trade.[2]

1 In *News Ltd v Australian Rugby League* (1996) 135 ALR 33, *(No 2)* (1997) 139 ALR 193 (the 'Superleague' case) it was held that there was an implied term each season that the clubs and the League would do everything reasonably necessary to make the season's competition run smoothly. It was breach of this implied term by the clubs that the rival Superleague organisers were held to have induced. However, the restrictions imposed that went beyond that season (loyalty arrangements) were in restraint of trade and void. See also *Australian Rugby League v Cross* (1997) 39 IPR 111 (implied term that a competition would be organised of sufficient size to provide players with a proper opportunity to earn a living and that players would have the opportunity to be selected on merit).

2 *Newport Town Football Club v Football Association of Wales*, 12 April 1995 Blackburne J. This precludes the recovery of damages based on the restraint of trade doctrine and preserves that doctrine's status as a defence only (or basis for a declaration of invalidity).

D THE RELATIONSHIP BETWEEN EXPRESS AND IMPLIED CONTRACTUAL OBLIGATIONS

8.18   In a normal contractual context, express terms take precedence over implied terms, subject to legislative intervention. This will be the case in the context of sport when it comes to straightforward implied terms. The situation is more complex however where the implied term is that the equivalent of the public law standard of review applies to the governing body's actions. It appears that the grounds for review cannot be excluded by express terms. A sports governing body cannot for example exclude the requirement to comply with the principle of natural justice by refusing to inform a player, club or other participant of the disciplinary charges against him, her or it.[1] Equally however, it is likely that the content of the rules, which were entered into consensually (at least nominally), will strongly influence the court's evaluation of what amounts to adequate procedural protection and fair treatment in a given context.[2]

1 See para **7.7** note 3.
2 Express terms imposing some limitations will be taken into account in deciding what the content of the obligation is in any given case. See *Modahl v BAF* (28 July 1997, unreported), CA per Lord Woolf MR at pp 20–26.

CHAPTER 9

Tort

9.1 The law of tort has been used by practitioners in the context of sport not so much to mount challenges to the actions of governing bodies, but rather in relation to personal injury negligence actions brought by players or spectators against other players or the organisers of events. The tort of inducing breach of contract or unlawful interference with contractual relations has also been put to use in disputes between clubs when players have been enticed away. The few tort actions that have been brought against governing bodies have generally arisen in similar contexts.

A ACTIONS IN NEGLIGENCE AGAINST SPORTS GOVERNING BODIES

9.2 Players injured while participating in a sport have often brought actions against another player who for example tackled them illegally, or against the referee who for example failed to prevent repeated scrum collapses. Alternative defendants include the club for which the offending player was appearing[1] or the governing body of the sport concerned. The limits of the responsibility of governing bodies in this context are uncertain and developing. Where a sports governing body actually organises an event itself, it may well owe a duty of care on normal principles to, for example, spectators in relation to the safety of stands, or to a participant not to place an archery contest too close to the discus throwers.[2] It may owe a duty where it licenses a race-course, as in *Wattleworth*.[3] A sports governing body may also be vicariously responsible for the actions of a referee as his employer, as in *Vowles v WRU*,[4] or for the actions of a player, for example on international duty.[5]

1 In *Gravil v Carroll* [2008] ICR 1222, the Court of Appeal held that a semi-professional rugby player's punch to another player was so closely connected with the course of the former's employment that it was fair and just to hold the club, Redruth RFC, vicariously liable for it.
2 *Morrell v Owen*, 1 December 1993 Mitchell J, (1993) Times, 14 December. See also *Horne and Marlow v RAC Motor Sports Association*, 24 May 1989 CA; *Stratton v Hughes and RAC*, 17 March 1998 CA.
3 *Wattleworth (Widow and administratrix of the estate of Simon Wattleworth (deceased)) v Goodwood Road Racing Company Limited, Royal Automobile Club Motor Sports Association Limited and Fédération Internationale de l'Automobile* [2004] EWHC 140 (QB) 4 Feb 2004 Davis J, [2004] All ER (D) 51.
4 *Vowles v Evans and WRU* [2002] EWHC 2612 QBD (Cardiff), 13 Dec 02, Morland J, [2002] All ER (D) 210, [2003] EWCA Civ 318 CA 11 March 2003, [2003] 1 WLR 1607, (2003) Times, 13 March, [2003] All ER (D) 134, [2003] ISLR iss 2 SLR-50 (a referee of an adult amateur rugby match owed a duty of

care to the players to take reasonable care for their safety when carrying out his refereeing duties and his breach of that duty caused the claimant's injury. The basis for the allegation, and finding, against the WRU as governing body was simply that it was vicariously liable for the actions of the referee as its employee, and not that it had itself failed to act in a particular way in the introduction or application of rules).

5 *Dean Ashton v Wright-Phillips, The FA, and Chelsea*, resolved by mediation (vicarious liability claim by Ashton based on the Chelsea player Wright-Phillips, whose tackle had injured Ashton, being on England international duty at the time).

9.3 More difficult is the situation where what is being impugned is not the sports governing body's own actions (or at least not its own immediate actions), or the actions of those for whom it is vicariously responsible, but rather the quality of its control through its rules over the actions of others, in order to ensure a safe sport. In *Agar v Hyde*,[1] two injured rugby players argued that the International Rugby Board owed a duty 'to take reasonable care in monitoring the operation of the rules of the game to avoid the risk of unnecessary harm to players' and 'to take reasonable care to ensure that the rules did not provide for circumstances where risks of serious injury were taken unnecessarily'. It was held that the sports governing body did not owe such duties of care to the many thousands of people who participated in the sport; indeed it was held to be unarguable that such duties of care existed.

1 (2000) 201 CLR 552, [2000] HCA 41, 173 ALR 665.

9.4 In contrast, in *Watson v British Boxing Board of Control*[1] the governing body was held to owe a licensed boxer a duty of care to ensure that rules were in place providing for adequate ringside medical assistance, and was also held to be in breach of that duty. The duty of care arose out of the particular circumstances of the sport, and in particular the fact that the BBBC licensed a relatively small number of boxers. Therefore, there was sufficient proximity to give rise to a duty of care, and it was fair and just to impose such a duty. The governing body set out by its rules, directions and guidance to make comprehensive provision for the services to be provided to safeguard the health of professional boxers taking part in the sport, the object of the sport was to inflict physical injury, and all those involved in a boxing contest were obliged to accept and comply with the board's requirements. The BBBC was a governing body with specialist knowledge giving advice to a defined class of persons in the knowledge that that class would rely upon that advice in boxing contests, and the boxer in fact relied on the BBBC to exercise skill and care in ensuring his safety during a fight. The boxer belonged to a class of persons within the contemplation of the governing body, which was itself involved in an activity that gave it complete control over and a responsibility for a boxing contest that would be liable to result in injury to the claimant if reasonable care were not exercised by the governing body. The BBBC was held to be in breach for failing to make it a requirement that ringside resuscitation be available.

1 (1999) 143 Sol Jo LB 235, (1999) Times, 12 October, [2001] QB 1134, CA. See also *Fox v Ministry of Defence* [2002] EWCA Civ 435, 6 March 2002, CA, for the responsibility of organisers for the actions of their doctor at boxing match.

9.5 In *Wright v Jockey Club*,[1] the jockey alleged that the Jockey Club owed him a duty of care and skill in carrying out the medical tests that would ascertain whether he was fit to ride. The claim in tort was withdrawn in argument and the court rejected the implication of a contractual term that the Jockey Club owed such a duty. The Jockey Club's duty was held simply to be to act fairly. At the very outset in *Modahl*, consideration was given to alleging a general duty of care to ensure that a drugs test is properly taken and dealt with and not mixed up or mishandled.[2] In the event, however, such a claim was not pursued. Outside the sports context, it has been held that claims do not lie for negligent prosecution of disciplinary charges,[3] or even for malicious prosecution of disciplinary charges.[4] Rather, the only claim in such circumstances would be for defamation.[5]

1 15 May 1995 Sir Haydn Tudor Evans QB, (1995) Times, 16 June, at p 8 of the Lexis transcript.
2 Cf [2002] 1 WLR 1192, CA per Latham LJ para 4.
3 See *Calveley v Chief Constable of the Merseyside Police* [1989] AC 1228, HL (no claim lies against police force for bringing disciplinary proceedings negligently).
4 In *Gregory v Portsmouth City Council* [2000] 1 AC 419, a claim against a Council for bringing disciplinary charges maliciously was rejected, the House of Lords ruling that recourse, if any, must be found in the tort of defamation. This must now be treated with some caution in view of the Privy Council's decision in *Crawford Adjusters (Cayman) Ltd v Sagicor* [2014] AC 366, in which the majority recognised a tort of malicious prosecution of civil proceedings under Cayman law. In *Willers v Gubay* [2015] EWHC 1315, the High Court held that it was bound by *Gregory* to decline to apply *Crawford Adjusters*, but gave permission to appeal. A decision is awaited from the Supreme Court.
5 See n 4 above.

B INDUCING BREACH OF CONTRACT AND THE ECONOMIC TORTS

9.6   The claim in tort of inducing breach of contract or unlawful interference with contractual relations[1] has been deployed in actions brought against sports governing bodies, particularly where there has been a battle over control of the sport. In *Greig v Insole*,[2] a number of cricket players decided to sign up for Kerry Packer's alternative tournament, which challenged the ICC's established control over the sport. In a defensive response, the ICC and the TCCB made a number of changes to their rules that effectively banned players that played for Kerry Packer from playing not only in tests for their country, but also from playing first class cricket. Importantly, the changes were introduced after the players had already concluded contracts with Kerry Packer, and were applied retrospectively. The court concluded that the rule changes constituted inducement of the players to breach their contracts and unlawful interference with contractual relations.[3] The argument is not however confined to battles for control. In *Walker v UKA and IAAF*,[4] the athlete accused the IAAF of seeking to induce UKA to breach their contract with the athlete by requiring them to participate in an arbitration brought by the IAAF to review the validity of their own decision. UKA was said to owe a contractual obligation to treat its disciplinary process as final. The argument there was flawed because not only was there no breach of any contract between UKA and the athlete, but also because the IAAF rules that UKA sought to enforce were pre-existing rules (in contrast to the position in *Greig v Insole*). In *Mohammed v The FA and FIFA*, an action alleging that the introduction of the player-agent licensing system was an unlawful interference with existing contractual relations between players and agents, and in breach of the competition rules, survived a summary judgment application by the governing bodies, at least in part, but appears to have gone unresolved.[5] In other contexts less well established economic torts have been valiantly argued, but to little effect.[6]

1 For the ingredients of the torts, see *OBG Ltd v Allen* [2007] UKHL 21.
2 [1978] 1 WLR 302.
3 Cf *News Ltd v Australian Rugby Football League Ltd* (1996) 135 ALR 33, *(No 2)* (1997) 139 ALR 193. See also *Fisher v NGRC (No 2)*, 25 July 1991, unreported, CA.
4 *Walker v UKA and IAAF*, 3 July 2000 Toulson J, 25 July 2000 Hallett J, IAAF Arbitration Award 20 August 2000 reported at [2001] 4 ISLR 264, see also [2000] 2 ISLR 41.

5 *Mohammed v Rougier (and two others) and FA and FIFA*, [2002] EWHC 287 QB, Field J, 21 February 2002 (dispute between agents also involving the validity of the introduction of the licensing regime itself on the basis that it was an interference with existing contractual relations and in breach of competition law).

6 See for example *Currie v Barton*, 26 March 1987, unreported, Scott J; 11 February 1988, unreported, CA, (1988) Times, 12 February (tennis player banned by his county association for three years for refusing to play in a county match and was consequently ruled ineligible to play for England by the LTA. Among other things the player relied on a tort of interference by unlawful means with his profession of tennis player and coach, but the argument was rejected: see p 12 of the Lexis transcript of Scott J's judgment).

C ACTIONS AGAINST SPORTS GOVERNING BODIES BASED ON OTHER TORTS?

9.7   The range of actions by sports governing bodies is wide and may therefore throw up particular factual circumstances revealing the commission of a variety of other torts. At least hypothetically there could be cases ranging from defamation[1] to nuisance.[2]

1 Certain authorities suggest that defamation would be the most suitable cause of action in the event that disciplinary charges are brought against an athlete without basis. See Taylor 'Disciplinary charges brought maliciously and without reasonable basis; What are the remedies?' (2000) 7(2) Sports Law Administration and Practice; above, para **9.5** note 4.

2 See for instance *Lawrence v Fen Tigers Ltd (No 2)* [2015] AC 106 in which the claimant house owners succeeded in a private nuisance claim against the operators of a noisy speedway track.

CHAPTER 10

Common law restraint of trade

10.1   The common law doctrine of restraint of trade[1] has provided a useful mechanism (particularly in the absence of a contract) for challenging the actions of sports governing bodies, principally where access has been refused to a sport, where the governing body has refused a particular request of a player, club or other participant, where disciplinary action has been taken on the basis of a rule that is restrictive, and where restrictive rules such as transfer rules have been challenged in their entirety. The doctrine has also been used in the context of challenges by players to the contractual constraints imposed upon them by the clubs employing them, although that topic falls outside the scope of this chapter. The doctrine of restraint of trade is a defensive mechanism: if a rule or action restrains trade without justification, it is void and unenforceable. The doctrine does not give rise to any action for damages,[2] although an action can be brought for a declaration that a particular rule or term or decision is void.

1 See generally Kamerling *Restraint of Trade and Business Secrets* (4th edn, Sweet & Maxwell, 2002).
  For a general analysis of the application of the doctrine to sport, see Stewart [1996] 6(3) SATLJ 41.
2 Nor is it possible to circumvent this position by arguing that an implied contractual obligation arises not
  to act in restraint of trade: see *Newport v FAW*, 12 April 1995 Blackburne J.

10.2   The developments in the availability of the grounds for review based on the public law standard discussed in Chapter 7 above, and the developments in competition law, throw into doubt however whether a conceptually distinct basis for challenge in the form of restraint of trade continues to exist. The discussion below addresses the basis for and extent of the doctrine, its historical application in the context of sport, and the possibility that it no longer provides a distinct basis for challenge.

A THE BASIS FOR AND EXTENT OF THE DOCTRINE

(a) The basis for the doctrine

10.3   The basis for the doctrine of restraint of trade is that as a matter of public policy a person should not be restricted in his or her ability to earn a living by an obligation that goes beyond what is necessary to achieve some legitimate and desirable aim.[1] It is in the interests of the individual or companies involved, and the public, that the individual should be free to be as productive as possible, so long as that does not prevent some equally worthwhile benefit being achieved. The doctrine is therefore based on similar premises to those on which the competition law rules are based, and to a lesser extent to those on which the equivalent of the public law grounds for review are based, and it is likely that the approaches will produce the same result in many instances.[2] If an individual term falls foul of the doctrine, it is unenforceable. If the offending clause cannot be 'severed' from the contract without losing the commercial benefit intended, then the whole contract will be unenforceable. It is generally not illegal to perform a contract in restraint of trade if both parties choose to abide by it, but either party to the contract, or a third party injured by the operation of the agreement, can seek a declaration that it is unenforceable.[3]

1 See *Herbert Morris v Saxelby* [1916] 1 AC 688; *Esso Petroleum v Harper's Garage* [1968] AC 269. The restriction need not be, but may be, contained in a contract between claimant and defendant.
2 Indeed, a different result under restraint of trade from the result reached by application of EU competition law is impermissible: *Days Medical Aids* [2004] EWHC 44 (Comm) Langley J, 29 January 2004, [2004] 1 All ER (Comm) 991.
3 See *Eastham v Newcastle United* [1964] Ch 413; *Greig v Insole* [1978] 1 WLR 302; and *Nagle v Feilden* [1966] 2 QB 633.

(b) The stages in the analysis

10.4   The constituents of the restraint of trade argument, in its conventional form, are set out in *Nordenfelt v Maxim Nordenfelt Guns.*[1] The starting point is that all restraints of trade are void unless justified. In the first stage of the analysis, the onus falls on the party advancing the argument (here the player, club or other participant) to prove that there is a restraint of trade, in other words that an obligation has been imposed on the player by the sports governing body that prevents him from earning, or limits him in his ability to earn, a living at his chosen occupation. Governing bodies have often argued that their rules and actions are not in restraint of trade in the first place, on the basis that the obligation does not affect the complainant's ability to earn a living at his occupation to a sufficiently substantial extent,[2] or on the basis that what the obligation affects is not the ability to earn a living, but to pursue a particular recreational activity, such as an amateur sport,[3] or on the basis that rules essential to the creation of a competitive sport should not be regarded as a restraint of trade but rather as encouraging trade,[4] or on the basis that the doctrine cannot apply to the rules of an international governing body regulating participants from around the world, who would not be subject to the doctrine in their home countries,[5] or on the basis that the restraint does not operate on trade within the geographic jurisdiction of the court,[6] or on the basis that it is not the claimant's trade that is restrained.[7]

1 [1894] AC 535. Other leading cases include *Herbert Morris v Saxelby* [1916] 1 AC 688 and *Esso Petroleum v Harper's Garage* [1968] AC 269, HL.
2 See eg *Newport v Football Association of Wales* interlocutory hearing Jacob J [1995] 2 All ER 87, trial Blackburne J 12 April 1995, a restriction on a club's ability to play in the League of its choice was caught.
3 *Chambers v British Olympic Association* [2008] EWHC 2028 (QB).
4 An approach which is analogous to the 'rule of reason' or 'ancillary restraint' doctrines in competition law. The approach was rejected in *Buckley v Tutty* (1971) 125 CLR 353.
5 Rejected in *Gasser v Stinson*, 15 June 1988, Scott J, at p 35F to 36H of the shorthand writers' transcript of Scott J's judgment.
6 Rejected in *Blackler v NZRFL* [1968] NZLR 547 at 555 and 571.
7 *Tonga National Rugby League v Rugby League International Federation* [2008] NSWSC 1173, 27 October 2008, Supreme Court of New South Wales.

10.5   If a restraint of trade is established, then in the second stage of the analysis (at least in the conventional form of the doctrine[1]) the onus switches to the party resisting the argument and seeking to uphold the obligation, here the governing body, to show that the restraint is reasonable and justified in the interests of the parties. This is the first limb of the *Nordenfelt v Maxim Nordenfelt* reasonableness test.[2] To be reasonable and justified in the interests of the parties, the restraint must: (a) pursue a legitimate aim which is worthy of protection; and (b) do so in a reasonable and proportionate manner. To be proportionate the restraint must not only be necessary to achieve the governing body's legitimate aim, but it must also go no further than is reasonably necessary to achieve that aim: the governing body must show that there is no less onerous alternative course of action available to it to achieve its legitimate aim.[3] Furthermore, the harm caused to the player, club, or other participant by the imposition of the obligation must not be out of proportion to the benefit secured by the governing body. Accordingly the quality of the legitimate aim must be assessed and balanced against the effect of the obligation. If the aim is actually not that important, or even if it is important but it would not be substantially undermined if the restriction were not applied, it will not justify a substantial detriment to the player, club or other participant. In the sports context, the principal justifications offered by sports governing bodies for restrictions have included the need to maintain competitive balance between clubs and thus public interest in the sport;[4] the need to encourage new entrants (whether players or clubs);[5] the need to generate revenue for reinvestment in the sport at grass roots level;[6] the need to maintain the integrity of the pyramidical and geographic structure of the sport;[7] the need to have a workable and deterrent system of doping control;[8] the need to improve the quality of the domestic league in order to improve the quality of the players from which the national team can be selected;[9] the need to have a commercially viable competition;[10] and the need to satisfy and respond to the demands of media companies, support from which is crucial to the particular sport's survival.[11]

1 *Stevenage* can be argued to be authority that in the context of a challenge on restraint of trade grounds to the rules of a sports governing body, the doctrine is adapted so that the second stage of the analysis is effectively omitted, leaving the challenger to establish both that there is a restraint, and that it does not operate reasonably in the interests of the public. The proposition that restraint of trade has ceased to be a distinct basis for challenge is based on that starting point.

2 [1894] AC 535 at 565.

3 Cf *Esso Petroleum v Harper's Garage* [1968] AC 269, HL.

4 This is the chief justification offered in respect of restrictions on the ability of players to move and in respect of rules requiring transfer fees, drafts and salary caps.

5 See *Adamson v NSWRL* (1991) 100 ALR 479; on appeal 103 ALR 319, 31 FCR 242 (draft arrangement) (1991) 27 FCR 535 on appeal.

6 See for example Rugby World Cup 1999: Pugh and Martin, 'How the Rugby World Cup Plays by the Rules' Sportvision (Autumn 1999), p 72; and Whitehead, 'Anatomy of a Tournament' (1999) 6(3) Sports Law Administration & Practice 1 (Rugby World Cup 1999).

7 See *Wimbledon Football Club v Football League* unreported FA Arbitration Panel decision dated 29 January 2002, FA Commission May 2002.

8 See *Gasser v Stinson*, 15 June 1988 Scott J; *Johnson v Athletics Canada and IAAF* (1997) 41 OTC 95 (where it was also held reasonable as necessary to protect Ben Johnson from himself).

9 See *Williams and Cardiff RFC v Pugh*, 23 July 1997 Popplewell J and 1 August 1997 CA; subsequently known as *Williams and Cardiff RFC v WRU (IRB intervening)*, 17 March 1998 Buckley J, [1999] Eu LR 195.

10 The argument that it was legitimate for one competition to defend itself against another seeking to take players away from its events because it would make them unviable failed on the facts in *Pilkadaris v Asian Tour (Tournament Players Division) Pte Ltd* [2012] SGHC 236 (HC (Sing)), 27 November 2012. The restrictions imposed were held to go too far. See also *South Sydney District Rugby League Football Club v News Ltd* [2000] FCA 1541, [2001] FCA 862.

11 See *South Sydney District Rugby League Football Club v News Ltd*, n 10 above; *Williams and Cardiff RFC v Pugh* subsequently known as *Williams and Cardiff RFC v WRU (IRB intervening)*, n 9 above.

10.6 If the governing body establishes that the restraint is reasonable and justified in the interests of the parties, in the third stage of the analysis (again in the conventional form of the doctrine) the party seeking to challenge the imposition of the obligation has a last chance. The doctrine requires restraints to be reasonable not only in the interests of the parties but also in the interests of the *public*. The onus of proving that an obligation is *not* reasonable in the interests of the public lies on the party challenging the obligation, here the player, club or other participant. This is the second limb of the *Nordenfelt v Maxim Nordenfelt* reasonableness test.[1]

1 [1894] AC 535 at 565.

(c) Questions raised

10.7 The particular circumstances of sport have meant that some of the cases applying the doctrine in that context have introduced additional elements to the standard restraint of trade analysis set out above at paras **10.4–10.6**. In particular, the debate as to whether sports governing bodies are in reality public bodies, or at least quasi-public, and the development in the law on the applicability of the equivalent of the public law grounds for review to the actions of sports governing bodies led Carnwath J to suggest[1] that the three-stage analysis set out above should be adapted. He suggested that if a rule or decision of a sports governing body is established to be in restraint of trade, the first limb of the *Nordenfelt v Maxim Nordenfelt* reasonableness test (whether the restraint is in the interests of the parties) should be omitted, leaving the court to apply only the second limb, shifting the onus onto the player, club or other participant to prove why the restraint is not in the public interest. As part of the same analysis, Carnwath J concluded that the standard of unreasonableness to be shown by the challenger should be the public law standard, in other words 'Wednesbury' unreasonableness, or irrationality. This approach constituted a marked departure from the previous approach in most sports law cases, under which the full *Nordenfelt v Maxim Nordenfelt* test was applied without adaptation.[2] It throws into doubt whether restraint of trade remains a conceptually distinct basis for challenging governing bodies' actions to the grounds of review based on the public law standard. Similar questions are raised by the requirement that EU competition law must not be circumvented by the application of the restraint of trade doctrine. These questions are addressed below in the discussion of the courts' application of the doctrine in sports contexts, and in the last section.

1 Technically obiter, in *Stevenage Borough Football Club v Football League Ltd*, Carnwath J (1996) Times, 1 August. For the Court of Appeal, see (1997) 9 Admin LR 109, CA.
2 Notably and relatively recently by Blackburne J at trial in *Newport v Football Association of Wales*, 12 April 1995.

10.8 Before that, however, two more immediate questions are addressed: (a) does the doctrine apply to rules of governing bodies that do not have contractual force in a particular instance? and (b) does the doctrine apply to governing bodies' decisions as well as to their rules?

(d) The restraint need not be imposed by contract

10.9 Although in the normal course the restraint of trade doctrine is applied to render specific contractual clauses unenforceable, the doctrine does have wider applicability. Even where there is no contractual relationship, a specific rule of a body with power to affect the ability of a person to trade can be declared incompatible with the doctrine.[1] In the sports context, this means that even where no contract arises between a governing body and an individual player, rules of the governing body that affect the player will nevertheless be subject to the doctrine.

1 *Pharmaceutical Society of Great Britain v Dickson* [1970] AC 403, HL per Lord Wilberforce at 440C; *Eastham v Newcastle United Football Club and the FA* [1964] Ch 413 at 443; *Greig v Insole (for the TCCB)* [1978] 1 WLR 302; *Buckley v Tutty* (1971) 125 CLR 353.

(e)   The doctrine applies to the decisions, as well as the rules, of sports governing bodies

10.10   Nor does the obligation, or the restraint, have to arise out of a sports governing body's rules. It may arise out of a particular decision of the sports governing body to apply in an unjustifiably restrictive way rules that in themselves are valid. For example, it may be perfectly appropriate to have a rule affording a sports governing body a discretion, but if the body seeks to exercise that discretion in an unreasonable way that restricts the ability of a person or company to trade, that exercise of discretion is reviewable on the basis of restraint of trade.[1] If this were not the case, any contractual exercise of power on the basis of a discretion would escape review by reference to the doctrine. Nor does the fact that a discretion exists to disapply a rule save a rule that is prima facie a restraint, since the party affected cannot be expected to rely on the favourable application of that discretion.[2]

1 *Newport v FAW* [1995] 2 All ER 87 at 97g–97h per Jacob J at the interim hearing; at trial Blackburne J 12 April 1995 at 24, 33–35 and 45 of the New Law Online transcript. See also *Stinnato v Auckland Boxing Association* [1978] 1 NZLR 1 (decision to refuse a licence capable of being a restraint of trade).
2 *Buckley v Tutty* (1971) 125 CLR 353.

B   APPLICATION TO THE RULES AND ACTIONS OF SPORTS GOVERNING BODIES

10.11   The starting point in relation to the application of the restraint of trade doctrine to the rules and actions of sports governing bodies is *Eastham v Newcastle United Football Club and The Football Association*.[1] At issue in that case was (inter alia) the validity of The Football League's then transfer and retention rules. The rules allowed a club to retain a player's registration, notwithstanding that his contract with the club had expired, until a transfer fee was paid by a new club. Wilberforce J held[2] that:

> 'the two systems when combined were in restraint of trade and, since [the League] had not discharged the onus on them of showing that the restraints were no more than was reasonable to protect their interests, were in unjustifiable restraint of trade, and ... as such they were ultra vires.'

The burden was therefore regarded as being on the governing body to show that the restraint was reasonably necessary in the interests of the parties.[3] The test applied was the first limb of the *Nordenfelt v Maxim Nordenfelt* reasonableness test, and Wilberforce J did not go on to the second limb. No doubt, however, if the governing body had established the reasonableness of the transfer rules as between the parties, the question would have moved on to whether the player could establish that the rules were not reasonably necessary in the public interest. The rules were held to be in restraint of trade because notwithstanding that the governing body and the clubs supported them, and notwithstanding that they had some benefits, the value of the benefit was wholly outweighed by the detriment to players, and the restraint went further than was necessary to protect the governing body's legitimate interests. The case is also authority for the proposition that the rules of a governing body should where possible be construed so as not to give rise to a restraint of trade.[4]

1 [1964] Ch 413. The application of the *Nordenfelt v Maxim Nordenfelt* test in *Eastham* has been followed in the Commonwealth: see *Blackler v New Zealand Rugby Football League* [1968] NZLR 547; and *Buckley v Tutty* (1971) 125 CLR 353.
2 See the headnote in *Eastham* [1964] Ch 413.
3 See [1964] Ch 413 at 431 and 439.
4 See [1964] Ch 413 at 440.

10.12   In *Greig v Insole*,[1] the ICC and the TCCB changed their rules relating to qualification to play in test matches and county cricket. The new rules provided that any player who played in a match that had been disapproved by the ICC or TCCB would be ineligible to play in any test match or county cricket match without the consent of the ICC or TCCB, such consent only to be given on the application of the player's national governing body. The ICC and TCCB then passed resolutions disapproving the World Series matches organised by Kerry Packer. The players thereby rendered ineligible for ICC and TCCB matches brought a challenge. The court held that the ICC and TCCB had legitimate interests in the proper administration of cricket, but that they had failed to discharge the burden on them of showing that the new rules were reasonable in the circumstances, due in particular to their retrospectivity. The test applied was the *Nordenfelt v Maxim Nordenfelt* reasonableness test.[2]

1 [1978] 1 WLR 302.
2 [1978] 1 WLR 302 at 345.

10.13   In *Gasser v Stinson*,[1] the court concluded that even if the anti-doping rules that the IAAF applied to Ms Gasser were a restraint of trade (although she was nominally amateur), they were proportionate and reasonable in the interests not only of the parties but also the public. Scott J concluded that although the relevant IAAF rules imposed a strict liability offence, that was justified in the particular circumstances of the threat to sport posed by drug taking and the difficulties in detecting and proving an offence. Scott J examined simultaneously the reasonableness of the rules in the interests of the public and in the interests of athletes, and introduced the concept of judicial reluctance to intervene into the restraint of trade analysis.[2]

1 15 June 1988 Scott J. See also *Wilander v Tobin*, 19 March 1996 Lightman J; 8 April 1996 CA, where an argument that the anti-doping rules were in restraint of trade was struck out as unarguable.
2 See pp 37H to 40E of the shorthand writers' transcript. Although *Gasser v Stinson* was not cited by Carnwath J in *Stevenage*, it provides some support for his analysis there, in particular Scott J's reliance on *McInnes v Onslow-Fane* [1978] 1 WLR 1520, on which Carnwath J also placed reliance. That said, Scott J did not suggest that he was departing from the conventional approach to restraint of trade. See also Scott J's analysis in *Currie v Barton*, 26 March 1987 Scott J (which involved collateral reliance on the restraint of trade doctrine in order to support a natural justice argument, as in *Nagle v Feilden* [1966] 2 QB 633), and his statement in *Watson v Prager* [1991] 1 WLR 726.

10.14   In *R v Jockey Club, ex p RAM Racecourses*,[1] a prospective racecourse developer sought judicial review of a decision by the Jockey Club not to allocate any racing dates to the proposed racecourse. The court stated that were it not for authority to the contrary, it would have held that the Jockey Club was amenable to judicial review. On the facts, it was decided that the developer could not have had a legitimate expectation of being granted any races. The court did, however, conclude obiter that it could have interfered if the exercise of power had been unlawful, even though the action ought to have been a private one. Stuart Smith LJ recorded that the Jockey Club '...accepted that in an appropriate case where a body enjoys a monopoly position such that it can prevent a person from earning his living by not admitting him or from conducting a legitimate business, in restraint of trade, it will be amenable to a declaratory judgment in an action begun by writ, if it has acted in an arbitrary and capricious way in refusing to permit the applicant's activities...'.[2] The test thus formulated (at least on the basis of the Jockey Club's concession) involved arbitrariness and caprice.

1   [1993] 2 All ER 225, DC.
2   [1993] 2 All ER 225 at 243f.

10.15   In *Newport v Football Association of Wales*, the issue was whether the Football Association of Wales (FAW) could stop ex-members playing home games in Wales in a competition not controlled by the FAW. The source of the problem was a resolution of the FAW that no Welsh clubs would henceforth be sanctioned under rule 57 of the FAW Rules to play home games in Wales as part of the English league pyramid (excepting those clubs already playing in The Football League itself). In essence the decision was to refuse consent to the non-league Welsh clubs that wished to continue to play in the English pyramid to play their home games in Wales. Certain clubs resigned and joined up with The FA. The FAW responded with sanctions, causing The FA to ban the three clubs from playing their home English league games in Wales. The three clubs then challenged the decisions of the FAW to exclude them from playing at home as being in restraint of trade. There were two hearings, at each of which the clubs succeeded. At the interlocutory hearing,[1] Jacob J granted an interim injunction in support of an action for a declaration alone. He also held that there was a serious issue to be tried, namely whether the FAW had by its decisions fettered the free choice of Welsh clubs as to where to play.[2] Jacob J proceeded on the basis that unreasonable 'arrangements' as well as contracts could fall foul of the restraint of trade doctrine. He also pointed out that making the clubs play away from home reduced their income to the point at which they would ultimately go into liquidation. Jacob J was not impressed with an argument that the three clubs ought to have sued The FA rather than the FAW. He took the view that The FA's decision was at the behest of the FAW, and that the FAW was the operator of the restraint. Jacob J held that the doctrine of restraint of trade is not technical and looks to substance not form.[3] He asked himself whether the decisions involved restrained trade, and held that it was arguable that they did.[4] He held that the test for reasonableness (by which he measured whether there was a serious issue to be tried) was the *Nordenfelt v Maxim Nordenfelt* test.[5]

1   [1995] 2 All ER 87.
2   In that instance whether they could play home games within the English pyramid non-league system (ie below the Football League) in Wales.
3   [1995] 2 All ER 87 at 95f.
4   [1995] 2 All ER 87 at 97g–97h.
5   [1995] 2 All ER 87 at 97j–98d.

10.16   The trial in *Newport v FAW* was before Blackburne J,[1] who held that the FAW resolution was in restraint of trade, and that it was not reasonably necessary to have the rule to protect the FAW's legitimate interests. In so doing he examined the compatibility of a decision, not a rule, against the doctrine,[2] and he specifically stated that this was what he was doing.[3] He applied the *Nordenfelt v Maxim Nordenfelt* reasonableness test.[4] He examined whether the FAW had discharged the burden of justifying the restraint.[5] He rejected an argument from the FAW that the very nature of the organisation of football within the UK, split into England, Wales, Scotland and Northern Ireland, gave rise to the restriction on the ability of clubs in one country to play home games for the league of another country.[6]

1 12 April 1995.
2 See pp 24 and 33–35 of the online transcript.
3 At p 45 of the online transcript.
4 At p 36 of the online transcript.
5 See pp 36 and 39 of the online transcript.
6 See pp 35–36 of the online transcript.

10.17   Soon after the decision in *Newport*, Lightman J and the Court of Appeal had to consider in *Wilander v Tobin*[1] whether it was arguable that the anti-doping rules of the International Tennis Federation were in restraint of trade. Lightman J followed Scott J's approach in *Gasser v Stinson*.[2] In the Court of Appeal, Neill LJ upheld Lightman J's decision, asking simply whether the rules in question were reasonable.[3] Subsequently the players attempted, ultimately unsuccessfully, to amend their claim to add arguments based on the free movement and the competition law rules.[4] In the Court of Appeal on the second occasion, Lord Woolf MR reached the conclusion, dealt with above, that it is implicit in the contract between players and a governing body contained in its rules that the governing body will be subject to grounds of review that mirror those to which a public body is subject.[5] It is arguable that in so concluding, Lord Woolf MR was setting the *upper*, as opposed to (or as well as) the *lower* limits, on a sports governing body's liability. In other words, if it is right that the equivalent of the public law standard should apply, then arguably that involves protecting the governing body from over-intrusive review just as much as ensuring a minimum level of review to claimants, and it ought not to be possible to circumvent this protection for the governing body by the application of a more intrusive test under the restraint of trade doctrine. Lord Woolf MR went on to say,[6] in assessing whether the free movement argument should be allowed in after the restraint of trade argument had been struck out, that:

> 'The requirement of proportionality [for the purposes of the free movement rules] may not be identical ... with reasonableness or natural justice but it is certainly close to these concepts.'

This leaves open the question of whether the test under the restraint of trade doctrine is the same as the quasi-public law test. If the reference to reasonableness here was a reference to reasonableness under the restraint of trade doctrine, Lord Woolf MR appears to have been equating it with the 'natural justice' test. On the other hand, he also appears to have contemplated that proportionality under the free movement rules is close to the appropriate test for the purposes of restraint of trade. At least until recently, the proportionality test under the free movement rules was not regarded as being the same as the traditional form of public law reasonableness: proportionality under the free movement rules is a more intrusive test than arbitrariness or capriciousness. It is possible that Lord Woolf MR was foreshadowing more recent developments that treat the reasonableness and proportionality tests as involving broadly similar considerations in a flexible and variable way dependent on the particular circumstances.[7]

1 19 March 1996 Lightman J, 8 April 1996 CA.
2 See p 20 of the online transcript of Lightman J's judgment.
3 See Lexis transcript of Neill LJ's judgment.
4 The action came back before Lightman J, [1997] 1 Lloyd's Law Rep 195, who gave leave to amend to add the free movement argument but refused leave to add the competition law argument on the basis that it was insufficiently particularised. The Court of Appeal refused leave to amend to add either argument, [1997] 2 Lloyd's Law Rep 296. The second Court of Appeal decision (December 1996) came after the decision in *Stevenage* (July 1996).
5 [1997] 2 Lloyd's Law Rep 296 per Lord Woolf MR at 300, col 1. Shortly thereafter (July 1997), Lord Woolf MR gave judgment in *Modahl v BAF*, where he held that the normal judicial review standard of fairness applied to the review of private body disciplinary decisions.
6 Per Lord Woolf MR at [1997] 2 Lloyd's Law Rep 301, col 1.
7 Summarised in *Kennedy v Charity Commission* [2015] AC 455 per Lord Mance at paras 51–55.

10.18   The position on the authorities following the *Newport* decision, and following the first round of *Wilander* decisions but before the judgment of Lord Woolf MR described above,[1] was that if a challenger established that a rule or decision of a sports governing body restricted his ability to earn a living at his chosen profession, the governing body would have to satisfy the first limb of the *Nordenfelt v Maxim Nordenfelt* reasonableness test by establishing that the restriction was necessary to achieve a legitimate aim of the governing body and that it was proportionate. It is against this background that Carnwath J's analysis in *Stevenage Borough Football Club v Football League Ltd*[2] is to be measured. In that case Carnwath J had to examine whether entry criteria for the club winning the Conference to gain promotion to The League were in unjustifiable restraint of trade. He decided the case on the basis that the club had delayed too long before making an application and that in its discretion the court should refuse relief since third party rights were affected.[3] He was upheld on this point by the Court of Appeal.[4] He also held obiter that a number of the criteria were in unreasonable restraint of trade,[5] and the consequence was that The Football League changed the rules that he had criticised. Although it is not certain, it appears that Carnwath J applied an adapted version of the restraint of trade doctrine in reaching this conclusion. Earlier in his judgment he suggested, technically obiter, that the test to be applied by the courts when considering whether a sports governing body is acting in restraint of trade was a rather different test to that used by the courts that had applied the doctrine in sports cases previously. It is arguable that Carnwath J did not reach a firm conclusion in relation to the test and how it applied in practice. The Court of Appeal[6] noted that in the context of one of the rules Carnwath J said that he 'would return later to consider whether this was the correct test', but that 'in the event, however, he did not do so' and instead dismissed the action on grounds of delay. The Court of Appeal appeared[7] to regard Carnwath J as evaluating whether The League had discharged the burden of showing that the restraints were necessary to protect its legitimate interests.[8]

1 The second Court of Appeal decision in *Wilander*, described above at para **10.17**, came after the *Stevenage* decision.
2 *Stevenage Borough Football Club v Football League Ltd* (1996) Times, 1 August; *affd* 9 Admin LR 109, CA.
3 At pp 34 to 35 of the online transcript.
4 At (1997) 9 Admin LR 109 at 117 to 121 per Millet LJ, at 122 to 123 per Hobhouse LJ.
5 At pp 26 to 33 of the online transcript. In the earlier FA arbitration, *Enfield v Football League*, the Panel had rejected a restraint of trade challenge to entry criteria: see Carnwath J at pp 31 to 32 of the online transcript.
6 (1997) 9 Admin LR 109 at 117E.

7 (1997) 9 Admin LR 109 at 117D.
8 The Court of Appeal's decision in *Stevenage* focuses on the question of delay, and specifically did not address the test for restraint of trade. See for example Hobhouse LJ at 121F–121H.

10.19   Carnwath J suggested[1] that because sports governing bodies (and specifically The League) exercise a quasi-public role, the appropriate test of justifiability is whether the restraint is justified in the *public* interest (the second as opposed to the first limb in the *Nordenfelt v Maxim Nordenfelt* reasonableness test), putting the burden onto the challenger to show why the restraint operated against the public interest, rather than on the governing body to show why it was justified in the interests of the parties. He regarded the test applied in *Greig* and in *Newport* (the first limb of the *Nordenfelt v Maxim Nordenfelt* reasonableness test) as misleading.[2] He also held[3] that the standard of unreasonableness for these purposes was the public law standard. In so doing he drew on the references to the words 'arbitrary or capricious' in *Nagle v Feilden* and in *McInnes v Onslow-Fane*. Carnwath J did state after examining the law that it was 'not the time to attempt a reconciliation of these various strands of authority'. In the authors' view, however, this does not undercut the status of his discussion of the doctrine,[4] to which weight should still be attached.

1 At p 25 of the online transcript.
2 At p 24 of the online transcript.
3 At pp 22 and 25–26 of the online transcript.
4 At pp 17–24 of the online transcript.

10.20   There has been academic support for Carnwath J's analysis from writers who believe that sports governing bodies fulfil a public role and that their decisions ought to be subject to judicial review rather than being dealt with in private law proceedings.[1] Carnwath J's analysis is useful to sports governing bodies seeking to defend actions brought against them on the basis of restraint of trade.[2]

1 Beloff et al. *Sports Law* (2nd edn, Hart, 2012) at para 3.63. The authors conclude at 3.64 that 'the upshot ... is that it is not always clear (1) where the onus of proof lies in a restraint of trade case involving a sporting body, or (2) precisely how the applicable standard of reasonableness should be formulated'.
2 Carnwath J's analysis was argued by the governing bodies, first in *Williams and Cardiff RFC v Pugh*, later known as *Williams and Cardiff RFC v WRU (IRB intervening)*, interim injunction hearings, 23 July 1997 Popplewell J, 1 August 1997 CA; application for a stay hearing 17 March 1998 Buckley J [1999] Eu LR 195, secondly in *Hendry v World Professional Billiards and Snooker Association Ltd*, Lloyd J 5 October 2001 [2002] 1 ISLR SLR-1, and thirdly in *Wimbledon v Football League* unreported FA Arbitration Panel 29 January 2002, in none of which was the issue decided.

10.21   On the other hand, an equally arguable analysis open to challengers is that the *Nordenfelt v Maxim Nordenfelt* reasonableness test continues to apply in full to the rules and decisions of sports governing bodies.[1] The courts have now categorically held that the decisions of sports governing bodies in situations such as this are not amenable to judicial review.[2] Until that position is overturned, it could be argued that the analysis in *Stevenage* starts from the wrong premise. While it is plain that the courts have drawn on public law considerations in identifying grounds for review implicit in any contract or enforceable by an action for a declaration, it could be argued that in doing so the courts have simply been endeavouring to define private law constraints on the actions of sports governing bodies. Arguably, the doctrine of restraint of trade applies precisely because the rules of a sports governing body, and their application, involve the domestic private law administration of a trade by those involved in it.

1 The argument would be put on the basis of *Eastham v Newcastle United* [1964] Ch 413, and *Newport v FAW* at trial Blackburne J 12 April 1995, interim hearing reported at [1995] 2 All ER 87, and the analysis in *Stevenage* would be refuted on the basis set out in this para and the following paras. The decision in *Stevenage* has been criticised. See Stewart [1996] 4(3) SATLJ 110; see also Alderson at p 107 in the same publication and Stewart [1998] 6(3) SATLJ 41. See also Dawn Oliver [1997] PL 630. Stewart argues, amongst other things, that Carnwath J relied on the absence of any contract in order to adapt the doctrine, yet there was no contract in *Newport* and that did not lead to the doctrine being adapted by Jacob J or Blackburne J; that Carnwath J was wrong to characterise the Football League as a sports governing body because that role is fulfilled by the FA, and the Football League is simply a group of commercial football clubs organising a competition; that Carnwath J was wrong to conclude that the earlier cases did not take into account the quasi-public role of governing bodies; that the analysis in *Stevenage* was complicated by the fact that the club was technically applying for membership, which has always been treated more restrictively by the courts; and that arguably Carnwath J did not formally decide the issue.
2 *R (Mullins) v Appeal Board of the Jockey Club (Jockey Club as an interested party)* [2005] EWHC 2197 Admin, 17 October 2005 Stanley Burnton J, reiterating what had been decided in *R v Jockey Club, ex p Aga Khan* [1993] 1 WLR 909 and *R v Football Association, ex p Football League* [1993] 2 All ER 833. In *Aga Khan* at 932H to 933A, Hoffmann LJ's test arguably presumes the full application of private law remedies such as the restraint of trade doctrine.

10.22   Subsequent cases have not significantly clarified the position, in part because of the increasingly decisive role played by EU competition law-based arguments. In the litigation between Cardiff RFC and the Welsh Rugby Union, Cardiff challenged (amongst other things) the WRU's attempt to introduce a rule under which a club that wished to play in the WRU's competitions was obliged to agree to do so for a fixed period of time.[1] Ultimately the WRU and International Rugby Board successfully applied to have the action stayed on the basis that the issue of compliance with the EU competition rules was pending before the European Commission as a result of notification by the governing bodies (a procedure that no longer applies[2]), and there was consequently a risk of conflicting decisions. In that context, Eady J approached the restraint of trade issue as being so analogous to the EU competition law issue that it was not safe to stay only that part of the action that related to EU competition law.[3]

1 *Williams and Cardiff RFC v Pugh*, later known as *Williams and Cardiff RFC v WRU (IRB intervening)*, interim injunction hearings 23 July 1997 Popplewell J, 1 August 1997 CA; application for a stay hearings 17 March 1998 Buckley J, [1999] Eu LR 195.
2 Modernisation of the European Commission's procedures removed the previous structure under which an Art 101(3) exemption from the prohibition in Art 101(TFEU) was only available from the Commission upon a notification to it, and national courts were confined to assessing whether there was a breach of Art 101(1). Where proceedings were pending in both places, national court proceedings might have to be stayed. Now national courts can apply Art 101(3), and there is no notification.
3 [1999] Eu LR 195 at 200.

10.23   Lloyd J took a similar approach in *Hendry v World Professional Billiards and Snooker Association*.[1] Having assessed in detail the arguments based on the competition rules, he appears to have considered there to be little room for a different conclusion under the restraint of trade doctrine, and he declined to decide whether the *Stevenage* case had altered the test to be applied.[2] Lloyd J examined whether the WPBSA's rule A5 (requiring players to have its permission to play in any snooker tournament, except in specified circumstances) was reasonably justified. The vice was of course that it gave the WPBSA the ability to limit the growth of rival organisations. Lloyd J held that Rule A5 was contrary to the competition rules and that 'even absent the constraints of competition law as such, WPBSA cannot justify this restriction as being no more than is reasonably required for the protection of its own legitimate interests'.[3] Other WBPSA rules that had been challenged were upheld both as a matter of the competition rules and the restraint of trade doctrine.[4]

1 Lloyd J 5 October 2001 [2002] 1 ISLR SLR-1.
2 At paras 114 to 116, 128 and 138.
3 A phrase that is more similar to the test in *Maxim Nordenfelt* than the test advanced by Carnwath J in *Stevenage*. Lloyd J not only appears to have contemplated the burden being on the WPBSA, but also addressed the issue from the point of view that the question was whether the WPBSA's interests, as opposed to the public's, were engaged. This is possibly a reflection of the fact that the WPBSA arguably has less of the hallmarks of a quasi-public body pursuing public functions than do some other governing bodies.
4 See para **11.9**, n 6.

10.24   In *Wimbledon Football Club v Football League*,[1] The Football League argued that the appropriate test was whether the club could establish first, that The League's decision to refuse permission for it to move to Milton Keynes was a restraint, and secondly that it was not reasonable in the interests of the public, applying a high standard (in other words Carnwath J's test in *Stevenage*). The club contended that once a restraint was established, the onus was on The League to justify its restrictive decision as being proportionate and in the reasonable interests of the parties (in other words the traditional test). In the event the FA Arbitration Panel ruled that The League's decision had been procedurally flawed, and remitted the matter to The League to consider again.[2] The Panel went on to say however[3] that a decision to refuse the club permission to move was a restraint, and that The League had to satisfy the court that preventing the club moving was proportionate, in the sense of no more than was reasonably necessary to protect the interests of the efficient organisation, administration and promotion of football as a whole.[4] Because the matter had been remitted on procedural grounds, the Arbitration Panel did not consider whether The League's refusal was proportionate.

1 29 January 2002 FA Arbitration Panel. The club had also pleaded a competition law argument, but reserved its position in relation to it at the hearing before the FA Arbitration Panel.
2 The League subsequently decided in April 2002 to refer the question to an FA Commission for de novo consideration in its place. The FA Commission decided in May 2002 that the club should be allowed to move, because the damage to it as a result of not moving outweighed any perceived damage to the football pyramid, as advanced by The Football League as a reason for refusing permission.
3 Following Blackburne J in *Newport v FAW*, 12 April 1995.
4 In so doing, the Arbitration Panel proceeded on the basis that in any event the doctrine of proportionality now forms part of domestic administrative law (cf Lord Slynn in *R (Alconbury) v Secretary of State for the Environment* [2001] UKHL 23, [2001] 2 All ER 929), that the proportionality test is as described by Lord Steyn in *R v Secretary of State for the Home Department, ex p Daly* [2001] UKHL 26, [2001] 2 AC 532, and that developments in administrative law are to be carried over into the content of the grounds for review to which sports governing bodies are subject by virtue of the analysis of the Court of Appeal in (at that time) *Modahl* and *Wilander* (and now *Bradley v Jockey Club* [2004] EWHC 2164 (QB), [2007] L.L.R. 543 (High Court), [2005] EWCA Civ 1056, [2006] L.L.R. 1 (Court of Appeal)).

10.25   In *Bradley*,[1] the former jockey's case as to why the sanction imposed upon him was unlawful and disproportionate was based at least in part on restraint of trade. Richards J however side-stepped the questions that arose as a result, rather stating:[2]

'The submissions of counsel touched on the question whether *Nagle v Feilden* is itself a restraint of trade case (I note that the present claimant's case was pleaded on the basis of restraint of trade) or whether the restraint of trade doctrine provides a jurisprudentially distinct basis for supervision by the court in a non-contractual context. Of the further authorities on restraint of trade to which I was referred, the most interesting was the detailed exposition by Carnwath J at first instance in the *Stevenage Borough Football Club* case (unreported judgment of 23 July 1996). What he said was dealt with only briefly by the Court of Appeal on appeal in the same case (9 Admin LR 109, referred to by Latham LJ in the passage from *Modahl (No 2)* quoted above). For present purposes, however, I think it unnecessary to get caught up in the subtleties of Carnwath J's analysis. It is sufficient that even in the absence of contract the court has a settled jurisdiction to grant declarations and injunctions in respect of decisions of domestic tribunals that affect a person's right to work. That applies both to 'application' cases such as *Nagle v Feilden* itself and to 'expulsion' or 'forfeiture' cases in which a person is deprived of a status previously enjoyed, though in the latter category of case it is likely in practice that a contractual relationship will also have been established. Moreover no challenge is made in the present case to the Rules themselves, only to the Appeal Board's decision reached in the application of those Rules, so I do not need to consider whether it is for the Jockey Club to justify the Rules or for a challenger to show that the Rules are unreasonable (an issue on which Carnwath J's conclusions are of particular interest).'

Although Richards J then went on to define the courts' consequent role as supervisory, and to decide the case accordingly, he did not purport expressly to endorse Carnwath J's approach or to hold that there was no distinct basis for challenge in restraint of trade.

1 Cited above at footnote 4 to para **10.24**.
2 Para 35.

10.26   In *Mullins*,[1] the Jockey Club argued that absent a contract jurisdiction to intervene only arose if a restraint of trade could be established, arguably suggesting that the availability of the grounds for review based on the public law standard are one and the same as the application of the restraint of trade doctrine. Stanley Burnton J rejected that proposition, stating:[2]

'… the Jockey Club … submitted that the jurisdiction of the Court … is limited to cases of restraint of trade (or the claimant's 'right to work') and those where the tribunal has acted unfairly …

… My provisional view is that there is no jurisdictional (in the narrow sense of the word) boundary to the power of the Court to grant declaratory relief in this context: the jurisdiction of the Court under CPR Part 40.20 to grant declaratory relief is unrestricted. The restrictions on the power are discretionary. The discretion will be exercised having regard to the respect and caution appropriate when considering the decision of an impartial qualified tribunal whose knowledge and experience of the subject matter in question is likely to exceed those of the Court. But the power to grant declaratory relief will not necessarily be excluded because, for example, the decision under challenge does not involve payment of a financial penalty.'

1 *R (Mullins) v The Appeal Board of the Jockey Club* [2005] EWHC 2197 (Admin), [2006] L.L.R. 151.
2 *Mullins v Mcfarlane* [2006] EWHC 986 (QB), [2006] L.L.R. 437 at paras 37 to 39.

10.27   In *Dwain Chambers v British Olympic Association*,[1] Mackay J treated *Bradley* as a restraint of trade case and approached the athlete's restraint of trade and irrationality challenges together,[2] assessing the extent to which there was a significant restriction on the right to work[3] and the extent to which the byelaw was proportionate[4] in the sense that it fell within the range of actions reasonably open to the BOA in pursuit of its aims. On the first question he concluded that the athlete would face an uphill struggle at trial, since the Olympics were a quadrennial amateur event with no prize money and the athlete had very limited prospects of securing a medal (which might lead to indirect benefits).[5] On the second he asked:[6]

'…Does the byelaw, when subjected to the intensity of review described in *Bradley*, go further than is reasonable or necessary to achieve the legitimate aims of the BOA?'

He concluded[7] that there was no evidence to demonstrate that the byelaw was disproportionate to the needs pursued through it by the BOA.[8]

1 [2008] EWHC 2028 (QB).
2 Cf *Park Promotion Ltd (t/a Pontypool Rugby Football Club) v Welsh Rugby Union Ltd* [2012] EWHC 1919 (QB), 11 July 2012, in which the club did not run a restraint of trade case distinct from the challenge under *Bradley*. Sir Raymond Jack at para 45 referred to both *Bradley* and *Stevenage* for the delineation of the supervisory jurisdiction.
3 At para 41 and following.
4 At para 48 and following.
5 Mackay J declined to discard *Currie v Barton*, 26 March 1987 Scott J; CA (1988) Times, 12 February, and *Gasser v Stinson* 15 June 1988 Scott J, which set a high standard for when a sportsman was restrained in his trade or had his right to work affected. Mackay J was not prepared to regard any effect adverse to the athlete as being sufficient.
6 Para 48.
7 Para 54.
8 He also held that the competition law argument was insufficiently separately developed to warrant separate analysis, and that he doubted that *Meca- Medina v Commission* (519/04) [2006] European Court of Justice, 18 July 2006 C-519/04P [2006] ECR I-699, [2006] ISLR SLR-175, [2006] All ER (EC) 1057, imposed a significantly different test.

10.28 In *Handsworth FC v FA*,[1] the lower league club alleged amongst other things that the decision to relegate it when it failed to meet a deadline imposed for it to improve its facilities and then sought to ground share to avoid the problem, was in unreasonable restraint of trade. The tribunal held that as the club was not involved in professional sport, it was to be doubted that there was any restraint of trade in the first place, but even if there were then 'the burden lies on a person challenging as a restraint of trade the lawfulness of a sporting rule not only to prove it is unlawful, but also to persuade the tribunal that, in the tribunal's discretion, the rule should be avoided', following Carnwath J in *Stevenage*. The tribunal was not persuaded that any restraint was unreasonable, and was not persuaded that it should grant a remedy in the light of the point in time when the application was made and the effect on third party clubs.

1 *Handsworth FC v FA* (FA Rule K arbitration, 6 and 11 July 2012, Mark Warby QC).

10.29 In the 2012 Singaporean decision, *Pilkadaris v Asian Tour*,[1] the traditional restraint of trade doctrine was applied. In *Pilkadaris*, the actions of the Asian Tour to prevent golfers playing on it from also playing on the OneAsia Tour were found to be in unreasonable restraint of trade. In 2009, the Asian Tour took the view that the OneAsia Tour, which had initially organised new tournaments on dates that did not conflict with Asian Tour events, was seeking to 'poach' tournaments that had previously formed part of the Asian Tour. The Asian Tour therefore imposed a requirement (Reg 1.10) on participants in its tournaments, that if they wished to play in OneAsia tournaments that conflicted or competed with Asian Tour tournaments, they had to obtain a 'release' from the Asian Tour Tournament Players' Committee, and if they played without a release they would be fined and banned from Asian Tour tournaments. Grant of release was at the discretion of the TPC, applying a release policy. The claimants applied for and were refused releases, nevertheless played, were fined, appealed, lost, and were informed that if their fines were not paid they would be banned. Interim injunctive relief was granted. The claimants sought declarations that Reg 1.10 was in unreasonable restraint of trade, that the application of it to them was capricious, arbitrary and in bad faith, and that the fines were unlawful as operating *in terrorem* and as being an unenforceable penalty. The Asian Tour defended on the basis that the members of the tour came together to create it in their interests and agreed to its rules; the board was obliged to protect the interests of the membership; and Reg 1.10 was a necessary and measured reaction to the actions of the OneAsia Tour, which were inimical to the interests of the Asian Tour members. The court decided that the regulations formed part of a contract between the Tour and its members, and that the doctrine of restraint of trade applied to render unenforceable any terms in them that were unreasonably restrictive of trade. The court rejected the suggestion that the doctrine did not apply to the Asian Tour because it was not a sports regulatory body, but an association of players who collectivised to achieve common career benefits, akin to a partnership. The court held that Reg 1.10 restrained professional golfers in their trade because it restricted their ability to play golf as they chose, in circumstances where they were independent contractors, they were not employed by the Asian Tour, the Asian Tour did not pay or train them, they in fact paid the Asian Tour, and the Asian Tour had no obligation to provide tournaments although golfers required access to tournaments to progress. The court rejected the argument that Reg 1.10 fell outside the restraint of trade doctrine on the basis that it simply required players who wanted the benefit of Asian Tour membership to accept the burden of limited ability to participate in a rival competition the actions of which were inimical to the interests of the Asian Tour. The court held the restraint to be unreasonable (applying the *Nordenfelt* test) because it went further than was necessary to protect existing Asian Tour tournaments. The court rejected the arguments that the provision was reasonable because it was made to protect the Asian Tour and its members from the assault of OneAsia, and it was not an absolute prohibition. The court also rejected the argument that the same provision was to be found in other golf associations' rules, because in fact such provisions only prevented golfers playing in tournaments that were on the same dates and/or within a particular distance. Finally the court rejected the argument that it was in the public interest to have a strong and vibrant Asian Tour, justifying action to restrict OneAsia: the public interest lay in competition. The court did not decide the remaining issues.

1 *Pilkadaris v Asian Tour (Tournament Players Division) Pte Ltd* [2012] SGHC 236 (HC (Sing)), 27 November 2012. See also the earlier, injunction, decision in the same case [2010] SGHC 294 (HC (Sing)), addressed in Alan Chalmers, Nick Fitzpatrick and Ella Russell, 'Participation in rival competitions: restraint of trade' (2010) 8(11) World Sports Law Report 14–16.

10.30   In *Baker v British Board of Boxing Control*,[1] the High Court rejected as unarguable the suggestion that rules of the BBBC that prevented a member promoter from participating in the organisation of events in the UK under the auspices of bodies other than the BBBC were (inter alia) a restraint of trade. As the High Court held, such rules were 'inherent in the organisation of the sport'.

1 [2014] EWHC 2074 (QB).

C   DOES THE DOCTRINE REMAIN A DISTINCT BASIS FOR CHALLENGE?

10.31   It is evident from the above discussion that the courts' election to subject sports governing bodies to grounds for review based on the equivalent of the public law standard notwithstanding that they also remain private law bodies subject to private law principles, including the restraint of trade doctrine, raises significant questions as to how those private law principles should be applied. This is compounded by the confirmation in *Days Medical Aids*[1] that the courts are in effect precluded from reaching a different result on the application of the restraint of trade doctrine (characterised as domestic competition law) to the result that would flow from the application of the competition law rules. Furthermore, the competition law rules themselves, or at least the antitrust rules, are designed primarily for application to the action of private law bodies.

1 *Days Medical Aids* [2004] EWHC 44 (Comm) Langley J, 29 January 2004, [2004] 1 All ER (Comm) 991. The reason is that domestic competition law must not conflict with EU competition law. In any event, as already identified, it is unlikely that the application of the competition law rules would produce a result different to that that would be produced by the application of the restraint of trade doctrine, as for example the *Hendry* decision demonstrates.

10.32 As things stand, it remains the case that there is a basis in the authorities for both the argument that restraint of trade should continue to be applied as a distinct doctrine, and the argument that it and the grounds for review based on the public law standard are in fact one and the same mechanism. In the view of the authors, the preferable conclusion is that the grounds for review based on the public law standard should not be regarded as founded in restraint of trade alone, and that the application of the restraint of trade doctrine should if anything mirror the application of the competition law rules rather than the application of those grounds for review. However, at least in the medium term, there may well remain some value for challengers in mounting their case in restraint of trade (assuming that there has been an effect on trade) and arguing that the doctrine should be applied in its conventional form. The courts remain more used to restraint of trade providing a level of review that is relatively intrusive in comparison for example to the irrationality ground for review. Further, restraint of trade is arguably better suited to address restrictions on particular individuals than competition law, which looks for a restrictive effect on competition itself.

CHAPTER 11

EU and domestic competition law

A   THE COMPETITION LAW RULES IN BRIEF 11.2
B   APPLICATION OF THE RULES BY THE ENGLISH
    COURTS IN THE CONTEXT OF SPORT 11.6

11.1   The EU competition rules and their domestic equivalent are an
important element of the legal control of the sports sector, particularly in the
context of challenges to the rules and decisions of sports governing bodies.[1] Much
of the application of the competition rules in the sports sector is conducted by
the regulatory authorities, the European Commission Competition Directorate and
the UK Competition and Markets Authority, which can act on a complaint or of their
own motion. On occasion the issue has arisen before the European Court of Justice.
Arguments based on the competition rules can however be made in the English
courts and in arbitral proceedings,[2] and increasingly parties challenging the actions
of sports governing bodies there have sought to base their attack (or defence), at least
in part, on competition law grounds. Decided English cases remain rare and have not
involved substantive success on the point[3] until in 2012 a club persuaded an arbitral
tribunal to overturn a governing body's decision to refuse promotion on the basis of
the competition law rules.[4] This chapter simply draws the reader's attention to the
availability of the argument in English proceedings, briefly mentions the substantive
rules, explains the extent to which, and the manner in which, they can be applied by
the English courts and arbitral tribunals, and then outlines the limited application of
the rules that there has been in the English courts and arbitral tribunals in the sports
sector.

1 Reference should be made to competition law texts, such as Bellamy and Child, *European Union Law
  of Competition* (7th edn, Oxford University Press, 2013).
2 The leading example of an English arbitral tribunal applying the competition law rules is now *London
  Welsh v Rugby Football Union* see note 4 below. On the international plane, the leading example is
  the CAS decision in *AEK Athens and Slavia Prague v UEFA* CAS arbitration 98/200 interim decision
  17 July 1998, final decision 20 August 1999, reported in *Digest of CAS Awards II 1998–2000*, p 36 and
  in [2001] 1 ISLR 122 (club failed in its challenge to the application to it of UEFA's Champions League
  rule prohibiting participation of clubs in common ownership with another participant).
3 For example *Hendry v World Professional Billiards and Snooker Association*, Lloyd J 5 October 2001
  [2002] 1 ISLR SLR-1, in which the rule found to be in breach had already been withdrawn by the
  governing body; *Adidas v Draper and others [representing the Grand Slams] and the International
  Tennis Federation* [2006] EWHC 1318 (ChD, Sir Andrew Morritt C, 7 June 2006) [2006] All ER
  (D) 30, in which it was held arguable at the interim stage that the governing bodies had breached
  competition law but the case was settled before a substantive hearing; *Attheraces v BHB* [2005] EWHC
  1553 Ch D (15 July 2005 Etherton J) [2005] All ER (D) 210; [2005] EWHC 3015 Ch D (21 December
  2005 Etherton J), [2005] All ER (D) 336; rvrsd on appeal, [2007] EWCA Civ 38 (2 February 2007,
  Mummery, Sedley and Lloyd LJJ), [2007] All ER (D) 26, in which the first instance decision that the
  governing body had abused its dominant position was overturned on appeal.
4 *London Welsh v Rugby Football Union, Newcastle Falcons intervening* (RFU Arbitration 29 June 2012,
  James Dingemans QC, Ian Mill QC and Tim Ward QC).

A   THE COMPETITION LAW RULES IN BRIEF

(a)   Article 101/the Chapter I prohibition

11.2   English courts and arbitral tribunals have jurisdiction to decide whether a sports governing body is in breach of Art 101 TFEU,[1] or its domestic equivalent under the Competition Act 1998 ('the Chapter I prohibition'). The EU and domestic provisions mirror one another. Article 101 and Chapter I prohibit agreements between undertakings, or decisions of associations of undertakings, that have the object or effect of appreciably restricting competition on the relevant market and affecting trade between Member States or within the UK. For these purposes, the rules of a sports governing body are an agreement, and its decisions are decisions of an association of undertakings. Side contracts with clubs and the normal commercial contracts entered into by governing bodies are caught as agreements between undertakings.[2] If a rule or decision or agreement appreciably restricts competition and affects trade and is therefore contrary to the prohibition in Art 101(1) or the Chapter I prohibition, it is void unless it can be justified under Art 101(3), or s 9. If it cannot be justified, then (subject to severance) it cannot be relied upon and there is a right to a declaration, an injunction and damages. The argument therefore operates both as a cause of action to challenge sports governing bodies' actions, and as a defence to the application of a particular rule.

1   Formerly Art 81, and before that Art 85. For the application of the EU competition rules by the English courts, see Bellamy and Child, *European Union Law of Competition* (7th edn, Oxford University Press, 2013), Ch 10.
2   Prior to the European Court of Justice decision *Meca-Medina v Commission*, Court of First Instance 30 September 2004 (T-313/02) [2004] ECR II-3291 [2004] 3 CMLR 1314 [2004] All ER (D) 184; European Court of Justice, 18 July 2006 (C-519/04P) [2006] ECR I-6991; [2006] ISLR SLR-175; [2006] All ER (EC) 1057, there was said to be a 'sporting exception' to the competition law rules, by which they did not apply to sports governing bodies' arrangements that related purely to how the sport was played, as opposed to how it was exploited economically. Since that decision there is no automatic exception, and the effect of arrangements must always be assessed against the competition law rules. See paras **6.10** and **6.11**.

(b)   Article 102/the Chapter II prohibition

11.3   English courts and arbitral tribunals have the power to decide whether a sports governing body is in breach of Art 102 TFEU or its domestic equivalent under the Competition Act 1998 ('the Chapter II prohibition').[1] Article 102 and Chapter II prohibit the abuse of a dominant position affecting trade between Member States or within the UK. Whether a sports governing body holds a dominant position depends on the definition of the relevant market in the particular context, and the body's position on it. Where the governing body is acting to regulate the particular sport, and is controlling access to it for players and clubs, it is likely to be held to be in a dominant position, as it has a de facto monopoly on the market for access to competition in the particular sport. If on the other hand the governing body is acting on a market where a number of sports compete with one another, then it may well not be in a dominant position. Where a governing body is in a dominant position, it must take care to ensure that it does not abuse that position by acting on the relevant market in such a way as to restrict competition without justification.[2] The English courts and arbitral tribunals may assess whether there has been an abuse, or rather whether the conduct impugned is justified.

1 Article 102 was formerly Art 82 and before that 86.
2 For example in *Motosykletistiki Omospondia Ellados NPID (MOTOE) v Greece* (C-49/07) [2008] ECR I-4863 (ECJ), [2009] All ER (EC) 150, [2008] 5 CMLR 11; [2008] CEC 1068, it was held that a state rule was unlawful because it gave a sports governing body the sole and unfettered right to authorise motorcycling events, although the body organised and commercially exploited such events itself, which could lead to it denying other operators access to the market contrary to Art 102.

(c)   When the issue is likely to arise

11.4   There are many factual circumstances when a competition law argument may arise.[1] Indeed, in many contexts, the most important controlling factor on a sports governing body's activities is the competition rules. This is particularly the case:

(a)   where a sports governing body enters into commercial arrangements to exploit economically the rights in the sport, and/or where some providers are chosen as commercial partners in preference to others;[2]

(b)   where a sports governing body adopts and enforces rules aimed at preserving its predominant position as the regulator of the sport and principal organiser of tournaments, competitions and events;[3]

(c)   where a sports governing body adopts and enforces rules which set restrictions on the way that participants organise themselves and take part in the sport;[4] and

(d)   where a sports governing body adopts and enforces entry or qualification criteria, for example on a club's ability to secure promotion.[5]

Attempts have been made to persuade the English courts to extend the competition rules to other contexts, such as the validity of the anti-doping rules.[6] Competition law issues may of course also arise in other litigation in the sports context but not involving the governing body.[7]

1 The Commission's approach to the application of the competition law rules in the sporting context is the subject of a lengthy analysis in its Staff Working Document SEC (2007) 935 accompanying the 2007 White Paper on Sport COM(2007) 391 Final.
2 For example in relation to the distribution and sale of tickets for major sports events, including the sale of tickets packaged with other products.
3 Sports governing bodies regularly rely on the proposition that in order to make an association work the members of the association can legitimately be prevented from belonging to other competing associations (citing *Gøttrup Klim* [1994] ECR I-5641, there an agricultural co-operative), but the Commission is astute to prevent rules and practices which might prevent rival competitions growing up. Cf the application of restraint of trade in this context: see para **10.30**.
4 For example, the imposition of transfer rules.
5 See for example in the English courts *Stevenage Borough Football Club v Football League Ltd* (see para **13.17**), and before an English arbitral tribunal *London Welsh v Rugby Football Union, Newcastle Falcons intervening* (RFU Arbitration 29 June 2012, James Dingemans QC, Ian Mill QC and Tim Ward QC).
6 See for example *Meca-Medina v Commission*, Court of First Instance 30 September 2004 (T-313/02) [2004] ECR II-3291 [2004] 3 CMLR 1314 [2004] All ER (D) 184; European Court of Justice, 18 July 2006 (C-519/04P) [2006] ECR I-6991; [2006] ISLR SLR-175; [2006] All ER (EC) 1057.
7 Notably in the context of replica shirts, see *JJB Sports Plc v Office of Fair Trading, All Sports Limited v Office of Fair Trading* [2004] CAT 17, 1 October 2004; Competition Appeals Tribunal [2004] All ER (D) 23; *Umbro v OFT, Manchester Utd v OFT, JJB Sports v OFT, All Sports v OFT* [2005] CAT 22; 19 May 2005, CAT (Sir Christopher Bellamy QC (President), B D Colgate, Richard Prosser) [2005] All ER (D) 323; *Argos, Littlewoods and JJB Sports v OFT* [2006] EWCA Civ 1318 19 Oct 06 [2006] All ER (D) 236.

(d) State aid

11.5 It is possible that unlawful state aid may be granted in the sports sector. Where state aid in the form of an intervention by the State or through State resources confers an economic advantage on selected recipients only, in a context where it distorts or threatens to distort competition in the market properly defined, and the advantage has a potential or actual effect on trade between Member States, that aid must be notified (so long as it is new aid or an alteration to existing aid). If it is not notified, then it cannot be implemented and the English courts will order its repayment by the recipient. If it is notified, it can be cleared on a number of grounds, but only by the Commission. Although the situations where the issue has arisen in the sports context are so far few and narrow, it is possible that the issue could arise in other situations, in particular where there is tax-advantageous treatment of or other assistance to sports clubs or governing bodies, lottery funding or the purchase of sports rights by publicly funded broadcasters such as the BBC. It is also possible (although probably unlikely) that grants from certain sports governing bodies themselves could be regarded as state aid. It would be a substantial development if the actions of sports governing bodies could be challenged on state aid grounds.

B APPLICATION OF THE RULES BY THE ENGLISH COURTS IN THE CONTEXT OF SPORT

11.6 Consideration by the English courts and arbitral bodies of competition law principles in the context of a challenge to the actions of a sports governing body has often occurred, in particular prior to the coming into force of the Competition Act 1998, at an interim stage and has not been detailed. In *Stevenage Borough Football Club v Football League*,[1] the club advanced a competition law argument in addition to its restraint of trade argument. Because the action pre-dated the Competition Act 1998, that argument had to be based on the EU rules. Carnwath J dealt with it in short order, stating that it was not established that there could be any effect on trade between Member States. In *Wilander v Tobin*,[2] Lightman J and the Court of Appeal had decided that the claimant tennis players did not have an arguable case that the ITF's anti-doping rules were in unreasonable restraint of trade and had refused to grant an interlocutory injunction. The plaintiffs then sought to amend to plead that the rules were contrary to the EU free movement and competition rules. Lightman J allowed the amendments in relation to free movement but refused permission to amend to add the case under the competition rules, ostensibly because the case was inadequately particularised, but also because he was not convinced that there was any basis for contending that the anti-doping rules restricted competition. The Court of Appeal did not allow either amendment. In *Williams and Cardiff RFC v WRU*,[3] the club challenged a wide range of actions, including a requirement that a club that wished to play in the WRU's competitions was obliged to agree to do so for ten years. Popplewell J held that it was arguable that this requirement was contrary to the competition rules, granted an injunction limited to the current season prohibiting the WRU from expelling the club for failing to enter into the ten-year commitment, and ordered a speedy trial. Before the case could be determined, it was stayed to avoid the risk of inconsistent decisions that arose when the IRB and the WRU notified the rules in question to the Commission. In *Mohammed v FA and FIFA*,[4] a claim that the introduction of the player-agent licensing system was an interference with existing contractual relations and in breach of the competition rules was the subject of an application for summary judgment by the governing bodies, which succeeded in part, but the case did not go further. In *BHB Enterprises v Victor Chandler*,[5] a competition law claim was struck out. In *Adidas*,[6] the clothing manufacturer obtained an interim injunction on competition law grounds restraining the defendants from applying their decision that the Adidas '3-Stripes' constituted manufacturer's identification that fell to be treated, for the purposes of the sport's limitations in its dress code on the size of such identification, in the same way as that of other manufacturers. Morritt C held that it was arguable that the governing bodies had abused a dominant position by applying a discriminatory approach.

1   24 January 1996 Scott V-C.
2   (1996) Times, 1 August; *affd* 9 Admin LR 109, CA. See also *Wimbledon v Football League*, where the governing body refused the club's application to establish a home ground in Milton Keynes. A competition law argument was available and was pleaded, but was reserved at the hearing before the Football Association Arbitration Panel.
3   *Williams and Cardiff RFC v Pugh*, 23 July 1997 Popplewell J, 1 August 1997, CA; subsequently known as *Williams and Cardiff RFC v WRU (IRB intervening)*, 17 March 1998 Buckley J, [1999] Eu LR 195.
4   *Mohammed v Rougier (and 2 others) and FA and FIFA*, [2002] EWHC 287 QB, 21 February 2002 Field J (dispute between agents also involving the validity of the introduction of the licensing regime itself on the basis that it was an interference with existing contractual relations and in breach of competition law).
5   *BHB Enterprises v Victor Chandler* [2005] EWHC 1074 (Ch) [2005] All ER (D) 445, [2005] UKCLR 787, [2005] ECC 40, [2005] Eu LR 924, 27 May 2005.
6   *Adidas v Draper and others [representing the Grand Slams] and the International Tennis Federation* [2006] EWHC 1318 (ChD, Sir Andrew Morritt C, 7 June 2006) [2006] All ER (D) 30.

11.7   In other cases, the arguments were developed, but the actions did not get to trial. In *Rugby Football Union v Westminster Hospitality and Events Ltd*,[1] for example, the RFU obtained undertakings from the reseller that it would cease to sell corporate hospitality packages including tickets to RFU matches pending trial. Westminster was owned and backed by the major US ticket re-seller RazorGator, and prepared to defend the action on the basis that restrictions on the black or 'secondary' market in the form of a ban on resale, and the RFU's arrangements for official providers, were contrary to competition law. However, RazorGator withdrew funding from Westminster before trial, and the company went into liquidation without the issue being resolved. In *R (Tottenham Hotspur and Leyton Orient) v Newham*,[2] a state aid challenge was made by the clubs to the council's funding of West Ham's successful bid for the Olympic stadium, but the acceptance of that bid was withdrawn when the hearing commenced but before decision, bringing the proceedings to an end. In *Leyton Orient v FA Premier League*,[3] a competition law case against the Premier League was withdrawn.

1   There was no reported judgment.
2   *R (on the application of Tottenham Hotspur FC and Leyton Orient FC) v Newham LBC, interested parties OPLC and Mayor of London*.
3   *Leyton Orient v FA Premier League* (FA Rule K arbitration, pending, in relation to the grant of permission by the Premier League to West Ham to move to the Olympic Stadium, in which a competition law case against the Premier League was withdrawn as a result of the body's markedly different tactic to that of the RFU, of denying every element of the competition law analysis and so raising costs. A league possibly stands in different position to a governing body such as the RFU or FA. The arbitration was

overtaken by events, when West Ham's bid together with Newham was the subject of judicial review proceedings for breach of the state aid rules, and the body inviting bids decided to start the process again. West Ham proved successful again).

11.8   In the first case where a competition law challenge was substantively considered, *Re an Agreement between the FA Premier League*,[1] the then Restrictive Practices Court considered at length the legality of the Premier League's broadcasting arrangements with BSkyB and the BBC under the UK's predecessor competition legislation, the Restrictive Trade Practices Act 1976. Although that Act was notoriously difficult to apply and its mechanistic test was very different from the current competition rules, the issues before the Restrictive Practices Court extended to basic competition law concepts, including whether the arrangements restricted competition and whether they were justified in the public interest. The court's conclusions in that context consequently retain considerable relevance. In summary, the court held that the Premier League's rule that its permission was required for any broadcast (which facilitated collective selling) and the exclusivity granted to the broadcasters each restricted competition between broadcasters on the market for football broadcasting rights, but that those restrictions were justified in the public interest. The court did however rule illegal the incumbent broadcaster's right to match the best offer received from elsewhere in the context of negotiation of the next contract.

1 *Re an Agreement between the FA Premier League* [2000] EMLR 78, [1999] UKCLR 258 (Restrictive Practices Court July 1999).

11.9   In *Hendry v World Professional Billiards and Snooker Association Ltd*,[1] Lloyd J for the first time in a trial before an English court applied the current competition rules to the rules and practices of a sports governing body, finding one rule illegal. Although the EU rules and the common law doctrine of restraint of trade were also in issue, Lloyd J concentrated on the Chapter I prohibition and the Chapter II prohibition under the Competition Act 1998. He appears to have approached both prohibitions on the basis that he could take into account the justification offered for any restrictions in the rules or practices of the sports governing body.[2] He carried out a detailed assessment of what the relevant market was, and decided that it was the market for the supply of services between snooker players and the organisers of snooker tournaments.[3] The WPBSA was such an organiser, although it was also a governing body; it was irrelevant that the money made by the WPBSA was reinvested in the sport. The WPBSA was dominant on the market: even though others could come in to rival it, they could not do so in the short or even medium term.[4] The WPBSA had abused that dominant position by the adoption of rule A5, which required the players (all of whom were members of the WPBSA) to obtain its permission to play in snooker matches, with some specific exceptions. The rule effectively allowed the WPBSA to restrict the ability of any rival organisation to gain a foothold, and it could not be justified on the basis that it was necessary in order to support the broadcasting and sponsorship revenue of the WPBSA for reinvestment in the sport, or to ensure that events were properly organised.[5] The rule was also held contrary to the Chapter I prohibition, to Arts 101 and 102, and to the common law doctrine of restraint of trade. Other WPBSA rules and practices were held valid.[6]

1 Lloyd J 5 October 2001 [2002] 1 ISLR SLR-1.
2 See [2002] 1 ISLR SLR-1, para 27 of the judgment of Lloyd J.
3 See [2002] 1 ISLR SLR-1, para 89.
4 See [2002] 1 ISLR SLR-1, paras 98.
5 See [2002] 1 ISLR SLR-1, para 110.

6 Rule P limiting the number of logos that could be worn by a player and requiring the WPBSA's approval was restrictive of competition but was justified because of broadcasting restrictions: para 128. Rule S requiring players to assist in the promotion of tournaments was not restrictive of competition and was not a restraint of trade: para 138. The criticism advanced of the WPBSA's ranking system, namely that it did not take into account results in competitions organised by other promoters (and thereby made it harder for them to compete) was held not to be established on the facts: para 141. The WPBSA's imposition of a deadline for the submission of entry forms for its competitions was also criticised as making it harder for rival organisers to compete. Lloyd J held that the imposition of the deadline was reasonable and justified and was not an abuse: para 154.

11.10   In *Racecourse Association v OFT; BHB v OFT*,[1] it was held that the collective sale of media rights by 49 of 59 British racecourses to a joint venture company did not infringe the Competition Act 1998, because the central negotiation in which the race courses had engaged was necessary for the achievement both by them and by the joint venture company of a legitimate commercial objective of creating a novel product that the joint venture company had proposed to exploit for the benefit of itself, punters, racecourses and racing generally.

1 [2005] CAT 29; CAT (Rimer J, Andrew Bain, Sheila Hewitt) [2005] All ER (D) 10, 2 August 2005.

11.11   In *Attheraces v BHB*[1] it was held at first instance that the defendant sports governing body had abused its market dominance by threatening to terminate the supply of pre-race data to the claimant company, which was an existing customer of the defendant, and without which supply the claimant would be eliminated from the market. In addition it was held at first instance that the prices specified by the defendant were excessive and unfair and amounted to an abuse of its dominant position. The Court of Appeal overturned Etherton J's decision that the BHB abused its dominant position by overcharging for race data. The judge had failed to apply the correct test when determining the issue of alleged excessive and unfair pricing of certain data, because he had applied the test of the cost to the supplier plus a reasonable return, whereas, in determining the economic value of the data, account should also have been taken of their value to the purchaser and how much the purchaser could make out of them as a source of income.

1 [2005] EWHC 1553 Ch D (15 July 2005 Etherton J) [2005] All ER (D) 210; [2005] EWHC 3015 Ch D (21 December 2005 Etherton J), [2005] All ER (D) 336; rvrsd on appeal, [2007] EWCA Civ 38 (2 February 2007, Mummery, Sedley and Lloyd LJJ), [2007] All ER (D) 26 Lloyd J 5 October 2001 [2002] 1 ISLR SLR-1.

11.12   In *British Sky Broadcasting Limited,* Ofcom's decision that Sky had to wholesale its core premium sports channels was overturned by the Competition Appeal Tribunal.[1] The CAT's decision was itself partially overturned by the Court of Appeal.[2] The matter is currently proceeding before the CAT on a remittal by the Court of Appeal.

1 *British Sky Broadcasting Limited, Virgin Media, The Football Association Premier League Limited, British Telecommunications Plc v Office of Communications* Competition Appeal Tribunal 8 August 2012 [2012] CAT 20 (non confidential summary only).
2 *British Sky Broadcasting Ltd v Office of Communications* 17 February 2014 [2014] EWCA Civ 133, [2014] 4 All ER 673, [2014] 2 All ER (Comm) 973, [2014] Bus LR 713.

11.13   The ability of sports rights holders effectively to prevent infringement of exclusive broadcast licences based on national territories was challenged, amongst other things on competition law grounds, in the *Murphy v Media Protection Services* and *FAPL v QC Leisure* litigation involving the use of foreign decoder cards to watch in England Premier League matches broadcast abroad. The Court of Justice held that national legislation making it illegal to import, sell or use foreign decoder cards infringed the freedom to provide services protected in Art 56 TFEU without justification and that prohibition in an exclusive licence agreement on the licensee supplying decoder cards for use outside their territory restricted cross-border competition contrary to Art 101 TFEU.[1] The Court of Justice took the view that people might well want to watch the television broadcasts of one country, in another country, and should be able to do so by taking a decoder card across borders. It held on the questions put to it: (a) that a decoder card was not an illicit device under Directive 98/84 just because it was used outside its licensed area; (b) Art 56 precluded Member State legislation making it illegal to import, sell or use a foreign decoder card, because that restriction on the freedom to provide services was not justified in the public interest: there was no need to protect the rights holders' territorial exclusivity premium which was unreasonably high, there was no copyright in the match itself to protect (although there might be in the surrounding programming); and it would have been possible to use contractual obligations to prevent matches being shown on television during the blackout period when they were actually being played; (c) the obligation in exclusive licence agreements on a broadcaster in one country not to supply decoder cards for use outside the country restricted cross-border competition contrary to Art 101 TFEU; (d) the internal workings of the decoder did not involve reproduction requiring the authorisation of the copyright holder; but (e) showing a programme in a pub was a 'communication to the public' which did require the authorisation of the copyright owner. The preliminary rulings were then implemented by the domestic courts.[2]

1 *Murphy v Media Protection Services Ltd* (C-429/08) and *Football Association Premier League Ltd v QC Leisure* (C-403/08) 04 October 2011 [2012] All ER (EC) 629, [2012] 1 CMLR 29, [2012] CEC 242, [2012] ECDR 8, [2012] FSR 1, [2012] Bus LR 1321, (2011) 108(40) LSG 22, (2011) 161 NLJ 1415; (2011) Times, 23 November; Advocate General's Opinion, 3 February 2011, [2011] ECDR 11; see also 16 December 2009 [2010] Eu LR 391.
2 The upshot of the preliminary rulings was that in *Murphy v Media Protection Services Ltd* [2012] EWHC 466 (Admin), [2012] 3 CMLR 2, [2012] ECC 16, 24 February 2012, the Divisional Court allowed the publican's appeal by case stated, and quashed her convictions under the Copyright, Designs and Patents Act 1988 for using a foreign decoder card to screen football matches in her public house. She was also awarded a substantial proportion of her costs on the civil basis [2012] EWHC 529 (Admin), [2012] 3 CMLR 3, [2012] FSR 13, 8 March 2012. In contrast in *Football Association Premier League Ltd v QC Leisure* [2012] EWHC 108 (Ch), [2012] 2 CMLR 16, [2012] FSR 12, the Chancery Division held that publicans who used a foreign decoder card still infringed copyright in the broadcast of a match (although not the match itself). This judgment was upheld in the Court of Appeal: *Football Association Premier League Ltd v QC Leisure* 20 December 2012 [2012] EWCA Civ 1708, [2013] Bus LR 866, [2012] Info. TLR 397, [2013] FSR 20.

11.14   In *London Welsh v Rugby Football Union*,[1] the club challenged on EU and UK competition law grounds the RFU's decision to refuse it promotion to the Premiership on the grounds that it did not have 'primacy of tenure' at its ground. Newcastle Falcons stood to stay up if the decision was lawful, and was given narrow permission to intervene. The RFU made wide-ranging concessions,[2] and defended solely on the basis that under the test in *Meca Medina*, it had pursued legitimate sporting aims and had not stepped outside the range of decisions reasonably open to it in so doing, in adopting and applying rules under which there could only be three clubs at any time with an exception to the primacy of tenure requirement, and any club being promoted had to satisfy the requirement, unless the club being relegated did not.[3] The RFU maintained that the primacy of tenure rule was necessary in order to provide a dependable calendar, which was required by the broadcasters whose fees were essential to the development of the sport, and that the current exceptions were an appropriate balance between that requirement and the difficulties faced by some clubs in securing primacy of tenure. The club contended that the aims pursued were in fact only commercial ones not inherent in the sport, and that therefore the margin of appreciation to be afforded to the RFU was considerably less, and that in any event the rule and decision went much further than was necessary to protect those aims.[4] The tribunal decided that the rules and their application were hybrids, but that they had a sufficient sporting aim to engage the wide margin of appreciation.[5] However, on the evidence the rules and their application went further than was necessary, whatever test was applied, because it had already been evaluated between Premiership clubs that there could be five clubs without primacy of tenure[6] without too much harm to the calendar. Contrary to Newcastle's submission, the answer to the unlawfulness of the three-club exception was not to sever that exception, but to rule that the entire primacy of tenure requirement as currently constituted was unlawful,[7] in effect removing the obligation on any and all clubs in the Premiership to comply with it. Lastly, the club could not be deprived of relief on the basis of delay or effect on third parties because under EU and UK competition law an anti-competitive rule is automatically void, and the tribunal was left with no discretion as to relief.[8]

1 *London Welsh v Rugby Football Union, Newcastle Falcons intervening* (RFU Arbitration Decision 29 June 2012, James Dingemans QC, Ian Mill QC and Tim Ward QC).
2 In order to achieve a resolution of the dispute in the short time available. Paras 39, 46.
3 Paras 41–43, 45.
4 Para 44.
5 Paras 46, 47.
6 Paras 70–74.
7 Para 82.
8 Paras 92–95.

11.15 In January 2015, competition law provided the foundation for the Higher Regional Court of Munich to bring into question the system of arbitration of doping cases before the Court of Arbitration for Sport, or CAS, in the *Pechstein* case.[1] The claimant had been found, in 2009, to have doped. The ISU banned her from all competitions for two years. The claimant unsuccessfully appealed the ban to the CAS, based on an arbitration agreement included in her licence with the national and international federations. She started an action for damages before the German Courts. The Higher Regional Court of Munich held that the arbitration agreement was void pursuant to German competition law – which formed a public policy basis for refusing to recognise the award – since the claimant had been forced into the arbitration agreement in circumstances in which the CAS procedures, in particular for arbitrators, incorporated a tendency for bias towards the governing bodies. Given the possibility for the same argument to be advanced under Article 102 TFEU, the case is being closely watched and is due to be heard by the Bundesgerichtshof in March 2016.

1 *Pechstein v International Skating Union*, Oberlandesgericht München, judgment dated 15 January 2015.

CHAPTER 12

The EU free movement rules

12.1   The EU free movement rules are also of importance for the legal control of the actions of sports governing bodies. There have been a number of further cases in the European Court of Justice in relation to the application of the rules in the sports sector, since the *Bosman* case itself. Other aspects of EU law apart from competition law and the free movement rules may of course form a basis for litigation in some sports contexts. There has been considerable litigation in relation to the listing by governments of sports events under Directive 89/552 with the result that the holders of the live rights in the events have to make them available to free to air broadcasters,[1] and in relation to whether there is a database right under Directive 96/9 in sports governing bodies' schedules of matches or races.[2]

1 *FIFA v European Commission* (T-385/07) 17 February 2011 (GC) (Belgian listing); *FIFA v European Commission* (T-68/08) 17 February 2011 (GC) (UK listing); *UEFA v European Commission* (T-55/08) 17 February 2011 (GC) (UK listing). An appeal (Cases C-201/11 P, C-204/11 P and C-205/11 P) was heard before the General Court in September 2012, and the football bodies' appeal was rejected by the General Court in July 2013: Cases C-201/11 P, C-204/11 P and C-205/11 P *UEFA, FIFA v European Commission*.

2 *Football Dataco Ltd v Yahoo! UK Ltd* (C-604/10) [2012] 2 CMLR 24, [2012] ECDR 10, 1 March 2012, Advocate General's Opinion, 15 December 2011 [2012] ECDR 7.

A   THE FREE MOVEMENT RULES IN BRIEF

12.2   The EU free movement rules contained in Arts 45, 49 and 56 TFEU[1] prohibit respectively, restrictions on the ability of workers to move from one Member State to another, on the ability of persons to establish a business in another Member State, and on the ability of persons from one Member State to provide services in another. While direct discrimination on grounds of nationality is incapable of justification, less stark restrictions may be lawful if they pursue a legitimate aim proportionately. The EU free movement rules apply in the context of sport,[2] but only to the extent that a commercial activity is affected. In the light of *Meca-Medina*,[3] however, there is no 'sporting exception' to the free movement rules. Nominally the rules are addressed to Member States, but they extend to public authorities, and sports governing bodies have been held to be included. Most sporting bodies are sufficiently public for these purposes to be governed by the rules, although it is possible that many may not be. The dividing line may be whether the sport actually involves any commercial activity at all. If it is such a marginal interest sport that there is no real economic activity associated with it, it may not be caught by the rules. The protection of the free movement principles may extend beyond nationals of other Member States to workers from third countries already within the EU, where those countries have treaty arrangements with the EU requiring equal treatment of workers.[4]

1 Formerly respectively Arts 39 (and before that 48), 43 (and before that 52) and 49 (and before that 59).
2 The principal European Court of Justice decisions on the application of the free movement rules in the context of sport are *Walrave and Koch v Association Union Cycliste Internationale* [1974] ECR 1405 (restriction based on nationality permissible in relation to national team); *Donà v Mantero* [1976] ECR 1333 (restrictions based on nationality otherwise not permissible); *Union Royal Belge des Sociétés de Football Association v Bosman* [1995] ECR I-4921 (nationality quota and transfer restrictions following end of contract impermissible); *Deliège v Ligue Francophone de Judo* [2000] ECR I-2549 (restriction on number of contestants from each country permissible); *Lehtonen v Fédération Royale Belge des Sociétés de Basketball* [2000] ECR I–2681 (player transfer deadlines permissible so long as not discriminatory); *Bacardi France SAS v TF1* [2004] ECR I-6613 and *Commission v France* [2004] ECR I-6569 (prohibition on alcohol advertising justified) and *Olympique Lyonnais SASP v Olivier Bernard and Newcastle United FC* (C-325/08) European Court of Justice [2010] All ER (EC) 615; [2010] 3 CMLR 14; [2011] CEC 60.
3 *Meca-Medina v Commission* Court of First Instance, 30 September 2004 (T-313/02) [2004] ECR II-3291, [2004] 3 CMLR 1314, [2004] All ER (D) 184; European Court of Justice, 18 July 2006 (C-519/04P) [2006] ECR I-6991, [2006] ISLR SLR-175, [2006] All ER (EC) 1057. See paras **6.10– 6.11**. *Meca-Medina* was an unsuccessful challenge on both completion and free movement grounds, to the legality of the anti-doping rules.
4 The *Bosman* decision that quotas based on nationality (or 'foreign player' rules) are unlawful if they exclude players from other Member States was extended in *Kolpak* and cases following it to cover players from outside the EU if they come from states that have a treaty arrangement with the EU requiring equal treatment of workers: *Deutscher Handballbund v Kolpak* [2003] ECR I-4135; *Simuntekov* [2005] ECR I-2579; *Real Sociedad de Fútbol SAD and Nihat Kahveci v Consejo Superior de Deportes and Real Federación Española de Fútbol* (C-152/08), order of 25 July 2008.

12.3   The free movement rules can be relied upon before the English courts and arbitral tribunals. Indeed the lack of any procedural regulation equivalent to that which applies to the competition rules means that the European Commission is less able itself to tackle breaches of the free movement rules by individual governing bodies, still less by international associations. It would have to bring proceedings against the relevant Member State.

12.4   As in the context of the competition rules, a restriction on the free movement of players, whether as employees or in order to provide services, may be justified and therefore permissible if it pursues a legitimate aim[1] and is proportionate in the sense that it goes no further than is necessary to achieve that aim. Again therefore, the exercise is similar to that carried out under the restraint of trade doctrine and under the competition rules. Indeed the Advocate General in *Bosman*[2] expressed the view that the entire analysis could equally well be put on the basis of the competition rules as the free movement rules, and Lord Woolf MR suggested in *Wilander*[3] that the proportionality test under the free movement rules was equivalent to the reasonableness test under the domestic doctrine of restraint of trade and to the test under the grounds for review based on the public law standard.

1 The legitimate aims available in this context are arguably more limited than in the context of the competition rules. The party seeking to justify its actions must bring its motivation within the specific aims listed in the relevant Treaty articles in respect of each freedom. It is however apparent from the *Bosman* case that the justifications that would generally be advanced by sports governing bodies can be raised in the context of the free movement rules, albeit in that case they were insufficient to sustain the previous transfer system.
2 *Union Royal Belge des Sociétés de Football Association v Bosman* [1995] ECR I-4921 at para 262 et seq. In *Tibor Balog v Royal Charleroi* (C–264/98), a Hungarian player challenged on competition law grounds the validity of the post-*Bosman* rules which required the payment of a transfer fee for a non-EU/EEA national who was out of contract. The Advocate General's opinion (29 March 2001)

was released and then withdrawn the same day when the action was settled. She had held that the then transfer system was contrary to the competition rules to the extent that it allowed a club in the EU/EEA to insist on a transfer fee to sell a non-EU out of contract player whether it be to a club in the EU or EEA or in a third country.

3 At [1997] 2 Lloyd's Rep 296 at 301, col 1.

B APPLICATION OF THE RULES BY THE ENGLISH COURTS IN THE CONTEXT OF SPORT

12.5   As with the competition rules, the English courts' consideration of the free movement rules in the sports context has been largely at the interim stage of proceedings and therefore generally relatively cursory. In *Williams and Cardiff v WRU*,[1] the club included in its pleadings a challenge on free movement grounds to the WRU rule requiring a minimum number of players at a club to be eligible for Wales. The issue was never resolved because the proceedings as a whole were stayed for fear that there would be inconsistent decisions on the competition law aspects, and the judgments do not address the issue of free movement. In *Wilander v Tobin*,[2] an amendment to add an argument that the ITF's anti-doping rules were contrary to the free movement rules was allowed by Lightman J, only to be disallowed by the Court of Appeal. Lord Woolf MR took the view that the test of proportionality under the free movement rules was sufficiently similar to 'reasonableness or natural justice', on the basis of which the player had previously advanced an unsuccessful case, to allow the court to conclude that the new amendment was also unarguable.[3] He was not, however, prepared to hold that the anti-doping rules were necessarily within the sporting exception that was then said to exist, although he saw 'considerable force' in the submission.[4] In *Edwards v BAF and IAAF*,[5] which is probably no longer good law after the European Court of Justice held in *Meca-Medina* that there is no sporting exception, the athlete complained that he had been unfairly discriminated against on grounds of nationality and had been unlawfully prevented from exercising his free movement rights, since the BAF enforced the IAAF's requirement of a mandatory four-year ban for a first doping offence, but other national associations were allowed not to do so by the IAAF if their local laws regarded such a ban as illegal. Lightman J held that the BAF and IAAF anti-doping rules fell within the sporting exception that was then said to exist, as rules that related to how the sport was played and not to its commercial exploitation. Lightman J went on to hold that the anti-doping provisions were in any event proportionate and necessary to stop cheating. He also held that there was no discrimination on grounds of nationality: the rule was that the ban should be for four years, but that if the law of a particular state made this unlawful, the last two years would be remitted. Lightman J held that the vice arose in the difference in national laws, not in any discrimination by the sports governing bodies. In *Bacardi v Newcastle*,[6] the English courts were prepared to grant an Art 234 (now Art 267) reference in relation to whether the French 'Loi Evin' contravened the free movement rules by restricting the provision of cross-border broadcasting services by restricting French broadcasters from showing coverage on French television of sports events played outside France in venues with alcohol advertising in them. In *Gough v Chief Constable of the Derbyshire Constabulary*,[7] the courts held football spectator banning orders to be compatible with the EU free movement rules. In 2007, some agents threatened to challenge the compatibility with the free movement rules of the proposed FA Football Players' Agents Regulations, which require foreign agents to register with the FA.[8]

1 *Williams and Cardiff RFC v Pugh*, 23 July 1997 Popplewell J; 1 August 1997 CA; subsequently known as *Williams and Cardiff RFC v WRU (IRB intervening)*, 17 March 1998 Buckley J, [1999] Eu LR 195.
2 *Wilander and Novacek v Tobin and Jude*, in relation to restraint of trade 19 March 1996 Lightman J; 8 April 1996, unreported, CA; in relation to the competition and free movement rules [1997] 1 Lloyd's Rep 195; revsd [1997] 2 Lloyd's Rep 296, CA.
3 [1997] 2 Lloyd's Rep 296 at 301 col 1 per Lord Woolf MR where he said that the concept of proportionality for the purposes of the free movement and competition rules was not identical with reasonableness or natural justice but it was certainly close to these concepts. The court proceeded on the basis that the ITF was bound by the free movement rules.
4 [1997] 2 Lloyd's Rep 296 at 300, col 2.
5 *Edwards v British Athletics Federation and the International Amateur Athletics Federation* [1998] 2 CMLR 363, [1997] Eu LR 721. Again, the court proceeded on the basis that the BAF and the IAAF were bound by the free movement rules.
6 *Bacardi-Martini SAS and Cellier des Dauphins v Newcastle United Football Club* [2001] Eu LR 45, 26 July 2000 Gray J. Newcastle had removed Bacardi's advertising for a game against a French side, because the French broadcasters took the position that they could not broadcast matches into France if there was alcohol advertising visible at the venue. Bacardi alleged that in so doing, Newcastle had induced the marketing company, with which Bacardi had a contract for the advertising, to breach that contract. The validity of the Loi Evin was regarded as critical to the outcome of the proceedings, even if not necessarily determinative. The reference was made before trial. Much of the reason for the court's approach appears to have been that it was not felt appropriate that an English court should consider the validity of a French law when the European Court of Justice was available to do this instead. The Court of Justice however rejected the reference: *Bacardi-Martini v Newcastle United Football Club* [2003] ECR I-905. It however went on later to uphold the validity of the Loi Evin in *Bacardi France SAS v TFI* [2004] ECR I-6613 and *Commission v France* [2004] ECR I-6569.
7 Divisional Court [2001] EWHC Admin 554, [2002] QB 459, [2001] 4 All ER 289; CA [2002] EWCA Civ 351, [2002] 3 WLR 289.
8 In the event the Regulations came into effect on 1 September 2007 without a challenge having been mounted.

CHAPTER 13

Remedies

13.1   This chapter addresses the remedies by which the courts enforce the requirements imposed on sports governing bodies, and the remedies that they grant to claimants where those requirements have not been met. The discussion is limited to the remedies available in the courts and does not address remedies that may be available under any internal processes of the sports governing body or as a consequence of a referral to any external arbitral body, though the latter may be able, depending on the terms of the arbitration agreement, to offer at least some of the remedies available to a court. The possible availability of such remedies through internal mechanisms or effective arbitration agreements may also be relevant to the stage at which an application to the court can be made and to the issues (if any) that the court may be asked, or will be willing, to consider. While it is too absolute a statement to say that the courts will not intervene if an internal dispute resolution process is in place that has not been exhausted, intervention in such circumstances will require the claimant to show a real risk of prejudice if he is confined to his domestic remedies, or that pursuing those remedies would be futile.[1] Where there is an arbitration agreement, if the defendant sports governing body insists that that process be followed it will almost always succeed in obtaining a stay of any litigation.

1 See *Enderby Town Football Club v Football Association* [1971] Ch 591, where Lord Denning MR suggested (at 605) that a party could bring an action either before or after disciplinary proceedings, and would not be disadvantaged either way; *Modahl v BAF*, 28 July 1997 CA per Morritt LJ at 39A–C; *Stevenage Borough Football Club v Football League Ltd* (1997) 9 Admin LR 109 at 119C, CA; *Collins v Lane*, 22 June 1999 CA at p 12 of the shorthand writers' transcript.

13.2   The same private law remedies are available on the causes of action dealt with in Chapters 7 to 12 in the context of challenges to the actions of sports governing bodies as in any other context. The discussion in this section is limited to the particular issues that arise in the sports context where what is challenged is the exercise of a regulatory function by the sports governing body. The discussion does not deal with the remedies available in the normal course in respect of the commercial, non-regulatory activities of sports governing bodies, where the usual principles apply. The remedies available are the private law remedies because, as described above, the courts at present refuse to treat the actions of sports governing bodies as susceptible to public law challenge by way of CPR Pt 54 judicial review.

13.3   The available private law remedies include in particular the grant of an injunction,[1] either in mandatory form (requiring a positive action to be taken) or in prohibitory form (preventing an action from being taken), the grant of a declaration as to the parties' rights and obligations,[2] and the award of damages.[3] Where appropriate there may be orders for specific performance or restitution, as in other contexts, and the remedies available under the Human Rights Act 1998[4] are adapted to that particular context. In particular instances of regulatory action, other specialised remedies may of course be available. For example, sports governing bodies that are companies may be the subject of the forms of relief available under the Companies legislation.[5] In respect of non-regulatory actions, still other remedies may on particular occasions be appropriate. Furthermore, as in other contexts, some relief may be available at an interim stage pending a final resolution of the dispute.[6]

1 See paras **13.4–13.19**.
2 See para **13.20–13.25**.
3 See para **13.28–13.39**.
4 See para **13.40**.
5 See **13.41–13.43**.
6 See **13.4–13.15, 13.20–13.22**.

A   INTERIM INJUNCTIONS

(a)   Availability of the remedy

13.4   The primary form of interim relief is the interim injunction, which either prevents a party doing something or requires a party to do something, in the period leading up to the final resolution of the dispute. The basis on which the court will grant an interim injunction and the procedure for applying for one are well established, and are not addressed in detail here. The claimant must show that there is an arguable case on the merits, including an entitlement to the relief ultimately sought, and that the 'balance of convenience' lies in favour of the grant of an injunction. The court then has a discretion, the exercise of which the Court of Appeal will be slow to overturn. In considering the claimant's case, the court will frequently take into account the principle that the courts should be slow to interfere in the exercise of discretion by the sports governing body in the regulatory areas entrusted to it. In considering the balance of convenience, the court will examine whether damages will or will not provide an adequate remedy for either party, as well as all other relevant circumstances. The overall aim is where possible to ensure that a claimant is not deprived of the fruits of a putative victory, whilst still ensuring that a defendant is not unfairly prevented from doing something that it might ultimately prove to be entitled to have done. The threshold may be regarded as relatively low, and is certainly lower than the threshold to be achieved at trial. In specific instances, however, the court may raise the threshold. First, although the way in which the test is expressed involves little difference dependent upon whether the relief sought is prohibitory or mandatory,[1] the balance of convenience may well be affected in practice if the governing body is to be required actively to do something, rather than not to do something. Certainly it is something to be taken into account, and there is an inclination to maintain the status quo. Secondly, it is also possible to argue in some instances that the court should be satisfied that the claimant's case is rather better than arguable, for example where the interim relief sought is in effect dispositive of the action.[2] This would arise where for instance interim relief is sought to allow the claimant to do something in the short term (such as to compete in an event), which once done cannot be undone subsequently even if there were a trial. The price of an interim injunction is a cross-undertaking in damages.[3]

1 *National Commercial Bank Jamaica Ltd v Olint Corporation Ltd* [2009] 1 WLR 1405 at paragraphs 19–20 per Lord Hoffmann, cited with approval in the Court of Appeal in *HMRC v Rochdale Drinks* [2011] EWCA Civ 1116 at paragraph 109 per Lewison LJ.
2 The hearing of the application for an interim injunction is in many cases in effect the end of the case. In these circumstances it may be appropriate to apply a higher standard. See *Dwain Chambers v British Olympic Association* [2008] EWHC 2028 QB, Mackay J, 9, 17 and 18 July 2008 and also at (2008) 16(2) Sport and Law Journal vol 16 iss 2, SLJR 4.
3 See para **13.12**.

(b) Particular factors in favour of interim relief in the sports context

13.5   A number of factors operate in favour of a claimant seeking an interim injunction in the sports context. First, it is often impossible to assess the loss likely to be suffered consequent upon the regulatory actions of a sports governing body. For example if a player or a club is excluded from the opportunity of competing, what quantifiable financial loss have they suffered? Damages are therefore arguably often unlikely to be an adequate remedy.[1] Secondly, individual participants may have a relatively short time at the top of their sport. Any delay may affect them disproportionately. Thirdly, the specific effect on an individual or club of their inability to compete on a given occasion may well be wider than the immediate effects of being excluded on that occasion. Fourthly it has sometimes been contended that the absence of interim relief would actually lead to a club going out of business: finances are on occasion on a knife edge.[2]

1 As in *Phoenix v FIA and FOM* [2002] EWHC 1028 Ch, 22 May 2002 Morritt VC, at paras 65 to 66; *Williams and Cardiff RFC v Pugh*, 23 July 1997 Popplewell J at p 10 of the shorthand writers' transcript; *Jones v WRU*, 27 February 1997 Ebsworth J (1997) Times, 6 March, 17 November 1997 Potts J, 19 December 1997 CA (1998) Times, 6 January, p 9 of the Lexis transcript of Ebsworth J's judgment.
2 Accepted in *Newport v WFA* [1995] 2 All ER 87.

(c) Particular factors against interim relief in the sports context

13.6   While the relatively low threshold on an application for an interim injunction may operate against the defendant sports governing body and in favour of the claimant seeking the relief, other factors may incline the court against the grant of the remedy in the sports context. Two major, and connected, factors (which may also prevent the grant of a final injunction) are delay in making the application[1] and the effect on third parties of the relief sought.[2] Both of these factors are material to the exercise of the court's discretion as to whether to grant interim relief. It is in the nature of the sports sector that the regulatory actions of sports governing bodies are likely to affect not only the challenger but also the other participants, with which the challenger is in sporting competition. An obvious example is that if one club is denied promotion, another either stays up or goes up in its stead. The longer that a challenger delays in making an application, the more likely that third parties will have acted on the basis that the unchallenged state of affairs will continue.

1 Compare *Stevenage Borough Football Club v Football League Ltd* (1996) Times, 1 August, affd 9 Admin LR 109 CA, where delay precluded relief because the club had waited to see if it would otherwise qualify for promotion before challenging the ground requirements that prevented it going up, and *Newport v FAW* [1995] 2 All ER 87, where a very substantial delay did not preclude interim relief in the light of the other powerful factors in favour of relief. See also *Dwain Chambers v British Olympic Association* [2008] EWHC 2028 QB, Mackay J, 9, 17 and 18 July 2008 and also at (2008) 16(2) Sport and Law Journal vol 16 iss 2, SLJR 4 (relief refused amongst other things because Dwain Chambers had waited to see if he would qualify for the Beijing Olympics before mounting his challenge to the BOA's byelaw excluding him from selection, despite the BOA pointing out to him repeatedly that if he was going to mount a challenge he should do so straightaway).
2 See *Stevenage Borough Football Club v The Football League Ltd* (1996) Times, 1 August; affd 9 Admin LR 109, CA (allowing the club promotion would mean that another club was denied it); *Phoenix v FIA and FOM* [2002] EWHC 1028 Ch, 22 May 2002 Morritt VC, para 67 (Morritt VC considered that allowing Phoenix to compete on an interim basis was not possible because although the points (if any) that they took away from other competitors could be restored if the team failed at trial, it would not be possible to take away the effect of other factors such as the team securing a better grid position at the start than other teams, or a Phoenix car shunting another car off the track).

13.7   Delay and effect on third parties cannot however preclude relief where the cause of action leaves no discretion as to the grant of relief. For example where a rule is contrary to Art 101 TFEU and s 2 of the Competition Act 1998, it is automatically void and must be so declared and cannot thereafter be applied or relied upon. So in *London Welsh v RFU*,[1] the club established that the RFU's decision to refuse it promotion to the Premiership on the grounds that it did not have 'primacy of tenure' at its ground, was contrary to EU and UK competition law. Newcastle Falcons stood to stay up if London Welsh did not succeed on that challenge, and argued in reliance on *Stevenage* and the cases that followed it, that London Welsh had long known of the rules, yet had chosen not to mount is challenge until the last moment, to the detriment of Newcastle Falcons, and so should not be granted any declaration or injunction. It was held that London Welsh could not be deprived of relief on the basis of delay or effect on third parties because under EU and UK competition law an anti-competitive rule is automatically void, and the tribunal was left with no discretion as to relief.[2] Once the rule was declared void, as it must be, it could not be applied by the RFU, irrespective of the absence of any injunction.

1 *London Welsh v Rugby Football Union, Newcastle Falcons intervening* (RFU Arbitration 29 June 2012, James Dingemans QC, Ian Mill QC and Tim Ward QC).
2 At paras 92–95.

13.8   A third factor in the sports context is that the inclination of the courts to maintain the status quo is informed by the distinction in *McInnes v Onslow-Fane*[1] between forfeiture, application and expectation cases. If a player or club already has a right that is being taken away, the inclination will be to prevent that happening in the interim pending trial; if on the other hand the challenger is seeking to gain a right in the interim, the courts will be much harder to convince.[2]

1 [1978] 1 WLR 1520
2 Compare *Tyrrell Racing Organisation v RAC Motor Sports Association and the Fédération Internationale de l'Automobile*, 20 July 1984 Hirst J, where an existing team was allowed to compete in an event pending the challenge to its suspension, and *Phoenix v FIA and FOM* [2002] EWHC 1028 Ch, 22 May 2002 Morritt VC, para 71: 'Finally there is the all important consideration of the status quo. Phoenix has not hitherto competed in any Formula One event. It would require a strong case on the merits to justify disturbing that position in anticipation of a trial'.

13.9   Fourth, a sports governing body will often seek to resist an interim injunction on the basis that judicial reluctance to intervene and the requirement that sports governing bodies be afforded a wide margin of appreciation in their regulatory decisions, mean that there is an insufficiently arguable case on the merits to warrant relief. This argument succeeds on occasion,[1] but is harder to run at the interim stage[2] than at trial, at least if the normal (as opposed to elevated) interim test is applied, and at least if it is the sole basis for resisting an injunction.

1 See for example *Chambers* [2008] EWHC 2028 QB (insufficient case established of breach of the *Bradley* grounds for review, or of competition law under the principles in *Meca-Medina*).
2 See for example *Adidas v Draper and others [representing the Grand Slams] and the International Tennis Federation* [2006] EWHC 1318 (ChD), Sir Andrew Morritt C, 7 June 2006 [2006] All ER (D) 30 (the governing bodies unsuccessfully sought to resist Adidas' application for an interim injunction to restrain an alleged breach of the competition law rules, on the basis that the manufacturer's case was unarguable in the light of the margin of appreciation to be afforded to sports governing bodies. The court held that the *Bradley* principles did not translate over directly to the competition law context, and that the margin of appreciation in competition law was an insufficient basis in the circumstances of the case to deny relief).

13.10   Fifth, the inadequacy of damages of course cuts both ways in the sports sector: in many if not most instances, damages will not be an adequate remedy for a sports governing body if it sees its careful regulation of the sport temporarily and wrongly upset.[1]

1 *Phoenix v FIA and FOM* [2002] EWHC 1028 Ch, 22 May 2002 Morritt VC, at para 65, where Morritt VC concluded that damages would not be an adequate remedy for either the team or the sports governing body.

(d)   Interim injunction when the action is for a declaration in respect of the grounds for review based on the equivalent of the public law standard

13.11   It appears that an interim injunction is available where the final relief sought is a declaration in respect of the grounds for review of the decisions of a sports governing body based on the equivalent of the public law standard. In *Newport v FAW*,[1] there was no contract; rather, the claim was simply for a final declaration, and was based solely on the grounds for review of a sports governing body arising out of its control of the sport, and on the restraint of trade doctrine. Jacob J had to deal with the question of whether an interim injunction could be granted in such circumstances. He granted the injunction on the basis that if he could grant a declaration at trial then he must be able to protect that position pending trial:[2] a sensible and practical conclusion.

1 [1995] 2 All ER 87.
2 [1995] 2 All ER 87 at 92b–92e. The contrary may, however, remain arguable: Hoffmann LJ in *R v Jockey Club, ex p Aga Khan* [1993] 1 WLR 909 stated (at 933) that the ability to grant an injunction in the circumstances of *Nagle v Feilden* had 'probably not survived' *The Siskina* [1979] AC 210.

(e)   Cross-undertakings in damages in the sports context

13.12   The price of obtaining the relief is that the court will almost always[1] require the claimant to provide a cross-undertaking to pay any loss or damage incurred by the defendant or by any third party as a consequence of the grant of the injunction should it appear to the court at full trial that the injunction should not have been granted. The claimant must produce evidence of its ability to meet the cost of this undertaking being called upon, and may be required to put up security. In the context of sport this hurdle may be difficult for the claimant to clear.[2] That said, it may be that the likelihood of any effective enforcement of the cross-undertaking in many sports cases is relatively low, since often a successful defendant sports governing body will be unlikely to be able to establish that it has suffered quantifiable loss by reason of the interim injunction. Further, the arguably quasi-public nature of at least some sports governing bodies and the often general applicability and importance of challenges of principle made to their regulatory actions, may raise an argument that in some contexts the court should perhaps not insist upon a cross-undertaking. It may be arguable that the challenger is fulfilling a useful function that will allow a point of principle of general importance to be determined, but will only do so if interim relief is granted (for example because otherwise the benefit will be lost) and that therefore the challenge should go ahead notwithstanding the impecuniosity of the challenger and the risk to the defendant governing body.[3] It would however have to be a strong case before such an argument would succeed.

1 But not always. See for example *Barnard v Australian Soccer Federation and FIFA* (1988) 81 ALR 51.
2 Inadequacy of the cross-undertaking offered was one of the reasons that relief was refused in *Phoenix v FIA and FOM* [2002] EWHC 1028 Ch, 22 May 2002 Morritt VC.
3 A similar argument might arise in the context of security for costs. In the public law context the principle has been so far extended in relation to costs that in particular circumstances a public law body may be made subject to a prior order that even if it succeeds in defending a Pt 54 Judicial Review application, it will not be able to recover costs from the claimant.

(f)   Interim injunction in support of sports arbitration

13.13   In many instances in the sports context, the substantive dispute falls to be decided by an arbitral body, which may have its seat in or outside the jurisdiction. Although such arbitral bodies generally have jurisdiction to grant interim relief themselves,[1] in some instances the body may not have yet been convened and the matter may be too urgent to wait. The English courts have jurisdiction in these circumstances to grant interim relief in support of the arbitration, but only if the particular requirements of s 44 of the Arbitration Act 1996 are satisfied.

1 While some arbitral tribunals do not have the power to grant interim relief, at least expressly, the recent trend has been not only to ensure that a mechanism for interim relief exists in the body's rules, but also that it can be quickly implemented: see the detailed provisions in the current FA Rule K, for example.

(g)   Dealing with an interim injunction by curing the vice identified

13.14   As set out above, it may be that an interim injunction is obtained on the basis only that the challenge is arguable. In these circumstances, the sports governing body has to decide how to deal with the situation. It can accept the position as ordered at the interim stage and settle the action, or it can fight the action at trial, which may be some considerable time (and quantity of money) later. On occasion there is however a third approach, which is for the governing body to take its own steps to cure the vice identified, and spike the guns of the challenger. This approach was successfully pursued by the WRU in *Jones v WRU*.[1] Having had an interim injunction granted against it on the basis of arguable flaws in a disciplinary procedure, the WRU decided to amend its procedures and to reconvene the disciplinary committee to hear the case in a manner that cured the alleged defects. It invited the player to participate but he declined. In his absence at the next hearing he was again suspended for four weeks. A further injunction was sought by the player and obtained.[2] On this occasion the WRU appealed. The Court of Appeal held[3] that the original interim injunction had been properly granted, but that the WRU could not be prevented from reopening the matter and dealing with it properly.

1 *Jones v WRU*, 27 February 1997 Ebsworth J, (1997) Times, 6 March; 17 November 1997 Potts J and 19 December 1997 CA, (1998) Times, 6 January.
2 17 November 1997, Potts J.
3 19 December 1997 CA, (1998) Times, 6 January.

(h)   Norwich Pharmacal relief

13.15   Where appropriate, specific forms of interim relief will be available in the sporting context, such as *Norwich Pharmacal* relief requiring disclosure from third parties.[1]

1 See for example *Rugby Football Union v Viagogo Ltd* [2012] UKSC 55, [2012] 1 WLR 3333 (Lord Kerr with whom the remainder of the Supreme Court agreed) and *Brady v PKF & Hill* [2011] EWHC 3178 (QB).

B   FINAL INJUNCTIONS

(a)   Availability of the remedy

13.16   If a challenge has succeeded on the merits then a claimant may seek a final injunction. Some of the factors that may preclude interim relief will have fallen by the wayside once a final hearing is reached. The 'balance of justice' as between the parties will have been determined by the determination of the merits. There can be no question of maintaining an incorrect status quo. Equally it will probably make little difference whether the order is mandatory or prohibitory. That said the remedy remains discretionary. Although final injunctions are an effective method of ensuring that sports governing bodies alter existing approaches and comply with their obligations in the future, there are limits to the availability of the remedy.[1]

1 For a complete analysis of factors to be taken into account in the grant of a final injunction, see Spry, *The Principles of Equitable Remedies* (Lawbook Company, 2010), pp 382–444. A court may be unwilling to injunct an international sports governing body outside the jurisdiction and made up of associations from many foreign countries: cf *Cowley v Heatley* (1986) Times, 24 July.

(b)   Delay and retrospective effect

13.17   Delay in the making of a challenge may even preclude final relief. In the *Stevenage* case,[1] the claimant football club succeeded in showing that a number of the League's entry criteria on promotion were in unreasonable restraint of trade, but Carnwath J nevertheless refused a final injunction following a speedy trial, primarily on the basis that the club could have challenged the criteria earlier, instead of leaving it to the eleventh hour after it had won the Conference and was eligible for promotion. The Court of Appeal agreed with Carnwath J and noted[2] the undesirability of granting relief which would have retrospective effect:

'What was in issue was the validity of the rules for promotion and relegation to and from the League, not merely whether Stevenage should be promoted to the League. In such a case the Court is concerned with three questions: (i) whether any and if so which of the rules is invalid; (ii) if so, whether it should grant a declaration to that effect; and

(iii) if so, whether it should make an order (whether by way of injunction or declaration) giving effect to the rules as modified by the excision of those which it finds to be invalid. Even where it is satisfied that each of these questions requires an affirmative answer, it would be an exceptional case in which it would be right to give retrospective effect to the modified rules.

In the present case Stevenage has known of the position since at least August 1994. It had sixteen months in which to bring its ground up to the required standard if it wished to be considered for promotion to the League in time for the 1996–7 season. It did not do so. By November 1995 Mr Green knew that Stevenage could not meet the criteria by the deadline of 31st December 1995 and that the League would not grant an extension of time. He knew that Stevenage would not qualify for promotion in 1996–7 unless it won the Conference championship and succeeded in challenging the criteria. He decided to mount a legal challenge but only if Stevenage won the championship and to conceal his intentions in the meantime. The inevitable consequence was that he was compelled to ask the Court, not merely to declare the parties' 'rights' for the future, but retrospectively to upset the basis upon which the previous season's competitions had been held. In my judgment the Court should be extremely slow to accede to such an invitation.'

In the context of final injunctions, however, a delay that does not involve the court in effectively granting retrospective relief ought not to matter. If the effect of the order is only as to the future, and there is a good basis for it, then it ought to be made. And, as described above at para **13.7**, final relief cannot be denied on this basis if the cause of action leaves no discretion.

1 *Stevenage Borough Football Club v Football League Ltd* (1986) Times, 1 August.
2 (1997) 9 Admin LR 109, CA.

(c) Adverse effect on third parties

13.18   Also as mentioned above, an adverse effect on third parties may lead a court to refuse final relief.[1] In the *Stevenage* case this was again a major factor in the refusal of Carnwath J and the Court of Appeal to grant a final injunction. As Carnwath J put it:[2]

'The position of Torquay is of special relevance. They are the club which will be relegated if Stevenage is promoted. Although they could not complain of that, provided they were given adequate notice, the scheme of the rules of both the League and Conference entitle them to be notified of that shortly after the end of the season, so that they can make their arrangements. The change from the League to the Conference necessarily affects sponsorship, players' contracts and the planning of the season. It is unfair to them that they should be left in uncertainty until very shortly before the new season. The mere fact that they were made aware at an early stage of this litigation, and indeed even made parties to it at one stage, did not give them any certainty as to the outcome. Mr Bateson, chairman of Torquay, gave evidence of the arrangements which have been made, including negotiations with the 18 members of the first team who have been signed to play third division football, the pricing of season tickets, and contracts of commercial sponsorship including the catering franchise.'

Again, as described above at para **13.7**, final relief cannot be denied on this basis if the cause of action leaves no discretion, as is the case for example with the competition law rules.

1 In *Miller v Jackson* [1977] QB 966, a majority of the Court of Appeal (Denning and Cumming Bruce LJJ) overturned the grant of an injunction to prevent the playing of cricket at a village club, notwithstanding

an ongoing nuisance, on the basis that the public interest in the playing of cricket outweighed the private interest of the claimant. The Court substituted damages for past and future inconvenience

2 *Stevenage Borough Football Club v Football League Ltd* (1996) Times, 1 August.

(d) Injunction not available to force membership or participation

13.19 It is well established that as a matter of English law the courts will not force a person to work for an employer or an employer to employ an employee and will not force parties into a contractual relationship of membership against their will.[1] There are two parallel principles at work here: first that a contract involving mutual trust and confidence will not be specifically enforced, and secondly that parties will not be forced into a contractual relationship that did not previously exist with a new member. As Carnwath J put it in the *Stevenage* case,[2] where the club ultimately unsuccessfully sought to force its way into the League (and where, on the *McInnes v Onslow-Fane* classification, the case was an application case):

'Even if a case in principle is established, the question of remedies poses difficulties in an application case. No case has been cited in which the Court has forced a private organisation to admit a member against its will, even where the organisation controls the member's right to work...'.

Carnwath J did not decide the point. However, if he had not dismissed the case on grounds of the lateness of the application and effect on third parties, it is to be doubted that he would have balked at forcing Stevenage's admission. It seems likely that the courts would enforce an individual's or a club's right to compete at their suit, but would not grant a governing body an injunction at its suit requiring the individual or club to compete. Be that as it may, the principle still appears to apply even in a context where there is a contractual entitlement and the issue is not as stark as in the *Stevenage* case.

1 *Lee v Showmen's Guild* [1952] 2 QB 329 per Denning LJ at 342; *Faramus v Film Artistes' Association* [1964] AC 925 at 941 per Lord Evershed.
2 *Stevenage Borough Football Club v Football League Ltd* (1996) Times, 1 August, at p 23 of the online transcript.

C INTERIM DECLARATIONS

(a) Jurisdiction

13.20 In *Newport v FAW*,[1] Jacob J held that the submission that 'an interlocutory declaration cannot be granted because it is a juridical nonsense ... you cannot have a provisional determination of the final rights of the parties' was 'manifestly right'. The opposite view had long been taken by Lord Woolf,[2] and the CPR introduced an express power to grant an interim declaration.[3]

1 *Newport Association Football Club v Football Association of Wales* [1995] 2 All ER 87 at 92a and 93e. There is also Court of Appeal authority to the effect that an interim declaration is 'a creature unknown to English law': *Riverside Mental Health NHS Trust v Fox* [1994] 1 FLR 614.
2 In the leading text on declaratory relief, Zamir and Woolf, *The Declaratory Judgment* (4th edn, Sweet & Maxwell, 2011) at paras 3.094–3.099 and 9.05, Lord Woolf concludes that the jurisdiction is advantageous because it gives the courts greater flexibility.
3 Under CPR Pt 25.1(1)(b).

13.21   It would however be wise not to confine any interim relief application to an application for interim declaratory relief. This is especially the case if Jacob J's approach in *Newport v FAW*[1] of filling the gap by granting an interim injunction is valid. If there is an interim injunction there is generally little need for an interim declaration. The possibility of the relief can therefore only be useful in circumstances where for some reason an interim injunction might not be available or sufficient. Examples of this situation in the sports context might include where a party is seeking membership of an association without any contractual right, where a cross-undertaking in damages cannot be substantiated, where a court is unwilling to injunct an international sports governing body, where an effect on a wider audience than the other party is desirable, or where the court is unwilling to grant an injunction in the light of the difficulties of enforcement. It might also be useful in circumstances where a party has an arguable case of breach of the competition law rules warranting interim relief, but for some reason (such as delay or effect on third parties) ought not to be granted at trial anything more than the declaration that must follow upon success on that cause of action.

1   *Newport v Football Association of Wales* [1995] 2 All ER 87 at 92b–92e.

(b)   Availability of the remedy

13.22   An interim declaration, like an interim injunction, can only be made if a prima facie case is established and if the balance of convenience justifies granting the relief.[1] Declarations, like injunctions, are discretionary remedies and many of the same factors will apply. The relief has rarely been granted.[2]

1   Zamir and Woolf, *The Declaratory Judgment* (4th edn, Sweet & Maxwell, 2011) at para E1.8 et seq.
2   The one sports-related instance known to the authors of an interim declaration being granted was in *R v ITC, ex p TVDanmark 1 Ltd* [2001] UKHL 42, [2001] 1 WLR 1604.

D   FINAL DECLARATIONS

(a)   Availability of the remedy

13.23   A final declaration is granted by the court after a matter is resolved on the merits and reflects a central conclusion of the court on an issue that it has determined. It affords the parties certainty as to their respective relevant rights. The declaration can be positive or negative. The remedy is available not only in cases where the claimant has a contractual right (where the declaration is as to the existence, extent and ambit of those rights), but also where there is no contract and the claim is based on the doctrine of restraint of trade as a free-standing principle[1] or on the grounds for review of the decisions of sports governing bodies in the absence of a contract (where the declaration is likely to be couched in terms of the constraints on the freedom of action of the sports governing body): in *Bradley*, Richards J held that:[2]

> 'Even in the absence of contract the court has a settled jurisdiction to grant declarations and injunctions in respect of decisions of domestic tribunals that affect a person's right to work. That applies both to "application" cases such as *Nagle v Feilden* itself and to "expulsion" or "forfeiture" cases in which a person is deprived of a status previously enjoyed, though in the latter category of case it is likely in practice that a contractual relationship will also have been established.'

As to whether the jurisdiction to grant a declaration is restricted to cases in which there is an effect on the right to work, see above at para **7.6**.

Declarations are also available in the context of other causes of action, such as breach of the competition or free movement rules.[3]

1 Under the doctrine of restraint of trade, a declaration is available against a person or body who does not stand in a contractual relationship with the claimant. See for example *Eastham v Newcastle and the FA* [1964] Ch 413; *Greig v Insole (for the TCCB)* [1978] 1 WLR 302.
2 Para 35.
3 See *Hendry v WPBSA*, 5 October 2001 Lloyd J, [2002] 1 ISLR SLR-1; *Bacardi-Martini SAS and Cellier des Dauphins v Newcastle United FC* [2001] Eu LR 45, QBD.

13.24 Because the remedy is discretionary, many of the considerations that defeat a claim for a final injunction may also defeat a claim for a final declaration,[1] even where the claimant has succeeded. If some other remedy is appropriate, that may be preferred to the granting of a declaration.

1 See Zamir and Woolf, *The Declaratory Judgment* (4th edn, Sweet & Maxwell, 2011) for analysis of when a final declaration will be granted.

(b) The reasons for granting a final declaration should be explained

13.25 A declaration without a judgment explaining it may be inadequate. In *Hendry v WPBSA*,[1] the WPBSA made a tactical retreat and withdrew its Rule E1 which it regarded as being the most vulnerable of the rules challenged, and which in the event was the only one overturned. The WPBSA stated that it would accede to a declaration of invalidity in respect of that rule alone, and that the trial should not continue in respect of it. Lloyd J however held that the claimant was entitled to know the reasons why Rule E1 was void, as it was only against such reasons that future conduct could be measured. A declaration alone would not be adequate. Lloyd J eventually granted a declaration that Rule E1, as in force between specified dates, was void under Arts 101 (ex 81) and 102 (ex 82) and ss 2 and 18 of the Competition Act 1998. His judgment explained the reasons why it was void.

1 Lloyd J, 5 October 2001 [2002] 1 ISLR SLR-1.

E REMISSION FOR A FRESH DECISION

13.26 A consequence of the adoption of grounds for review equivalent to the public law grounds in relation to the decisions of sports governing bodies (and in particular their independent disciplinary bodies) is that the court may feel that it is on occasion appropriate to order the remission of a question to the domestic body for a fresh decision.[1] Such a fresh decision might for example be by the same panel but now acting in accordance with the court's declaration as to what the sport's rules require, or as to what the substantive law is, but is more likely to be where there has been a failure to provide a proper procedure, and a fresh decision is required for example by the same panel affording procedural fairness, or by a new panel not tainted by apparent bias.

1 See Fordham, *Judicial Review* (6th edn, Hart, 2012), Ch P3.

13.27   The approach to remittals was addressed in *McKeown v British Horseracing Authority*.[1] Stadlen J rejected the majority of the jockey's arguments, but did decide that he had been wrongly prevented from taking two points before the domestic appeal board. One of those points could not have made a difference to the result, and it did not therefore need to be remitted. The other point however might have made a difference, and the appropriate course for the court in that instance was not to seek to predict what the domestic appeal board would have done, but to remit the question to it for a fresh decision. In that case, as in many others, the fresh decision was to the same effect.[2]

1 *McKeown v British Horseracing Authority* [2010] EWHC 508 (QB), 12 March 2010. Note that there is a main judgment and a subsidiary judgment given on the same day with the same reference. On remission the relevant judgment is the subsidiary one.
2 On the basis that there was other sufficient evidence that led to the same conclusion as had originally been reached, namely that the jockey was at least also the source of the information: see British Horseracing Authority Disciplinary Panel: decision on penalty reconsideration of Dean McKeown (2010) 3/4 International Sports Law Review, SLR157-158.

F   DAMAGES

13.28   Generally the player's or club's concern is not to recover damages in respect of regulatory action but rather to stop or undo that action. It is however relatively common for athletes and clubs to include claims for damages in their pleadings. The losses generally claimed focus on the loss of sponsorship and advertising opportunities, as well as the loss of a chance to win prize money. The practical ability to recover such damages is however limited for a number of reasons.

(a)   Compensation only available where there is a cause of action that sounds in damages

13.29   Damages compensating a claimant for loss will only be available for breach of an obligation that gives a right to damages. Most obviously this is breach of contract, but it could also be negligence or some other tortious cause of action, and damages are available for breach of the competition rules, and if applicable the Human Rights Act 1998. This is of particular importance in the sports context, because two of the major bases for challenge in that context do not sound in damages.

(b)   No damages in respect of the grounds for review based on the equivalent of the public law standard, in the absence of a contract

13.30   Damages are not available where an action has been found to be unlawful under the grounds for review of the decisions of sports governing bodies based on the equivalent of the public law standard, unless a contract can be said to arise between claimant and defendant sports governing body. If there is a contract, for example on the basis of the sport's rules, between claimant and defendant sports governing body then breach of the express terms of that contract by the governing body will, subject to the proper construction of the contract, sound in damages. But, first, many claimants are not in that position, and secondly, the ground for review engaged in a particular case may not be breach of an express term. The trainer in *Nagle v Feilden*[1] could not have recovered damages as she had no contract with the Jockey Club on the basis of its rules, but even if she had, it is not clear that there would have been a breach of any express term in it. She was confined to a declaration.

1 [1966] 2 QB 633.

13.31 It was this problem that confronted Diane Modahl in her action against the BAF. She had no express contract with the BAF and her complaints related to the way the decision had been taken against her. After protracted litigation it was ultimately held by the Court of Appeal[1] that a contract did arise between the athlete and the BAF, but of a limited character in the light of the separateness and independence of the disciplinary body that made the actual decision, for the decisions of which the BAF should not be taken to be wholly responsible, or at least not to the extent of being liable in damages. There was no implied contractual obligation on the BAF that the decisions of its separate disciplinary body would be correct and not reviewable. The limit of the obligation on the BAF was to establish a fair process, and not to guarantee the right result. There was no contract between the athlete and the independent disciplinary body. A breach was not established on the facts, and in any event there were causation problems that would have stood in the way of recovery.

1 [2001] EWCA Civ 1447, [2002] 1 WLR 1192, [2001] All ER (D) 181) 8 October 2001.

13.32 The nature and extent of the implicit contractual obligations was further analysed in *Bradley*,[1] although no claim for damages arose in that case. Richards J again regarded the disciplinary body that took the actual decision as separate and independent from the governing body sued, but went further than *Modahl*[2] by holding that the governing body would be implicitly contractually bound not to enforce a decision other than one reached by the separate disciplinary body, and not to enforce a decision reached by the separate disciplinary body that fell foul of the grounds for review based on the equivalent of the public law standard of review. Although Richards J did not so state, it would appear that if the governing body acted in this way, it would be in breach of contract, and that would in the normal course sound in damages.

1 [2004] EWHC 2164 (QB), [2007] L.L.R. 543 (High Court), [2005] EWCA Civ 1056, [2006] L.L.R. 1 (Court of Appeal).
2 See para **13.31** above.

13.33 In the authors' view, the current position is as follows. First, absent a contract there is no right to damages. Secondly, where a contract exists between the defendant sports governing body and the claimant on the terms of the rules and regulations, damages are available for a breach of the express terms of them by the sports governing body *itself*, as opposed to by a separate disciplinary body. Thirdly, where a sports governing body has been found *itself* to have acted in a way that is impermissible under one of the grounds for review *other* than breach of an express rule, by reference to the same supervisory standard that would apply irrespective of contract, and proceeds to enforce that action, it would appear that the sports governing body is in breach of an implied requirement in the contract that it should not do so, and a cause of action in damages will arise. Fourth where a *disciplinary body* created by, but separate from, the sports governing body takes a decision that has been found to be impermissible under *any* of the grounds for review, by reference to the same supervisory standard that would apply irrespective of contract, whether a cause of action in damages arises against the sports governing body depends upon the extent of the implicit contract between it and the claimant. There is no contract with the separate disciplinary body, so no claim in damages against it. While prior to *Bradley*,[1] the limit of the governing body's implicit contractual obligation in these circumstances was said to be to establish a fair process, Richards J arguably established obligations sounding in damages first to enforce the decision made by the separate disciplinary body and nothing else, and secondly not to enforce such a decision if it was reached in breach of the supervisory standard of review.

1 [2004] EWHC 2164 (QB), [2007] L.L.R. 543 (High Court), [2005] EWCA Civ 1056, [2006] L.L.R. 1 (Court of Appeal).

13.34   The availability of damages for anything other than a breach of an express contractual obligation is subject to counter arguments. Where a sports governing body has itself acted in a way reviewable under one of the grounds for review *other* than breach of an express rule, it could be said that the extent of what is implicit in its contract with the claimant is that such action should be subject to the equivalent of public law review, and not that a cause of action in damages arises. It could be said that the proposition that there should be the same standard of review irrespective of implied contractual obligation, means that the *remedies* available should also be the same, consequently excluding damages. Where a separate disciplinary body is involved, there are additional arguments against an implicit obligation sounding in damages: the basis for that obligation in such circumstances lies in Richards J's judgment in *Bradley*,[1] and he did not expressly state that breach of his implied terms sounded in damages, there was no claim for damages before him, his statement of the existence of the second implied term was arguably equivocal, and such a result would arguably go further than what had been contemplated in the cases on which he relied.

1 [2004] EWHC 2164 (QB), [2007] L.L.R. 543 (High Court), [2005] EWCA Civ 1056, [2006] L.L.R. 1 (Court of Appeal).

(c)   Damages are not available under the restraint of trade doctrine

13.35   It is well established that the restraint of trade doctrine does not sound in damages.[1] Nor can this principle be avoided by seeking to identify a breach of an implied term. In the *Newport* case, Blackburne J rejected the proposition that there is an implied term that a party will not act in restraint of trade, thereby heading off the attempt to circumvent the principle.[2]

1 *Eastham v Newcastle and the FA* [1964] Ch 413 at 452.
2 *Newport v Football Association of Wales*, trial, 12 April 1995 Blackburne J, p 45 of the online transcript.

(d)   Damages are available for breach of contract

13.36   If a contract exists, damages are recoverable if the claimant establishes the existence of a term in it, breach of that term by the defendant, a foreseeable financial loss caused by that breach, and that on its proper construction, a remedy in damages was not excluded.

(e)   Damages are available in tort

13.37   Damages will be available against sports governing bodies in tort in the ordinary way. In *Watson v BBBC*,[1] the sports governing body was held liable in damages for its negligent failure to ensure adequate medical facilities were available at the ringside.

1 *Watson v BBBC* (1999) 143 Sol Jo LB 235, (1999) Times, 12 October, Court of Appeal [2001] QB 1134, CA, 19 December 2000. For a recent example of a tortious damages award against a sporting club, see *Hamed v Tottenham Hotspur Football Club and Athletic Limited* [2015] EWHC 298 (QB).

(f)   Damages are available for breach of the competition rules

13.38   If a rule or decision or agreement is contrary to the EU competition rules or their UK equivalents, and is not capable of exemption, it is void (subject to severance) and cannot be relied upon and there is a right to damages as well as to a declaration and an injunction. An individual or company that is party to the rule or decision or agreement challenged may find it harder to recover damages than third parties, but theoretically can do so in circumstances where the rule or decision has been forced on the party challenging it.[1]

1 See Bellamy and Child, *European Union Law of Competition* (7th edn, Oxford University Press, 2013), para 10-058. See also *Hendry v WPBSA*, Lloyd J 5 October 2001 [2002] 1 ISLR SLR-1 at para 159.

(g)   Assessment of damages and the particular problem of causation

13.39   The normal principles of assessment of damages apply in the sports context as in other contexts, and they are not set out here.[1] The usual limitations, such as the requirement of establishing causation, will also apply. So, for example, it would not be enough for the claimant to establish simply that there was a breach of contract; it must also be shown that that breach of contract caused the loss for which the claimant seeks compensation. In the *Modahl* case the Court of Appeal[2] decided that a finding of apparent bias in one member of the initial tribunal did not cause any loss. In the context of amateur sport, there is a real risk that nothing more than nominal damages will be recoverable even if a player is successful in his action.[3]

1 See *McGregor on Damages* (19th edn, Sweet and Maxwell, 2014).
2 [2002] 1 WLR 1192 CA, per Latham LJ at para 68 and Mance LJ at paras 132 to 135.
3 See *Collins v Lane* 22 June 1999 CA at pp 12–14 of the shorthand writers' transcript where £250 was awarded for wrongful expulsion from a shooting club. Membership would not be reinstated.

G   REMEDIES UNDER THE HUMAN RIGHTS ACT 1998

13.40   The remedies available under the Human Rights Act 1998 are adapted to the particular circumstances of that legislation. Where there is a breach of a Convention right, the court has a discretion under s 8 of the Act to grant such relief as falls within its powers and as it considers just and appropriate in order to afford 'just satisfaction' to the victim. This may be damages, or it may be confined to a finding that there has been a violation.

H   UNFAIR PREJUDICE PETITIONS UNDER SECTION 994 OF THE COMPANIES ACT 2006

13.41   Section 994 of the Companies Act 2006[1] provides a mechanism by which a member of a company can object if the company is being operated in a way that is unfairly prejudicial to its interests. The member can petition the court to secure suitable relief: the court has a wide range to choose from, including ultimately winding up the company. Many sports governing bodies are companies of which each of the clubs under their jurisdiction is a member. In particular, leagues such as the FA Premier League are companies made up of the clubs who play in the league from time to time. What is more, such leagues are operated in a way that is akin to a joint venture in the interests of all the members. In these circumstances, there is a basis for contending that the decisions of the governing body that affect individual members disproportionately, trigger the unfair prejudice jurisdiction.

1 Previously s 459 of the Companies Act 1985, as amended.

13.42   In an Australian case, *Wayde v New South Wales Rugby League*,[1] the claimant relied unsuccessfully on the equivalent of s 994 in the relevant legislation when the sports governing body decided to reduce the size of the top division, depriving the claimant of its place. The claim was unsuccessful because the measure of unfairness for the purposes of the section was held to be equivalent to the measure applicable under the ground for review based on the equivalent of the public law standard that the sports governing body should act reasonably in its handling of issues relating to the governance of the sport. On the basis of that authority it would be unlikely that resort to the particular mechanisms of the Companies Act would achieve a different result to that which could be achieved in any event on the basis of the grounds for review based on the equivalent of the public law standard. The court ought to feel the same constraints in relation to intervention in the actions of a sports governing body in both contexts.

1 (1985) 61 ALR 225.

13.43   This has not stopped imaginative practitioners seeking to use the mechanism in England against sports governing bodies, in reliance on the proposition that the English courts are not in general restrictive when considering what is 'unfair' under s 994. Most such attempts have been abandoned early. In *Fulham v Richards and FAPL*,[1] the Court of Appeal held that a s 994 petition, like any other action, falls to be stayed under s 9 of the Arbitration Act 1996 if there is an arbitration agreement covering the dispute.

1 *Fulham Football Club (1987) Ltd v Richards and FAPL* [2011] EWCA Civ 855, [2012] Ch 333, [2012] 2 WLR 1008, [2012] 1 All ER 414, [2012] 1 All ER (Comm) 1148, [2012] Bus LR 606, [2011] BCC 910, [2012] 1 BCLC 335, 21 July 2011, on appeal from [2010] EWHC 3111 (Ch), [2011] Ch. 208, [2011] 2 WLR 1055, [2011] 2 All ER 112, [2011] 1 All ER (Comm) 714, [2011] 1 BCLC 295.

Procedural aspects

14.1   A claim challenging the actions and rules of a sports governing body involves the same procedural considerations as any other action, and this section does not address all those considerations, since they will be obvious to the practitioner. This section is confined to addressing specific aspects of the courts' procedure that may prove to be of particular use to those making, or resisting, a claim brought against a sports governing body. After touching on questions relating to parties, it concentrates on those aspects of procedure that may enable the parties to obtain a speedy resolution of the matter in issue by the courts or in contrast to take the matter away from the courts.

A PARTIES

14.2   A claimant must identify the correct defendant against which to bring proceedings. This will include for example assessing whether the true author of a rule is an international as opposed to a national governing body. A claimant must also take care in the light of *Bradley*[1] to ensure that it sues the actual author of a decision, since some disciplinary decisions are taken by a body that although created by the governing body, is separate from it.[2] However as set out in that case, for some purposes the governing body may also still be sued.[3]

1 [2004] EWHC 2164 (QB), [2007] L.L.R. 543 (High Court), [2005] EWCA Civ 1056, [2006] L.L.R. 1 (Court of Appeal).
2 See paras **3.12–3.13**.
3 A prudent course may often be to sue both.

14.3   Some sports governing bodies, the decisions of which are to be challenged, do not have legal personality. Although this is decreasingly the case, there remain for example a number of sports governing bodies that are unincorporated associations. In these circumstances the sports governing body cannot be sued in its own right, and the action must be brought against its members, or one member who can stand as a representative defendant for the others.[1]

1 See CPR 19.6. See further para **3.14** above.

14.4   The problem is not confined to the proper identification of the respondent. It is also necessary to ensure that the appropriate claimant sues. For example, the decisions of a sports governing body in relation to a player may often affect his club, but it may be that the player should be a claimant in addition to or in place of the club.

B   OBTAINING A QUICKER RESOLUTION OF THE ISSUE

14.5   In the specific context of challenges to sports governing bodies' actions, the remedy of a final award of damages, declaration or final injunction, is often not really adequate. A faster solution is often required by the challenger and indeed on occasion by the sports governing body. The usual process of litigation involves exchange of statements of case setting out the parties' respective legal positions, the exchange of evidence in the form of relevant documents, written statements of the oral evidence that will be given at trial by witnesses of fact and by experts, for a trial in which the evidence will be given orally and subject to cross-examination. In any case of reasonable substance, this process inevitably may take several months even without taking account of the pressure on the court's time. A practitioner seeking to speed matters up must find procedural mechanisms to circumvent these delays. The following are offered as suggestions as to how this might be achieved.

(a)   Interim relief

14.6   The first, and most obvious method is to seek interim relief, as described above at paras **13.4–13.14**. While the test on an application for interim relief is not the same as at trial, it offers the claimant the prospect of some protection should he ultimately succeed. Equally, an application for interim relief by a claimant allows a defendant sports governing body to gain a fair understanding of the attitude of the court to its actions, which it can then reappraise on a more informed basis. The hearing can be brought on very quickly, even without pleadings, and the evidence is contained in witness statements on which there will generally be no cross-examination. The courts are prepared and able to show flexibility in the manner in which applications are heard and dealt with. Where urgency is essential, an order could be sought on immediate application to a judge, if necessary by telephone and without notice to the defendant. In such cases if the order is granted the claimant must undertake to issue proceedings and a formal application notice and evidence as soon as practical. Where orders are made without notice to the other side, the court will if necessary stipulate a return date when the matter will be heard again and the defendant given an opportunity to put its case. In practical terms however, the challenger would have been provided with protection in very short order. It should also be noted that the Court of Appeal is prepared to deal quickly with appeals from urgent interim decisions.

(b) Agreeing that an interim hearing disposes of the matter

14.7 Taking this a step further, it is possible for the parties, with the consent of the court, to agree that the interim hearing actually disposes of the matter. This has obvious costs advantages, but equally it has obvious risks for the sports governing body and indeed the challenger. It is a mechanism that is likely only to be of use where the case turns on a point of law (such as construction of the rules), which the court would in effect decide the same way whether the hearing was an interim hearing or a final hearing. Any agreement should be made on the basis that the test that the court will apply will be the balance of probabilities rather than the lower test (arguable case) applicable on an interim hearing.

(c) Summary judgment and striking out

14.8 A more aggressive approach for a defendant sports governing body to take would be to apply immediately for summary judgment or to strike out the claim. This could be done in response to an application for an interim injunction by the claimant,[1] or simply after the action is commenced. Either party may seek summary judgment under CPR Pt 24 on the grounds that the other has no 'real prospect of succeeding' on a claim or an issue, and there is no other compelling reason why the case should be disposed of at trial. A party may also apply to strike out an opponent's claim or defence if it discloses no reasonable grounds for bringing or defending the claim under CPR Pt 3, rule 3.4. Many cases falling within rule 3.4 are also the subject of applications under Pt 24. An application under CPR Pt 24 may not be made by a claimant until after a defendant has acknowledged service or served a defence. However, this is subject to the court giving permission and in cases of urgency permission can be sought from the court at the time that the claim is originally issued. If necessary this can be coupled with an application that will truncate the usual timescales for acknowledgment of service and service of evidence under Part 24. It may theoretically be possible, therefore, to commence a claim and have an application for summary judgment heard within a few weeks. Equally a strike out claim can be brought on quickly.

1 As in *Adidas v Draper and others [representing the Grand Slams] and the International Tennis Federation* [2006] EWHC 1318 (ChD), Sir Andrew Morritt C, 7 June 2006 [2006] All ER (D) 30.

(d) Preliminary issues

14.9 It may be possible to identify an issue or issues in a claim that if determined would effectively dispose of the whole case. In such circumstances, it may be possible to obtain an order from the court that these issues be dealt with in advance of the remainder of the claim. If these issues do not involve contested facts, this may speed up the process.

(e) CPR Part 8

14.10 CPR Pt 8 provides an 'alternative procedure for claims' that is most appropriate where there is unlikely to be a substantial dispute as to fact. The evidence is filed at the same time as the claim is issued and defence served. Since the relevant evidence is limited, cross-examination is likely to be unnecessary and it may be possible for the matter to come on for hearing relatively quickly. The procedure is particularly appropriate where an issue such as the interpretation of a contract or of rules is raised.

(f)   Expedited trial

14.11   Where there is an obvious need for urgency, the court may be asked to order that there be an expedited trial.[1] In that case there will usually be directions for the exchange of evidence that take account of the date for which the trial is fixed. Other orders may be sought which for example limit the issues on which evidence is required or limit the extent of the evidence needed on any issue. It may for instance be helpful to consider and specifically limit the extent of disclosure of documents on any issue. In seeking an expedited trial the parties will want to have in mind that the advantage of speed may be tempered by the disadvantage of over-hurried preparation. Many judgments delivered following a speedy trial, while expressly commending the parties for the speed with which matters were brought together, note that unfortunately specific points were not fully dealt with in the evidence.

1 In *Gasser v Stinson*, 15 June 198 Scott J at p 2B of the shorthand writers' transcript, Scott J said that the procedure to produce a speedy trial adopted in that case had been a model for what was possible.

14.12   Many disputes in the sports context, such as selection, exclusion, and promotion and relegation cases need ideally to be determined on an expedited basis so that the claimant is not deprived of the fruits of possible victory by lapse of time, and equally so that interim relief does not operate to disadvantage third parties. In *London Welsh v RFU and Newcastle*,[1] an extraordinary level of expedition of final resolution of a competition law claim by an arbitral body was achieved with the consent of the parties. So too in *Pontypool v WRU* case the High Court brought the matter on very quickly.[2]

1 *London Welsh v Rugby Football Union, Newcastle Falcons intervening* (RFU Arbitration 29 June 2012, James Dingemans QC, Ian Mill QC and Tim Ward QC). The RFU made a wide number of concessions in order to bring the case on quickly, limiting the issues to whether its actions were justified under the *Meca-Medina* test.
2 *Park Promotion Ltd (t/a Pontypool Rugby Football Club) v Welsh Rugby Union Ltd* [2012] EWHC 1919 (QB), 11 July 2012.

(g)   Limiting evidence

14.13   Other directions relating to evidence may be given in any case. For example it is possible to order that matters are dealt with on the basis of witness statements alone (analogous to CPR Pt 8 proceedings or Pt 54 judicial review) where the parties or the court can be satisfied that those issues will not be dealt with any more clearly through cross-examination.

(h)   Arbitration or alternative dispute resolution

14.14   Although this chapter is concerned with challenges in the courts rather than alternative forms of dispute resolution, the two are not entirely exclusive.

The CPR includes specific provisions that encourage the use of mediation and other ADR techniques even during the course of litigation. Successful mediation obviously achieves a swifter result. Furthermore, as described above, interim relief may be available from a court in support of arbitration and just as interim relief in court proceedings may speed up resolution, so may an injunction obtained in support of arbitration. Finally, it may be possible to achieve a faster resolution through resort to arbitration rather than the courts.

C   SECURITY FOR COSTS

14.15   A major preoccupation for sports governing bodies is the cost of litigation. Where possible, therefore, a sports governing body may seek at an early stage an order that the claimant provide security for costs.[1] This has the merit of forcing a claimant to assess at an early stage whether it is prepared to take the risk of losing the funds secured, and of protecting the governing body if the claimant decides that it does. It is however an established principle of the security for costs procedure that an order should not be made if it would defeat a genuine arguable claim by an impecunious claimant. Furthermore, the arguably quasi-public nature of at least some sports governing bodies, and the often general applicability and importance of challenges of principle made to their regulatory actions, may raise an argument that security for costs should not be used to prevent such challenges being resolved for the general good.

1 Normal principles will apply: see CPR Pt 25.

14.16   In *Pontypool v WRU*, it was held on an interim hearing[1] that a sports governing body has as much right to security for costs as ordinary litigants, in order to protect its stakeholders:

> 'It is necessary to bear in mind that the defendant has a duty to protect itself and those who are involved with it as employers and supporters. If it is out of pocket as a result of these proceedings, it will affect the money available for the support of rugby in Wales. It is entirely reasonable to take protective steps in those circumstances'.

This overrode the difficulties that the club would have in collecting together funds and the fact that it had an arguable claim.

1 *Park Promotion Ltd (t/a Pontypool Rugby Football Club) v Welsh Rugby Union Ltd*, 14 June 2012, Eady J.

D   STAY IN THE LIGHT OF AN ARBITRATION CLAUSE OR INTERNAL PROCEEDINGS

(a)   Arbitration clause

14.17   The most obvious method by which a sports governing body can seek to take a matter away from the courts is where there is a valid arbitration clause in an agreement between the challenger and the governing body, entitling the defendant to seek a stay of court proceedings. The same principles apply to the grant of such a stay in the sports context as in other contexts: if the criteria are met, the stay is mandatory.[1] In some circumstances, an analysis of the rules may lead a court to conclude there is no submission to arbitration, and so it can decide the matter itself, and refuse a stay where sought.[2]

1 Under s 9 of the Arbitration Act 1996. See *Stretford v The FA* [2007] EWCA Civ 238, 21 March 2007, Clarke MR, Waller and Sedley LJJ. See further para **7.26**.
2 See for example *Rangers Football Club Plc, Petitioner* [2012] CSOH 95; 2012 GWD 20-402; Court of Session (Outer House) 6 June 2012.

14.18   Conversely, if there is no arbitration clause in favour of a particular arbitral tribunal, the English courts will restrain an attempt to commence arbitral proceedings before it. In *Sheffield United Football Club Ltd v West Ham United Football Club Plc*,[1] the court granted Sheffield an anti-suit injunction restraining West Ham from seeking to raise before CAS a challenge to the decision of an FA Rule K arbitration. Rule K did not contemplate an appeal to CAS, but rather expressly stated that the award was final and binding (subject only to the Arbitration Act 1996).

1 [2008] EWHC 2855 (Comm), [2009] 1 Lloyd's Rep 167, [2008] 2 CLC 741, (2008) 16(2) Sport and Law Journal, SLJR 4, 26 November 2008.

14.19   Where a claimant seeking an interim injunction in the courts is met with an application for a stay, he may seek to persuade the court to grant the injunction in support of the arbitration, if a stay is granted.[1] The arbitration rules may however exclude such a possibility.[2]

1 As happened in *Sankofa and Charlton v The FA*, 12 January 2007 Comm Ct Simon J and *Phoenix v FIA and FOM* [2002] EWHC 1028 Ch, 22 May 2002 Morritt VC.
2 See FA Rule K, for example.

14.20   The courts will be slow to review the legality of an arbitration once it has taken place. The arbitration rules may purport to exclude all but the mandatory provisions of the Arbitration Act 1996. It will often be difficult for a third party to join an arbitration, or even to rely on what has been decided in it.

(b)   Internal proceedings

14.21   Whether the courts will intervene in internal proceedings of the sports governing body, or rather suspend their own proceedings in the light of them, will turn on the individual facts of the case. The party seeking such intervention would have to demonstrate that its challenge to the lawfulness of the internal proceedings was one that ought properly to be determined before those proceedings had concluded. The courts will be slow to stop ongoing internal proceedings, in the absence of the applicant showing real prejudice.[1] They may equally be unwilling to entertain challenges before the internal proceedings are commenced. This is because the sports governing body has a wider responsibility to all involved in the sport to enforce the rules as they are set down, and it is in the best position to enforce those rules. The integrity of regulation may be impeded if challenges can be made to the courts, interrupting or pre-empting internal proceedings. It is often the position that claimants have agreed to the internal proceedings by virtue of their agreement to the rules, and should be held to that agreement. Court proceedings may be premature before issues of fact are determined by the internal bodies. For the same reasons, the courts may also feel that it is appropriate to stay or suspend their own involvement until such internal proceedings have been completed: such a stay is discretionary.

1 *Modahl v BAF*, 28 July 1997 CA per Morritt LJ at 39A–39C.

E STAY IN THE LIGHT OF PENDING CRIMINAL PROCEEDINGS

14.22 The courts will not stay criminal proceedings in the light of pending civil proceedings or pending disciplinary proceedings. The court in the civil proceedings, or the disciplinary body or sports governing body, may however choose to stay those proceedings pending the criminal proceedings. Whether it will do so will depend on all the circumstances, including the particular rules, the likelihood of prejudice to the criminal process of early disciplinary proceedings, whether the player can be suspended on an interim basis pending criminal trial, how long the delay pending criminal trial will be, the dependency of the disciplinary proceedings on evidence held by the police, and how damaging the player continuing to play pending trial is perceived to be. The choice between proceeding with disciplinary proceedings despite criminal proceedings, staying disciplinary proceedings pending criminal proceedings, and staying the disciplinary proceedings but on the basis of an interim suspension is often a difficult one, with each course having advantages and disadvantages. In the *Fallon* case,[1] the jockey was suspended from riding pending criminal trial, only for the trial to be thrown out. The interim suspension, while protecting the sport, arguably had an unfair effect on the jockey. In the *John Terry* case,[2] the player continued playing (including at the Euro 2012 tournament, although he lost the captaincy), was acquitted in a criminal trial, but subsequently disciplined by The FA. Arguably, there the sport was insufficiently protected by the player's continued involvement. The three Pakistani cricketers Butt, Amir and Asif were first disciplined by the ICC, and subsequently convicted.[3] Proceeding with the disciplinary proceedings protected the sport, but arguably prejudiced the criminal proceedings.

1 *Fallon v Horseracing Regulatory Authority* [2006] EWHC 1898 (QB), 28 Jul 06, [2006] All ER (D) 427 (interim suspension by HRA of jockey's licence pending trial upheld).
2 *R v Terry*, Westminster Magistrates' Court, 13 July 2012; *FA v Terry*, FA Regulatory Commission decision dated 27 September 2012.
3 *ICC v Salman Butt, Mohammad Amir, and Mohammad Asif* ICC Disciplinary Tribunal (Michael Beloff QC), 5 February 2011 (bans of up to 10 years), appeals denied, *Asif v ICC*, CAS 2011/A/2362, award dated 17 April 2013; *Butt v ICC*, CAS 2011/A/2364, award dated 17 April 2013. For criminal cases see *R v Amir (Mohammad), R v Butt (Salman)* [2011] EWCA Crim 2914; [2012] 2 Cr App R (S) 17 (CA (Crim Div)).

F STAY IN THE LIGHT OF PENDING CHALLENGE

14.23 So too it will depend on the circumstances[1] whether a disciplinary disposal by a domestic disciplinary body should be stayed pending a challenge to that disposal in the courts, or an arbitral body. The extent to which that disposal can be undone if the appeal is successful is likely to be the determining factor.

1 In *Chelsea FC v RC Lens and FIFA (re Kakuta)* (CAS 2009/A/1976, February 2010), CAS stayed the FIFA DRC's sanction of a transfer ban imposed on the club for supposedly tapping up the player, pending its hearing of Chelsea's appeal. Following the presentation of argument and evidence that the player was not under valid contract with another club, FIFA withdrew its opposition to the appeal.

G STAY IN THE LIGHT OF PARALLEL REGULATORY COMPETITION PROCEEDINGS

(a) Discretionary stay where the regulatory authorities are also, or will also become, involved

14.24   A discretionary stay of court proceedings may be available where the same competition law subject matter of the proceedings is also being, or is likely to be, dealt with by the administrative or regulatory authorities.[1] Such a stay would be in order to avoid inconsistent decisions, to give due respect to the expertise of the regulatory authorities, and to allow the determination of factual issues. There have been a number of instances in the context of sport where the courts have stayed English proceedings in the light of pending European Commission proceedings. The courts also have discretion to stay, pending resolution of a matter by the CMA or CAT.[2] Such an application is less likely, however, since modernisation of the competition law rules. Now that jurisdiction to grant individual exemptions lies with the courts, it is rarer that the regulatory authorities and the courts will be engaged in parallel proceedings.

1 Council Regulation 1/2003 (16 December 2002), Art 16; *Masterfoods v HB Ice Creams Ltd* (C-344/98) [2000] ELR I-1369 (para 57); Commission Notice on Co-operation between the Commission and the Courts of the EU Member States [2004] OJ C101/03; Practice Direction – Competition Law paras 5.1–5.3.
2 *Synstar Computer Services v ICL* [2001] UKCLR 585, Lightman J, [2002] ICR 112.

(b) Jurisdiction of the English courts where the regulatory authorities have already made a decision

14.25   The jurisdiction of an English court to apply the EU competition rules effectively ceases if the European Commission has reached a formal decision in relation to the matter in question,[1] or at least the English court cannot take a decision inconsistent with that of the Commission. The same applies to domestic regulatory decisions.[2]

1 See Council Regulation 1/2003 (16 December 2002) Art 16; *Masterfoods v H B Ice Creams Ltd* (C-344/98) [2000] ER I-1369 (para 52); Commission Notice on Co-operation between the Commission and the Courts of the EU Member States 2004] OJ C101/03. Where a complaint has been rejected by the Commission, and the complainant has participated in the procedure, it will not be allowed as a matter of English domestic law to reopen the issue before the English courts (although as a matter of EU law it may technically be possible): see *Coal Authority v HJ Banks* [1997] Eu LR 610, (31 July 1998, unreported), CA. Where the EC Commission has decided that there *was* a breach of the competition rules, that is effectively binding before an English court on the party found to have acted in breach.
2 Under s 58 of the Competition Act 1998, a decision by the Competition and Markets Authority is binding as to the facts in subsequent private proceedings if it has not been appealed, 'unless the Court directs otherwise'.

H REFERENCES TO THE EUROPEAN COURT OF JUSTICE

(a) Reference to assist a court in reaching a decision

14.26   Courts will refer to the European Court of Justice broadly any question of EU law which they do not feel confident of dealing with themselves and which is necessary to their decision. It is possible that such questions will arise in the course of challenges to the legitimacy of a sports governing body's actions. It may be more likely that such issues would arise in the context of the free movement rules[1] than in the context of the competition rules.[2] The EU rules on intellectual property in the sports context have been the subject of references.[3]

1 See for example *Bacardi-Martini SAS and Cellier des Dauphins v Newcastle United FC* [2001] Eu LR 45, 26 July 2000 Gray J, albeit the reference was subsequently found inadmissible. A reference was the mechanism by which *Deutscher Handballbund v Kolpak* (C-438/00) [2003] ECR I-4135 and *Simutenkov (Igor) v Spanish Football Federation* (C-265/03) [2005] ECR I-2579, came before the ECJ.
2 Although this is plainly possible (the Belgian court made a reference in *Tibor Balog v Royal Charleroi* (C–264/98), Advocate General's opinion of 29 March 2001).
3 Most notably in the *Murphy v Media Protection Services* and *FAPL v QC Leisure* litigation, addressed in paras **2.48** and **11.13**.

(b) Reference where the dispute is referred to arbitration

14.27   A particular difficulty where a dispute involving EC law is referred to arbitration is whether, and if so how, a reference can be secured if it is necessary to allow the arbitrators to make a decision, as opposed to a court. Ostensibly, arbitrators cannot themselves refer. There is no specific power in the Arbitration Act 1996 for the court to make a reference at the request of the arbitrators. However, it appears that there may be a mechanism to secure a reference: a party may be able to appeal to the Commercial Court under s 68(2)(g) of the Arbitration Act 1996, if it can be established (if necessary with the help of a reference) that the award misapplies competition law. Public policy would preclude such an award standing.[1]

1 *Eco Swiss China Time Limited v Benetton International NV* (C-126/97) [1999] ECR I-3055, [1999] 2 All ER (Comm) 44.

I JURISDICTION AND APPLICABLE LAW

14.28   As in any other context involving contracts between parties based in different jurisdictions and subject to different legal systems, issues can arise as to which courts have jurisdiction to hear a particular matter, and as to which law should be applied. As sport becomes increasingly better organised, the role of international federations and associations is becoming pivotal. Again, as is the case in respect of the other procedural aspects addressed above, the general principles governing jurisdiction and applicable law in the sports context are the same as in other contexts, and they are not dealt with in detail here.[1]

1 See *Dicey, Morris & Collins on the Conflict of Laws* (15th edn, Sweet & Maxwell, 2012).

(a) Avoiding the jurisdiction and English law

14.29   International federations and associations have on occasion attempted to avoid the jurisdiction of the English courts and the application of English law. The IAAF is a good example of this approach. In *Reel v Holder*,[1] proceedings could be brought in England because the defendants actually sued were IAAF officers based in England. The court applied English law to the construction of the IAAF rules. Lord Denning MR's basis[2] for assuming jurisdiction and applying English law was that:

> 'We are simply concerned with the interpretation of the rules of the federation. The rules are in English. The head office of the federation is in England. It is right that, if the rules need to be construed, the matter should come to the English Courts to be decided.'

In *Gasser v Stinson*,[3] the IAAF was again sued through its officers present in the jurisdiction. English law was held to apply, chiefly on the basis that the organisation was based in England. The IAAF did not dispute that English law applied to the construction of the rules. The IAAF did however contend that English public policy rules such as the doctrine of restraint of trade could not apply to the IAAF because it was an association of foreign sports governing bodies. Scott J rejected this contention on the basis that English restraint of trade principles had been applied in *Greig v Insole* to the rules of the ICC, and that in order to prevent the IAAF escaping the rule of law, the full force of English law should apply to it. The IAAF subsequently moved to Monaco and took on Monegasque personality. Following that, in *Walker v UKA and IAAF*,[4] the IAAF sought to challenge the jurisdiction, but that challenge failed before Toulson J on 3 July 2000 on the basis inter alia that UKA had been validly sued and the IAAF was a proper party to be joined. Before the CAS, the IAAF was unsuccessful in disputing the jurisdiction in *Baumann*,[5] a case at the Olympic Games. The IAAF has since decided to provide for CAS jurisdiction in all its cases.[6]

1 *Reel v Holder (for IAAF)* [1979] 1 WLR 1252; affd [1981] 1 WLR 1226, CA (the Taiwanese athletics governing body obtained a declaration that the IAAF was not entitled to expel it from membership).
2 At p 1230. The assumption of jurisdiction on this basis in *Reel v Holder* was followed in *Cowley v Heatley*, 22 July 1986 Browne-Wilkinson VC, (1986) Times, 24 July at p 4 of the lexis transcript.
3 15 June 1988, Scott J. See also *Cooke v Football Association* [1972] CLY 516.
4 *Walker v UKA and IAAF*, 3 July 2000 Toulson J, 25 July 2000 Hallett J (no judgment), IAAF Arbitral Award 20 August 2000 reported at [2001] 4 ISLR 264, see also [2000] 2 ISLR 41 and para **8.12**.
5 In *Baumann* CAS Sydney 00/006, *Digest of CAS Awards II 1998–2000*, p 633, the German national governing body acquitted the athlete on a drugs charge. The IOC consequently accredited the athlete for the Olympics. The IAAF took the decision of the national governing body to the then IAAF Arbitral Panel. A two-year suspension was imposed. The IOC removed the accreditation. Baumann appealed to the CAS. The IAAF disputed the CAS's jurisdiction on the basis that there was no submission of IAAF decisions to CAS arbitration. The CAS rejected this argument holding both the IOC and the IAAF to be bound by its ad hoc jurisdiction at the Olympics.
6 *Reeb* [2001] 4 ISLR 246.

14.30   Equally, however, in an appropriate case, such as where the rules expressly provide for the courts of another country to have jurisdiction, the English courts are likely to decline jurisdiction. In *Lennox Lewis v World Boxing Council and Frank Bruno*,[1] permission to serve out on the World Boxing Council (based in Mexico) was originally given on the basis that it was a necessary and proper party to the action brought by Lewis against Bruno to restrain him from accepting a challenge from Tyson in place of Lewis. Rattee J however concluded that the substance of the action was against the WBC, and that Bruno had only been joined in order to form a basis for the action against the WBC in England. Rattee J enforced an exclusive jurisdiction clause in the WBC Rules in favour of Texas. It should however be remembered that even where the courts may not have jurisdiction over the substantive matter, in some circumstances they can grant interim relief.[2]

1 3 November 1995, Rattee J.
2 In *SPI v National Football Museum and FIFA*, 9 January 1998 Lloyd J, it was noted that even though the court did not have jurisdiction to grant substantive relief against FIFA in the light of pending proceedings in Switzerland, interim relief could be granted under s 25 of the Civil Jurisdiction and Judgments Act 1982.

14.31   The challenge to the jurisdiction may fall to be made in the courts of another country. In *Indian Cricket League v BCCI, ECB and ICC*,[1] English proceedings were stayed while an application for an injunction was made in India to restrain the ICL from suing the BCCI, the ECB and the ICC in England instead of India.

1 *Essel Sports Pvt Ltd (Indian Cricket League) v Board of Control for Cricket in India, England and Wales Cricket Board Ltd and International Cricket Council* [2011] INDLHC 1834, 31 March 2011, on appeal from [2010] INDLHC 642 and 643 (4 February 2010).

(b) Applicable law

14.32   As the involvement of international organisations becomes increasingly important, so too does the question of which law applies to challenges against their actions and rules. Again, the normal principles apply.[1] Where a governing body is made up of national governing bodies from around the world, it may be difficult in the absence of an express choice of law clause in the relevant rules to ascertain which law applies, and it appears that recourse can only be had to where the body is based. As a result, the majority of international governing bodies specify the law that governs their rules. The international nature of such bodies also raises the issue, addressed in *Gasser v Stinson*, of whether some of the specific public policy doctrines of a particular legal system should also be applied to such bodies. In the English courts, the answer appears to be that they should. A second, related issue arising out of the international nature of such governing bodies is the willingness of international arbitral bodies such as the CAS to apply 'general principles of law' which draw on the legal systems of all nations.[2]

1 See *Dicey, Morris & Collins on the Conflict of Laws* (15th edn, Sweet & Maxwell, 2012).
2 See *AEK Athens and Slavia Prague v UEFA* CAS 98/2000, interim decision 17 July 1998, final decision 20 August 1999 at paras 155–158, reported in Reeb, *Digest of CAS Awards II 1998 2000*, p 38 and in [2001] 1 ISLR 122. These general principles in the context of sports law have been referred to by a number of Latin tags such as the *lex sportiva* and the *lex ludica*.

Index

[all references are to paragraph number]